N. C. EDrALL
1977

Z .39ρλ

D0850635

Historical Problems:
Studies and Documents

Edited by

PROFESSOR G. R. ELTON
University of Cambridge

17

BRITISH ECONOMIC POLICY AND THE EMPIRE, 1919-1939

BRITISH ECONOMIC POLICY AND THE EMPIRE 1919-1939

Ian M. Drummond
Professor of Economics, University of Toronto

Our race would not have gotten far
Had we not learned to bluff it out
And look more certain than we are
Of what our motion is about . . .

W. H. Auden, *Reflections in a Forest*

LONDON: GEORGE ALLEN AND UNWIN LTD

BARNES & NOBLE BOOKS
(a division of Harper & Row Publishers, Inc.)

FIRST PUBLISHED IN 1972

This book is copyright under the Berne Convention. All rights are reserved. Apart from any fair dealing for the purpose of private study, research, criticism or review, as permitted under the Copyright Act, 1956, no part of this publication may be reproduced, stored in a retrieval system, or transmitted, in any form or by any means, electronic, electrical, chemical, mechanical, optical, photocopying, recording or otherwise, without the prior permission of the copyright owner. Enquiries should be addressed to the publishers.

© *George Allen and Unwin Ltd., 1972*

British ISBN 0 04 330208 4 HARDBACK
0 04 330209 2 PAPER

Published in the USA 1972 by
HARPER & ROW PUBLISHERS, INC.
BARNES & NOBLE IMPORT DIVISION

American ISBN 06 4 91782 7

Printed in Great Britain
in 10 on 11 Plantin type
by the Aldine Press, Letchworth

PREFACE

Many people and many organizations have helped me with this book. First I must thank the University of Toronto for a travel grant, and for so rearranging my teaching duties as to speed the research and writing. I also wish to thank the Canada Council, for a travel grant which allowed me to use research materials in Australia. I owe a great debt to the archivists and staffs of the Public Record Office, the University Libraries of Cambridge, Birmingham, Sheffield, and Newcastle, the Public Archives of Canada, the National Library of Australia, and the Commonwealth Archives Office in Canberra. I am grateful to the Australian National University, which, by making me an honorary fellow in the Department of Economic History, Research School of Social Studies, provided a comfortable and stimulating environment for my work in Canberra. I profited greatly from the comments I received in seminars at the Australian National University, Cambridge, and Sussex. My graduate students at the University of Toronto have often irritated me into further thought on the issues this book raises. Among the many individuals whose comments and conversation have helped me to avoid error and clarify argument, I must mention in particular Malcolm Knight, Donald Moggridge, L. S. Pressnell, Jennifer Roberts, J. H. Dales, L. Fitzhardinge, Boris Shchedvin, Sir Keith Hancock, Neville Cain, N. G. Butlin, and Donald Patterson. Perhaps my greatest debt is to Robert L. Patterson. His perceptive remarks have helped with the entire task of research and writing; his close reading has left its mark on the final draft. Finally, I must thank various archives and persons for permission to reproduce material in this volume. Errors, omissions, and confusions remain my own responsibility.

London, 1971   I.M.D.

In preparing the introduction, and the notes to the documents, I have used both primary sources and secondary works. Footnotes have been used to document statements or expand them—not, in general, to guide the reader through the secondary literature. No useful bibliography could be fitted into the space constraints of this volume. The following primary materials are actually cited:

Public Record Office, London: Cabinet Papers (CAB), Colonial Office Papers (CO), Dominions Office Papers (DO), and Treasury Papers (T).

Public Archives of Canada, Ottawa: WLM King Papers, RB Bennett Papers (microfilms of originals in the Harriet Irving Library, University of New Brunswick, Fredericton, Canada), HH Stevens Papers.

National Library of Australia, Canberra: Sir George Pearce Papers.

Commonwealth Archives Office, Canberra: miscellaneous papers relating to Imperial Conferences (CP).

University of Birmingham: Austen Chamberlain Papers.

University of Cambridge: Stanley Baldwin Papers.

University of Sheffield: W. A. S. Hewins Papers.

University of Newcastle upon Tyne: Walter Runciman (Lord Runciman of Doxford) Papers.

It is hard to write concisely about the inter-war 'British Empire' because the terminology was always changing, and almost always cumbersome. In the course of twenty years, the Empire became a Commonwealth. But Australia had also been a Commonwealth for several decades—ever since 1901. Also, the Dependent Empire was not part of the Commonwealth, and India was neither a Dominion nor Dependent in the same sense as, for example, Trinidad or Hong Kong. Further puzzles arise from the odd status of Southern Rhodesia after 1923, and of Newfoundland after the collapse of her responsible government. And then there is Ireland. I have decided to ignore the Irish Free State entirely, because its economic relations with the United Kingdom cannot be divorced from a political problem whose complexity is beyond the wit of the mere economic historian. Throughout I have written of the 'Empire', including all the other Dominions, India, protectorates, colonies, and mandated territories in this entity. I have written of Australia, not of 'the Commonwealth'. But there remains the problem of the governments themselves. I have often violated contemporary usage, and constitutional propriety, by writing 'British Government' in place of 'Imperial Government'—the usual form early in the twenties—or 'His Majesty's Government in the United Kingdom'—the correct usage from the mid-twenties onward. The difficulty was, of course, that *all* the Empire governments were equally 'British'—especially the ones of the self-governing Dominions. But it would be pedantic to retain such circumlocutions as 'His Majesty's Government in the Dominion of Canada', especially for a work of this sort. Hence I speak simply of Canadian, Australian, New Zealand, and South African Governments. I also ignore the complexity of the channels through which the Dominions communicated with the Government of the United Kingdom. The reader, however, should be aware that the channels were *not* those usually found among and between separate nation-states.

Until 1925, the United Kingdom Government communicated with the Dominions through the Colonial Office, and thereafter through the Dominions Office. In London there were High Commissioners for the several Dominions, but they did not function as proto-Ambassadors, and were by no means always informed about the relations between Whitehall and the several Dominion capitals. At the Dominion end, the primary channel was at first the Governor General. After 1928, the United Kingdom began to appoint High Commissioners in the

Dominions. But these officials were often remarkably intimate with the members of the governments to which they were accredited. And there were many informal contacts, both in London and in the Dominion capitals, between the civil servants and politicians of the several governments. The Imperial Conferences themselves, and the many less structured meetings of the nineteen-thirties, encouraged the development of direct correspondence between the various Prime Ministers, and, on occasion, between the more senior cabinet ministers of the many governments. Further, the Governors General continued to report, often direct to the politicians who had appointed them, and those personal friends they so frequently were. The Viceroys of India often stood in an identical relation to the statesmen of the United Kingdom.

Finally, a comment on oil. The reader should remember that to no significant extent did the inter-war Empire *have* an oil industry. In the twenties, the only significant production was in Trinidad, and in Burma. In Iraq, exploration went slowly, and production began only when Britain's mandate was being wound up. Further, the producing organization, the Iraq Petroleum Company, was an international consortium with very strong French and American elements. Iraq, and its oil, were important on the diplomatic and military stages. It is less clear that anybody thought them of economic significance. The whole matter merits closer study; the secondary literature, though often suggestive, has not considered the relevant primary materials, which, in turn, it has not been possible to examine for this study. However, what the author has seen convinces him that the oil question, whatever its significance for Iraq, was of remarkably little importance in Imperial economic policy as a whole.

CONTENTS

CONTENTS

CONTENTS

I should like to thank the following persons and bodies for permitting me to reproduce copyright material:

The Controller of H.M. Stationery Office with respect to materials at the Public Record Office in which Crown Copyright subsists.

The Hon. H. H. Stevens.

Sir Robert Menzies.

The Harriet Irving Library, University of New Brunswick.

The Public Archives of Canada.

The University of Newcastle upon Tyne.

Random House Inc.

PART I:
MAKING IMPERIAL ECONOMIC POLICY

Patterns of Trade, Migration, and Capital Movements

The Empire bulked large in British discussion and policy making during the inter-war period. It has become fashionable to ignore this fact. The imperial rhetoric which survived from Victorian times is now profoundly embarrassing to the intellectuals of a Britain whose role they now see in very different and more limited terms. For post-imperial Britain, Commonwealth Preferences, sugar and butter are now incumbrances which make it more difficult to enter the Common Market. It is hard for us to empathize with those who believed, in the aftermath of a bloody war, that Britain's military security could only be secured by the peopling of the Empire. In today's fashionable ideologics, 'population planning' means agricultural depopulation, abortion, birth control, and euthanasia—not agricultural settlement on virgin lands. We think we have learned to manage the British economy by monetary devices and by government spending and taxing—not by tariffs. Those who wish to make reputations and fees in the guiding of economic development would find it distressing to admit that their creative breakthroughs of the nineteen-sixties were the stock-in-trade of grey civil servants and flamboyant imperialist politicians in the nineteen-twenties. And there is the Britons' bad conscience with respect to the Empire. It is evil enough to have been willing—eager—to rule all those lesser breeds without the law. But had not Britain—somehow or other—grown rich by exploiting her Imperial subjects? How else could Britain be so rich while India is so poor and Tanzania so backward?

The reader will soon discover that the author has some sympathy with the imperial system. But on purely methodological grounds he thinks it wrong to proceed by compiling the errors of Imperial administrators and white settlers. All men are greedy and inclined to exploit other men; all administrators make mistakes; all governments mis-understand events and adopt foolish policies. To list these 'crimes' is a necessary part of nationalist agitation. Such lists may have a place in the political historiographies of the imperial successor states. They cannot form part of the present work. For this exclusion there are several reasons. First of all, in many cases the necessary historical work has not been done—or done properly. Secondly, the activities of local white settlers and local white officials are in no sense part of British government policy. Often Whitehall did not cause these activities; all too often it could not prevent them; only in the most emptily formal and legalistic sense can it be held responsible for them. Thirdly, as a matter of fact, in the inter-war period imperial economic policy making was much more concerned with the Dominions than with India or with the fully dependent Empire. The shape of economic thinking about the Empire, and the concerns of the politicians and their advisers, cannot be understood unless these matters are explored. For this exploration, space is needed.

The documents in this volume have been selected to illustrate the issues which actually dominated British imperial economic policy-making between 1917 and 1939. The introductory essay describes these policies and their development—first the expansionary and visionary phase of the nineteen-twenties, and then the protective and cautious phase of the thirties. Since the author is an economist, the essay also contains some comments on the sense or nonsense of these policies.

This chapter contains data on the patterns of British trade and Empire trade during the inter-war years. It also contains a discussion of the intra-imperial movements of capital and labour during this period. Both kinds of evidence are used to discuss the extent of Empire economic integration and the reasons for such integration as existed.

Graph One shows the values of the various trade flows between Britain, the several parts of the Empire, and foreign countries. Graph Three converts these flows into percentages. By 1938 the United Kingdom was sending 47 per cent of her exports to the Empire. In 1913 the percentage had been 22. Relative to foreign markets, Empire markets had become much more important to British industry. In the underemployed British economy of the period, these exports meant jobs and profits which would not otherwise have existed. However, it does not follow that the whole British economy had become more dependent upon the Empire market. To pursue this question we must relate Empire demand to all other demand—not just from foreigners but from domestic sources also. Graph Five does this. It relates the trade flows to British output—and, therefore, by implication, to British employment and general prosperity. It shows that, throughout the inter-war period, the Indian market was small and diminishing in overall importance—however great its significance for particular industries. In the twenties, the Dominions and the other dependent empire countries became

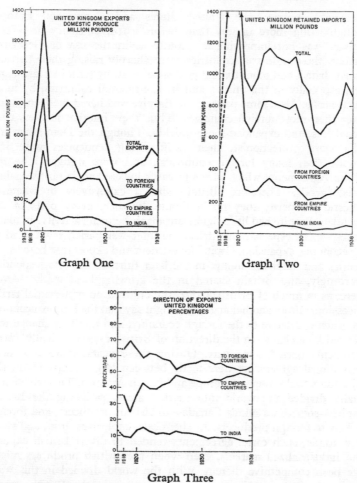

Graph One

Graph Two

Graph Three

Sources: See Note 12, page 35.

steadily more important, though they remained much less so than the export markets in foreign countries. In the thirties, as the British economy somewhat disengaged itself from its long involvement with external markets of all kinds, all export markets became sharply less important—in spite of devaluation and of the Ottawa Agreements. And Britain still sold more to foreign countries than to Empire countries.

Why did Empire markets become more important, relative to foreign markets, than they had been before the first world war? It was steadily harder for British goods to compete in the markets of the developed industrial countries—the United States and Continental Europe. Though rising more rapidly than before 1914, efficiency in British industry was not improving as rapidly as in the USA or Germany. Further, these industrial countries were sharply raising their barriers against British and other foreign goods—at first, by tariff increases, and later, especially in the thirties and in Continental countries, by more direct means. Also, some parts of the Empire weathered the Depression better than most foreign countries. Thus their internal markets contracted less, and expanded more quickly. Though the Dominions and India were protectionist, their tariff-raising tendencies were less extreme than many foreign countries', and were mitigated by the Ottawa Agreements which in many cases lowered their tariffs against British goods. Therefore, Britain shared extensively in whatever domestic prosperity they might attain. Further, many parts of the dependent Empire had little significant manufacturing activity. In many of these areas, especially in Africa, the inter-war period saw considerable economic expansion. Capital investment and export rose both in the twenties and, after the slump, in the later thirties. Imports responded accordingly, and Britain shared in the growing local market—even where, as in much of British Africa, she enjoyed no preferential tariff-concessions. From another angle, we might say that the Empire economy was growing relative to the foreign economy, and that this change was reflected by a change in the direction of British exports. Finally, cartel agreements played some part. During these years, more and more international agreements were made between large companies in the major industrial powers of Europe and North America. The agreements usually divided the world into market areas, assigning the British Empire—sometimes minus Canada—to British producers, and foreign markets to foreign producers. In chemicals, explosives, iron, and steel, for example, such cartel agreements tended to divert British exports from industrialized markets, even when the British producers might have been competitive therein. With the world divided in this way, Empire markets would naturally loom larger in the British export picture. To cartelized exporting firms like Imperial Chemical Industries, therefore, the Empire came to matter enormously and increasingly— even though in the *aggregate* export picture foreign markets were still more important, and even though domestic demand was becoming relatively much more important than in the past.

Graphs Two, Four and Six present similar data on British imports and relate them to the absorption of output within the United Kingdom. Foreign suppliers became less important relative to suppliers in the Dominions and in the other dependent parts of the Empire. This development reflects cartelization, British protectionism in manufacturing especially after 1932, and the Ottawa Agreements, by which Britain discriminated against foreign foodstuffs and in favour of Empire foodstuffs. Nevertheless, foreign supplies remained overwhelmingly

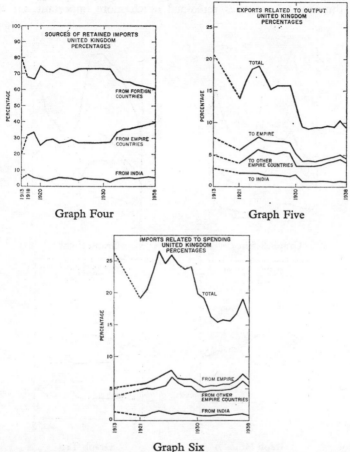

Graph Four

Graph Five

Graph Six

Sources: See Note 12, page 35

more important than Empire supplies. In 1913, 80 per cent of Britain's imports came from foreign countries. In 1938, after all these changes, foreigners still supplied 61 per cent of the import total. And both foreign supplies and Empire supplies contracted relative to British national expenditure. That is, even though the total value of British imports rose both in the nineteen-twenties and after 1933, overseas suppliers were making a smaller and smaller contribution to Britain's needs. Here again we see a tentative disengagement from the world economy.

In summary: between 1919 and 1939 Empire countries were gaining on foreign countries, both as markets for Britain and as suppliers for her. But foreign countries remained much more important, on the

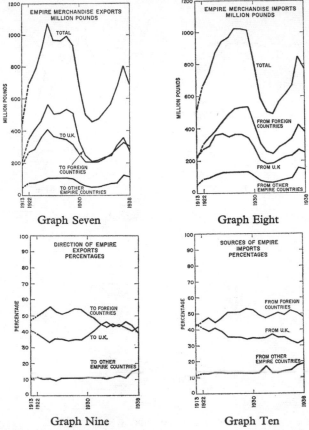

Graph Seven   Graph Eight

Graph Nine   Graph Ten

Sources: See Note 12, page 35.

export side and especially on the import side. Further, relative to British domestic economic activity, both foreign trade and Empire trade mattered less and less.

So much for Britain. What of the Empire countries? Graphs Seven through Ten summarize their trade data.

Both in the twenties and after 1933, the Empire increased its imports from the United Kingdom. But these imports represented a decreasing proportion of Empire imports. To some extent the slack was taken up by an expansion of trade between Empire countries themselves. In the twenties and after 1933 these trade flows increased both absolutely and relative to total Empire imports. The Ottawa Agreements made some contribution here. So did other bilateral tariff agreements between Empire countries. And something was owing to Canadian industrialization, which, for example, supplied most of the Empire with American-type cars. Nevertheless, the Empire was tending to fill more and more of its import needs from foreign sources. The trend was very slight but it was present—in spite of the 1931 devaluations and in spite of the intra-imperial trade agreements. Throughout our period, Empire countries supplied about half of Empire imports. In 1913, they had supplied 56 per cent. So far as imports were concerned, the Empire countries were becoming more integrated with one another but not with the United Kingdom, whose share in their imports, damaged by decreasing competitiveness both in old staple goods and new engineering products, fell steadily from 44 per cent in 1913 to 33 per cent in 1938.

On the export side, at first sight things were different. Only in the late thirties did Empire markets look more important to Empire exporters. The British market, however, became much more important relative to foreign markets during the slump of 1929–33. This fact reflects devaluations, the Ottawa Agreements, and new protective devices in the United States and Continental Europe. It also reflects the fact that the British economy, though less prosperous in 1929 than the other major industrial powers, did not contract nearly so drastically between 1929 and 1933. Thus British import-demand was better sustained, and so the British market bulked larger relative to foreign markets even though it too was contracting. The final effect, which appears in Graph Eight, is this: more and more of Empire exports to the United Kingdom and other Empire countries.

This fact may give the impression of tighter economic integration. But the impression is certainly spurious, because the percentages reflect the peculiar and transitory events of the thirties. If the United States and Continental markets had revived more quickly, or their governments had become less protective, Empire exports would have risen, and more of them would have been drawn to foreign markets. But in the structure of the Empire economy, or with respect to imperial economic integration, nothing fundamental would have changed.

Anyway, the percentages look rather different if we include gold production and export. In the thirties there was a world-wide boom in gold production. Because commodity-prices had fallen, and because the United States had raised the world price of gold, the industry became much more profitable than in the nineteen-twenties. Thus in 1926 the major Empire producers[1] exported £32·1 million in gold and silver bullion and coin, while in 1937 they exported £127·9 million. Almost all of the increase was gold. And though this gold flowed through the London metals markets, almost none of it was retained within the Empire. If we treat gold as a commodity, and regard foreign countries as its ultimate buyers, we sharply raise Empire exports and the

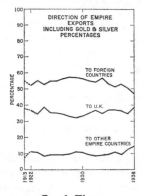

Graph Eleven

Source: See Note 12, page 35.

foreigners' share therein. For instance, for 1937 the foreigners would then be buying 54 per cent of Empire exports—not the 44 per cent of Graph Eight. Graph Eleven shows the results of treating gold in this way. Britain now appears to absorb a much more gently increasing fraction of Empire exports. Therefore, since exports were falling relative to domestic output in Canada, Australia, India, and probably New Zealand, as a generator of Empire employment and profits the British market mattered less and less.

Though its macro-importance was diminishing, the British market was still vital for some Empire products—Australian butter, wool, wine, beef, dried and canned fruits, sugar, and lamb; New Zealand butter, cheese, lamb and mutton; Rhodesian tobacco; West Indian and Mauritian sugar; South African sugar, wine and fruit; Canadian apples, tobacco, and canned salmon; Indian tea and jute; Ceylonese tea. These industries had been first established, especially in the Southern Hemisphere, with the British market in mind. In the twenties they had expanded rapidly, to serve this market. Governments had helped them, and some had borrowed heavily to do so. In the thirties, as old markets

---

[1] South Africa, Southern Rhodesia, Australia, and Canada.

were closed and no new ones opened, it became of overwhelming importance to secure the maximum possible share of the British market. For
tea and jute there was no problem: Britain had no alternative source of
supply. But the other products Britain herself could produce, and there
was strong foreign competition. The United States exported cheese,
dried fruit, canned fruit, canned salmon, ham, tobacco, and apples.
Denmark and the Baltic countries exported butter and bacon. Greece
exported currants. Argentina exported chilled beef and frozen lamb
and mutton. Cuba exported sugar. So did continental Europe, whose
nations also sent wine and brandy. Individually and collectively, these
goods accounted for a small share of Empire exports and British imports,
but the British market was a matter of life and death for the Empire
residents who produced these same products. Hence it is hardly surprising that Empire politicians spent so much time and effort on them.
To an extraordinary but understandable extent, the history of inter-
war imperial economic policy is the history of negotiation with respect
to objectively insignificant goods.

Though there were important changes during the inter-war period,
the Empire's trading patterns of the twenties and thirties were not
sharply different from those that the nineteenth century had shaped.
By developing her industry and allowing her agriculture to shrink,
Britain had become the world's largest importer of food and raw
materials. These were drawn from everywhere. In 1913, only 5·2 per
cent of British imports came from India, and 15·3 per cent from the
Dominions and the dependent Empire. The overwhelming bulk came
from foreign countries—wheat, oil and cotton from the United States,
meat from Argentina, butter and cheese from Denmark, timber from the
Baltic countries and Russia, wheat from Russia and continental Europe,
iron ore from Sweden and Spain, rubber and tin from the Dutch East
Indies, and so on. Within the British market, Empire products faced
competition from foreign products, and they generally competed on
equal terms, because before 1932 Britain imposed so few tariffs, and
before 1919 she levied the same rates on Empire and foreign goods.
Further, in some instances the Empire exports found foreign markets
more receptive. Thus Canadian cattle and timber exports went mostly
to the United States, while most Indian raw cotton went to continental
Europe and to Japan.

Within the British market, some Empire products were absolutely
dependent upon preferential tariff treatment. Australian meat and dairy
products would have moved to Britain in any event. But Empire wine,
brandy, dried fruit, canned fruit, and probably citrus fruit and timber
would not. Empire timber first received a preferential concession in the
Import Duties Act of 1932, which imposed duties only on foreign

timber. In the twenties, Canada had sold almost no timber to the United Kingdom. But in 1932 the Americans raised their timber duties and the British introduced the preferential system. Thereafter, Canada sent more and more timber to the United Kingdom. Without the preferences, there would certainly have been an even more drastic contraction in the British Columbia logging industry. As for wine, liquor and fruits, preferences were first granted in the Finance Act of 1919. Before that time, foreign goods held the British market—American canned and dried fruit, Greek currants, continental wine and brandy. But in the twenties, Empire production expanded rapidly, especially in Australia, where whole tracts of land were newly settled for fruit farming and grape-growing. Without the preferential system, these tracts would not have been put to this use. Indeed, if politicians had not thought they had a preferential market, the lands might not have been settled at all and governments would probably not have undertaken the large, loan-financed development outlays which settlement required. Further, since for these products the British preferences meant higher producer-prices, the preferences were probably essential to induce any white farmers to take up such extremely labour-intensive cultivation. Even with the preferences, many holdings were abandoned, and governments had to give constant artificial respiration. In the nineteen-twenties the Australian government was forced to subsidize the export of frozen beef and canned fruit. It connived at the creation of two-price systems for dried fruit, wine, and butter, by which export prices were kept much lower than domestic prices. And in effect it soon wrote off its settlement outlays. In Australia, New Zealand, and South Africa, the twenties saw the passage of legislation by which the exports of such products as butter, meat, wine and dried fruits were brought under 'control'. Though lacking any real power over prices in British markets, the export control boards tried to manage shipments, and to divide production between domestic and export markets, in such a way as to maximize producers' returns. They also became potent lobbies for 'their' producers' interests.

All the Dominions were 'development-minded'. Though in general their leaders wanted manufacturing industry in the nineteen-twenties, they thought that the path to development lay also through the export of primary products. In general, too, they equated development with the import of capital funds—chiefly though not exclusively from Britain. Further, development meant deliberately increasing the white population—in South Africa, preferably by natural increase; elsewhere by natural increase and planned immigration. Canada would and did welcome white migrants from anywhere; Australia and New Zealand were interested chiefly in British settlers. In Australia, by 1923 the national government had integrated these three elements into a philosophy of development: Australia, S. B. Bruce told the British, must have men, money and markets. That is, Britain must give these to Australia. The men were to settle on the land; the money was to finance extensive development of the land; the markets were to absorb the new primary production. Though Canadian and New Zealand politicians were less self-conscious about the strategy, during the twenties they shared the same assumptions and acted in accordance with similar imperatives. The South African situation was different. Boer agriculture and husbandry were backward. The country imported more foodstuffs than it exported. The whites were leaving agriculture; the problem was not to attract immigrants, but to create enough new urban jobs, so that there would be 'decent' livings for the Boers. Nevertheless, immigrants were tolerated, and capital-import was actively sought—especially for the mining industry. Further, the Government hoped that more and more of white agriculture could move to an export basis. In other words, it hoped that not only English-speaking but Afrikaans farmers could win some share in the British market. To this end it manipulated internal railway rates, and it was lavish with technical assistance.

These assumptions and policies were only too clearly derived from an extrapolation of pre-war economic history. Before 1914, the British market had in fact expanded enormously. Population had grown, and standards of living had risen enormously over a 70-year period. British politicians had allowed British agriculture to decline. To an enormous extent the countries of new settlement had developed by importing labour and capital from Europe, while exporting foodstuffs, gold, and raw materials to Europe—especially to Britain. Why should not these trends continue? And could not a clever politician expand or accelerate their impact on his own Dominion?

We now know that in all the Dominions before 1914, the development process had been far more complicated, and far more related to purely domestic conditions, than any politician could have known in the nineteen-twenties. Nevertheless, even today historians agree that the sketch was broadly accurate. Unfortunately when applied to the inter-war period its implicit assumptions were quickly found to be untrue.

British population would not continue to rise at the old rate. By 1932, demographers were expecting that it, like other European populations, would decline. Hence Britain could neither absorb goods nor pump out migrants on the old scale. Further, the pre-war boom in food imports had been connected with some special developments on the British scene. British agriculture, especially the grain-growing part, had shrunk enormously. After the War it was so small that its further shrinkage could not have had comparable effects on imports—even if British governments had still been willing to see British agriculture vanish. Wartime experience had somewhat changed British attitudes with respect to home agriculture; depression would shortly change them further. Before 1913, British food imports had risen in large part because of transport improvements and the overseas settlement process itself; these developments had radically cheapened food, both absolutely and relatively, but they could not be expected to recur on the same scale. Indeed, in the Dominions the frontiers of agricultural settlement were in many cases being reached: extra output could only be attracted at rising costs which would themselves tend to raise prices in Britain, and restrict sales. Per capita British food consumption could remain high only if most Britons had jobs. In the inter-war years all too many did not. Admittedly, among the employed, rising real productivity raised incomes. Some of the extra earnings were spent on more and better foodstuffs. But the dietary transformation of the pre-war years could not be repeated. And there were new things to buy—the 'consumer durables' which began to make a small but growing impact on the British mass market during the later twenties. Also, new technical changes were beginning to affect the demands for primary products. For instance, rayon helped the market for woodpulp but hurt the producers of wool, raw cotton, and silk.

Besides these basic changes in demand conditions, Continental Governments imposed artificial restrictions on a new and frightening scale. Even before 1914, these governments had not followed the British example: they had given some protection to domestic agriculture, and had even subsidized some agricultural exports—notably beet sugar and rye. But in the twenties and thirties they moved toward agricultural protectionism and export-subsidization with a new and striking vigour.

However gloomy the long run prospects might be, in the twenties the pre-war pattern revived. Empire governments strained to increase their outputs of primary products. Migrants left Britain for the Dominions in the hundreds of thousands, helped now, for the first time in a hundred years, by a United Kingdom subsidy. Between 1922 and 1931, the natural increase of the United Kingdom population was 2,678,000, but emigration removed 667,000—25 per cent—of this increase.[2] Two-thirds of these migrants went to Canada, Australia, and New Zealand. Almost all the rest settled in the USA; Kenya, Rhodesia, and South Africa absorbed less than 20,000.[3]

---

[2] HMSO, *Annual Abstract of Statistics*, No. 84, 1935–46.
[3] Calculated from 'net balance outward' statistics in Overseas Settlement Committee, annual *Reports*, for the period 1922–30.

Partly to finance their developmental spending, Empire Governments borrowed heavily in London, just as they had done before 1914. Empire public bodies raised £486 million in new money between 1920 and 1929. Also, Empire companies obtained £219 million. Almost 25 per cent of all the new capital issued in London went to the Empire. Foreign bodies and companies floated only 15 per cent of the total new issues. Additional large sums came from the London issues and the retained earnings of British companies which operated wholly or partly overseas—mines, oil companies, tea, coffee, and rubber plantations.[4]

As a result, Britain's 'foreign investment' was extraordinarily large relative to her 'domestic investment' during the nineteen-twenties. Between 1921 and 1929, the United Kingdom added £872 million to her claims against the rest of the world, while adding only £1127 million to her domestic plant, equipment and stocks.[5] Overseas investment continued to absorb a remarkably large share of total net investment, and more and more of this overseas investment was going to the Empire.

It is with respect to the movement of inputs, not outputs, that the Empire of the nineteen-twenties seems most integrated economically. Admittedly, there was little movement of people or capital between the Empire countries. Indians were not allowed to settle in the White dominions, and the Dominions' white populations rarely moved to other Dominions or invested much in them. Further, Canada attracted much American direct investment and portfolio investment; she also welcomed many settlers from continental Europe, and some from the United States. American funds were also placed in Rhodesian and South African mines. Nevertheless, in most of the Empire it was still British capital funds which were imported, and therefore to Britain that new obligations were being incurred. And it was British migrants who flocked to New Zealand and Australia.

In the thirties, this integration remained, but its forms were very different. Capital and labour were now flowing to the United Kingdom,

---

[4] Statistics as compiled at the time by the Midland Bank, and reproduced *inter alia* by T. Balogh, *Studies in Financial Organization* (Cambridge, 1938), Tables XLVIA, B. Include all public and private issues which came to the Bank's attention, but exclude refunding, bonus issues, United Kingdom government loans, bills, and issues made by private companies.

[5] Basic data from London and Cambridge Economic Service, *Key Statistics*, Tables A, N. Cumulating the balance-of-payments surplus on current account we get £872 million. Gross domestic fixed capital formation was £3656 million; physical addition to stocks was £187 million. Capital consumption was estimated at £2696 million, giving total net domestic physical investment of £1127 million (£3656 + 187 − 2696). All data in current prices. Current account surplus includes profits retained overseas for reinvestment.

not from it. The overseas Empire Governments still enjoyed the special 'trustee' status under the Colonial Stock Acts which gave them favourable terms in the new issue market. Further, the Treasury's informal control now systematically discriminated in their favour. But on balance they were repaying some loans and refinancing others at the new lower interest rates of the decade. From the beginning of 1931 to the end of 1938 they raised only £113 million in new money. Empire companies raised only £111 million. And the British economy as a whole was now importing capital. In 1931–38 the cumulative deficit on the current account of the balance of payments was £258 million, while net domestic physical investment was £1273 million.[6] As for population, from 1931 to 1939 natural increase added 1·2 million to Britain's population, and net immigration added a further 514,000. Many of these immigrants were the returning emigrants of the twenties— disappointed by overseas conditions, and impoverished by the collapse of primary product prices.[7] As yet, few were coming from India or the West Indies.

Nevertheless, for particular uses, Britain was still exporting capital. In 1934–37 there was a boom in gold-mining issues. The world price-fall, and the American devaluation, had enormously increased the profitability of gold mining. British capital responded, and so did gold output in South Africa, Rhodesia, Canada, and Australia. Rhodesian copper mining was also attractive, though largely financed outside Britain. Tropic plantations, their markets destroyed, attracted almost no new capital funds. Nor did oil. However, oil profits were now large enough to finance further expansion in the Middle East.[8] There was also some British direct investment in India and the Dominions, where protective tariffs caused difficulties to British exporters.

During the twenties and thirties, who cared about these trade and factor movements? Almost all British politicians were obsessed by them. Did anyone try to plan or regulate them? Not really. As we shall see in the next chapter, many British politicians, in both major parties, did have a vision of imperial economic development, and through the

---

[6] Sources and definitions as before. To some extent the United Kingdom could borrow automatically from the central banks and currency boards of the sterling area, which kept their external reserves in the form of claims on London. However, during the thirties Empire sterling balances were very volatile and on balance contributed little to the financing of the United Kingdom's international deficit.

[7] *Annual Abstract of Statistics*, No. 84, 1935–46.

[8] The British capital market provided only £8·3 million in new funds for oil in 1931–38. Tea, coffee, and rubber enterprises raised £8·7 million, but mines raised £68·3 million. Balogh, *Studies*, Table XLVIA, B.

Colonial Office they did something to make it concrete. Almost always, the result was an increase in the production of exportable primary products. Further, throughout the period the United Kingdom Government was willing to spend on emigration, and in the twenties the Exchequer disgorged several million pounds for it. Intermittently, too, there were controls on capital movements. For ten months in 1925, to ease the return to the gold standard, all new foreign issues were forbidden, and Empire issues[9] were given only limited access to the market. After 1931, foreign issues were in general forbidden, while Empire issues were not automatically permitted. These controls were operated informally, through private negotiations between issue houses, the Treasury, and the Bank of England.[10] But there was no general control or planning, either of capital movements or of population flows.

The British Government made spasmodic and purely verbal attempts to convince British industrialists that they should set up more branch plants overseas, and should cooperate with Empire industrialists. In private, Cabinet members and civil servants often deplored the Dominions' 'uneconomic' protected industrialization. Many of them believed that there was a natural division of Empire labour, by which Britain would supply manufactures, capital and migrants, while the rest of the Empire would supply foods and other primary products. But they never did anything systematic about these beliefs. Except in so far as the Ottawa negotiations may be thought to have had this effect, the United Kingdom made no systematic effort to prevent or retard Empire industrialization. Long before 1932, British politicians had publicly admitted that the Dominions and India had the right to industrialize. With respect to the colonial empire proper, this right was privately reiterated in 1934. Those who love industrialization should not accuse the United Kingdom of retarding it. The Empire of 1919–39 was not the Empire of 1776.

Throughout the period, Lord Beaverbrook and his newspapers campaigned for 'Empire Free Trade'. Britain, Beaverbrook thought, should tax all foreign goods, while in exchange the Empire countries should grant free entry to British and Empire goods. The result would be a free trade area. Each member country controlled its own tariffs on foreign goods, but only transport costs would impede the internal movement of goods. In 1930, Beaverbrook even tried to float a new political party on this platform. His manœuvres were of some importance with respect to the internal life of the Conservative Party. His

---

[9] On June 15, 1925, the Colonial Office cabled the Dominions, warning them of pressure on London and asking them for discretion in the offering of new issues. The controls were lifted on November 3, 1925. See CO 884/11.

[10] For details about the controls in their early stages, see DO 35/254/9099/182.

propaganda may have helped to prepare the electorate to accept the protective tariffs which the National Government imposed in 1931–32. But he was not responsible for the protectionist attitudes within the Conservative Party—or in the Labour Party, where, by 1931, protection enjoyed much support. Conservative landowners often grew up in the protectionist faith of their fathers. Conservative industrialists came to believe that a tariff system would mean more sales and more profits. Labour leaders increasingly suspected that tariffs would mean jobs, and that dearer food for the employed might be better than no food for the unemployed.

All these attitudes must have been strengthened during the twenties. Protectionist countries were booming, while free-trade Britain was recovering slowly and with difficulty. Within Britain, the booming industries were the protected ones. Though in fact explicable within the framework of rigorous economic theory, these results were not what the *vulgar* free trade arguments had led people to expect. Free trade virtue was supposed to be rewarded. Now the rewards were going to the evildoers. Might there not be something wrong with the free traders' case?

As the slump deepened after 1929, more and more people came to support protective tariffs because such tariffs would ever more obviously benefit them. The Conservative leaders were ready to articulate this change in public attitudes, because so many of them had been protectionists for decades. Many Labour leaders, too, were prepared to remain within a protectionist government. Other solutions were propounded, but party leaders neither understood nor accepted them. Thus the leaders of both major parties understood political and economic reality in terms which made a protective system inevitable.

Given the decision to impose tariffs, should Empire goods be admitted free of duty, or taxed more lightly than foreign goods? Imperial preferences had been on the Imperial agenda at least since 1897, when Canada unilaterally granted a lower duty on British goods. They had been discussed at every Imperial Conference in the century. Since 1919, Britain herself had taxed Empire goods at preferential rates. Because of these developments, which of course owed nothing to Beaverbrook, imperial preferences had become a kind of imperial habit. Except perhaps for Canadian motor cars, in the United Kingdom market, Empire manufacturers were not thought at all frightening. For Empire foodstuffs the case was different. But by offering preferential entry Britain might win better terms for her own manufactures in Empire markets. At the bottom of a slump such a strategy was to be expected. Further, for three decades Conservative politicians had been discussing the use of tariff offers as bargaining counters in general tariff-reduction.

And Stephen Runciman, the Liberal free trader who joined MacDonald's National Government to operate the new protective system, was passionately devoted to this strategy.

The Empire was not the only possible arena within which a preferential system could have been expanded. But the Empire did exist, its members already granted preferential tariffs, and its leaders were presumed to want more of them. Further, Empire countries could grant preferential tariff concessions to one another without automatically extending them to any foreign countries. Britain had signed many commercial agreements which contained the 'most-favoured-nation clause'. Unless such old agreements were denounced, Britain could not grant any preferential concessions to particular foreign countries; because of the most-favoured-nation clause, the new preferential rate would apply to goods from all the countries with whom the old agreements had been signed.

The protective and preferential system would have been introduced even if Lord Beaverbrook had never left the rivers and ponds of New Brunswick. But protection and preferences were not 'Empire Free Trade'. Actually, at no time in the inter-war period was Beaverbrook's scheme politically practicable. Neither in India nor in the Dominions would the politicians have stood for it. London civil servants were well aware of this fact. So were many leaders of the Conservative party. Long before 1900 it had become constitutionally impossible for the United Kingdom government to make tariff policy for the self-governing Dominions; after 1919 it could not do so for India. Hence Empire Free Trade was a matter for negotiation, not for imposition. No United Kingdom Government could 'introduce' it.

To Empire politicians there were two defects in 'Empire Free Trade'. First of all, the Dominions and India were industrializing behind protective tariffs. Few of these industries were thought to be competitive with British industry. Some Empire manufactures, such as Indian cotton goods and Canadian motor cars, were already exported to other Empire countries, to foreign countries, or to both. They, and other manufactures, undoubtedly would have survived tariff-free British competition at home, though with lower outputs, employments and profits. But Empire employers and trade unions had an obvious interest in convincing their politicians that British competition would destroy local manufacturing. And of course in many lines it would indeed have done so. Hence it was politically impossible to abolish duties on British manufactures. Secondly, the Dominions and India could not gain much from the British end of the 'Empire Free Trade' bargain—a British tariff on foreign food and raw materials. In 1903, if Britain had imposed a preferential wheat duty the Dominions would have received a higher price for every bushel of wheat they sold to the United Kingdom. But by 1920 their wheat outputs had increased enormously. Thereafter the Empire produced more wheat than it consumed. The same was true for wool, tea, jute, and most of the non-ferrous metals. Whenever this was the case, unless thwarted by some special 'management' of the world market, competitive forces would lower the realized price in Britain to the 'world' level.

For the Empire countries, preferential British tariffs meant higher prices and outputs only when Empire consumption exceeded Empire output. This point was well understood in the Dominions and India. Their politicians also knew that the United Kingdom would never impose duties on raw materials because these would raise the export prices of British manufactures. Hence many of the relevant imports would never be taxed under 'Empire Free Trade'. Only on a narrow range of construction goods and consumer goods—timber, meat, butter, fruit, cheese, tobacco, coffee, canned fish—did the scheme have anything to give. Understandably, these commodities dominated the discussions both in 1923 and at the Ottawa Conference itself. For the Empire's great staple exports—wheat, wool, lead, zinc, nickel, tea, jute, and of course gold—the scheme was simply irrelevant.

Lord Beaverbrook was neither stupid nor ill-informed. How can we explain his devotion to such a manifest nonsense? Perhaps he was simply being mischievous.[11] But his imperial devotion does seem to have been real. Perhaps he was extrapolating from his own extraordinary career.

Born in the Province of New Brunswick, a perpetual colony which has depended on subsidy ever since its first English settlement in the 1780s, Max Aitken began his business successes in Halifax, Nova Scotia, a maritime city with a vigorous merchant class and strong West Indian interests. There, he helped to promote and finance public utilities in the British West Indies. The management was largely Canadian, the money largely British. From Halifax he moved to Montreal, where his securities firm arranged an extraordinary series of mergers in Canadian manufacturing. Though the bridging finance came largely from Canadian banks, again the long-term funding came largely from Britain. Having made his fortune in three years, Aitken settled in Britain, bought a newspaper, and shortly became a peer and a political force. Beaverbrook's career superbly exemplifies 'Empire Free Trade', not in outputs

---

[11] Robert Blake, citing 'private information', says Beaverbrook simply wanted protection: he talked of 'Empire Free Trade' only because he thought the British electorate so wedded to free trade that Tariff Reformers could win only by using such a label. *The Conservative Party, from Peel to Churchill* (London, 1970), 233.

but in inputs—capital funds and entrepreneurial talent. It is hard not to see some link between his early achievements and his later opinions. Certainly, Beaverbrook was not the only man whose personal success on the wide Imperial stage conditioned his view of the Empire's economic potential.[12]

[12] The graphs in this chapter are constructed from: import and export data in United Kingdom, *Annual Abstracts of Statistics* and *Statistical Abstracts of the British Empire*, and output data in London and Cambridge Economic Service, *Key Statistics*, Tables A, N, K, L. Trade data exclude re-exports. Imports are valued c.i.f., and exports f.o.b.

2

The Imperial Vision: Dream and Action in the Nineteen-twenties

I

In the controversies about Britain's imperial economic policy during the nineteen-twenties, we find two battling points of view, those of the *laissez-faire* free traders and the Imperial Visionaries. The fight was not a party matter: important politicians in all three parties were devoted to free trade and to passivity with respect to the Empire, while the Conservatives and Labourites both included devotees of imperial development, overseas settlement, and a protective and preferential tariff system. Some of the most eminent, such as Lloyd George and Ramsay MacDonald, were not firmly committed to either viewpoint. Even Stanley Baldwin was only loosely settled in the Visionaries' camp.

The inter-war controversies echo earlier disputes—Joseph Chamberlain's Tariff Reform campaign, Milner's activities in South Africa, even the Corn Law debates of the 1840s. Most of the participants had formed their world views before 1914. Many had then become firmly committed to one side or the other—either by active involvement, like L. S. Amery or W. A. S. Hewins, or, like the Chamberlain brothers, by inheritance. However, after 1919 the discussion was taking place in a changed economic environment. Britain had emerged from the War with reduced economic strength. Unemployment was a chronic problem. The *laissez-faire* free traders may be said to have dominated the monetary reconstruction of the period, a reconstruction whose goal was to restore the good years before the war. With respect to any more innovative policy in Empire development or protection, they were primarily obstructive.

The Visionaries got their way to some degree. In 1917 the United Kingdom committed itself to tax Empire goods less heavily than foreign goods. In 1923 the first Baldwin Government promised to grant more preferences, partly by imposing new food-duties. It then lost an election, and, after returning to power, acted only to increase preferential margins, not to impose new taxes on foreign goods. These concessions were trivial in relation to Empire trade or Dominion demands. But they established the principle of Imperial Preference—a principle which was to exfoliate in the Ottawa Conference and in subsequent trade negotiations. Further, in 1919 the United Kingdom began to subsidize the emigration of ex-servicemen, and in 1922 Parliament provided funds for 'Empire Settlement'. It had not done this for many decades. Finally, both the Baldwin and the MacDonald Governments tried to encourage Empire investment.

To a limited extent it was the lessons of the War that made these schemes palatable. After so many lives had been lost, it made a kind of sense to retain population within the Empire. Should war come again, the emigrant Briton could not be conscripted, and might not volunteer, if he lived in the United States or South America. Similarly, the war had encouraged a preoccupation with raw materials, foods and self-sufficiency. The more self-sufficient the Empire could be, the easier it would be to control and maintain another major war effort.

Nevertheless, it was the unemployment problem which actually carried the Visionaries' schemes through Cabinet opposition—and over the fears of many civil servants. In the twenties, as much as in the thirties, unemployment dominated the British politicians' strategy with respect to the Empire. If governments had not feared this unemployment in 1921–23, 1925 and 1929 there would almost certainly have been no Empire Settlement Act, no Financial Cooperation scheme, no Guaranteed Loan to East Africa, no Colonial Development Act.

The Imperial Visionaries were of several kinds. Some, like Lord Beaverbrook and J. H. Thomas, were romantically attached to the idea of Empire. Others, like Sir Philip Cunliffe-Lister, saw the preferential tariff system and Empire development as good business propositions.[1] Still others, like W. A. S. Hewins, drew analogies with the protectionist Britain which had become rich and great in the seventeenth and

---

[1] See Lord Swinton, *I Remember* (London, 1949) 31: 'I have never been able to regard the issue of protection and free trade as other than a practical business proposition. Of course it does simplify the subject if you can persuade yourself that it is a moral and not an intellectual problem, and that only free traders are predestined to be saved. This specious profession of faith I have always found singularly unconvincing ... practical experience had long convinced me that tariff policy must be considered from 2 angles, British industry and Imperial trade, and that the two were in fact inseparable.' Lord Swinton (b. 1884), first as Sir Philip Lloyd-Graeme and then as Sir Philip Cunliffe-Lister, was President of the Board of Trade in 1922–23, 1924–29, and 1931. In 1931–35 he was Colonial Secretary, in 1935–38 Secretary of State for Air, and in 1952–55 Secretary of State for Commonwealth Affairs. He was ennobled in 1935.

eighteenth centuries. And still others, like Lord Milner and L. S. Amery, were in part the captives of their racial theories and their overseas experiences, and in part the perceptive critics of *laissez-faire* neo-classical economics.[2]

The Imperial Visionaries saw their world in the following terms. Neither natural resources nor labour were fully employed. Capital funds and labour flowed freely throughout the world. There was no guarantee that either capital funds or labour would spontaneously so distribute themselves as to maximize world output or Empire output. There were already many artificial and semi-natural encouragements and impediments to their free flow. Finally, the several parts of the Empire were more inclined to trade with one another than with foreign countries.[3]

These are factual propositions about the world. They make up a view of the economic order very different from that of ordinary neo-classical economics—the economics of Alfred Marshall, J. C. Pigou, or John Stuart Mill, or Liberal and Labour free trade politicians. In neo-classical economics all inputs are always fully employed. Capital and labour move perfectly within countries but not at all between them. Both spontaneously seek that use which maximizes their total contributions both to output and welfare, and, in the absence of artificial barriers, encouragements, or external effects, their private choices are also right from the social point of view. People always know what is good for

---

[2] Hewins (1865–1931) was under-secretary of state for the colonies, 1916–19, and a confidant of Baldwin at least in 1923. The first director of the London School of Economics (1895–1903), he had left that post, and his appointment as a professor of economics and economic history, to direct Joseph Chamberlain's unofficial Tariff Commission (1903–17) and to campaign with Chamberlain for Tariff Reform. Lord Milner (1854–1925) began as a journalist, became a highly successful civil servant, and was sent to South Africa as Governor and High Commissioner (1897–1905). While there, he gathered a 'Kindergarten' of bright young men to help him reconstruct the Boer colonies. On his return, with these and other men he formed the Round Table group (1909) to work in a semi-secret fashion for 'organic Empire union'. He was member of the War Cabinet 1916–18, Secretary of State for War 1918–19, and Colonial Secretary 1919–21. In 1923, he chaired Baldwin's Tariff Advisory Committee (see Doc. 10). L. S. Amery (1873–1955) began as a barrister and *Times* journalist, then entered politics (1911) to fight for Tariff Reform. At Milner's insistence he became parliamentary under-secretary of state for the colonies (1919–21). He chaired the government's Overseas Settlement Committee. In 1921–23 he was first Parliamentary and Financial Secretary to the Admiralty, and First Lord. In 1924–29 he was Colonial Secretary, and in 1925–29 Dominions Secretary. Out of office in the thirties, he returned in 1940 as Secretary of State for India and Burma (1940–45).

[3] More rigorously, each Empire country had two marginal propensities to import, and the propensity to import Empire goods exceeded the propensity to import foreign goods.

them, and what is good for each person is also good for society, so long as various technical conditions are satisfied. Though these conditions are never precisely satisfied in the real world, departures are sufficiently small and/or transitory, so that their effect can be ignored. So neo-classical economists assume.

From two such different world views two different sorts of prescription are bound to come. Even if their proponents agree fully about the ends of economic policy, the 'imperialists' are more likely to regard State interference as legitimate; neo-classicists are more likely to think that the market knows best. The former are disposed to think that the State can and should plan to improve its defence and development; the latter are inclined to believe that the unregulated market is the best developer, and that unregulated affluence is the best defence.

Further differences arose because in fact the imperialists and the neo-classicists wanted different things. The imperialists attached much more importance to military preparedness, and to development for its own sake. Some neo-classicists, like Philip Snowden and perhaps Lloyd George, were more interested in improving the distribution of income; others simply wanted a quiet life.

The Visionaries' programme was simple in outline though complex in detail. It involved the export of capital and people to the overseas Empire—both the white Dominions and the newer and more parti-coloured colonies. India would receive capital only. The exported capital and labour would cooperate with local raw materials and labour to raise total Empire output. Because all Empire countries tended to buy from the United Kingdom, British exports would necessarily rise in step with Empire output and imports. Thus there would be a short run fall in British unemployment, and also a longer-run tendency for greater prosperity in the UK. All these tendencies would be strengthened if Britain and the other Empire countries should adopt preferential tariffs, admitting Empire products free or at lower rates. Such tariffs would tend to make Empire development more profitable, thus directing British migrants and British capitalists toward Empire locations. They would also increase Britain's share in whatever overseas trade Empire development might generate. On Britain's side, preferential tariffs would make Empire goods displace foreign goods, especially foods. On the Empire side, preferences would preserve and raise Britain's share of a growing trade in manufactures. Since most parts of the Empire were on a sterling exchange standard, preferences would also support sterling vis-à-vis the American dollar.

Not surprisingly, Lord Milner was the most forceful advocate of the Imperial Vision. Arguing in 1923 that the United Kingdom starved and

neglected her colonies, especially in the Caribbean and Africa, he chose
a title which echoed Joseph Chamberlain. He explained:

> what these countries need ... is economic equipment—roads, rail-
> ways, engines, tractors, and in some cases, notably the Sudan,
> irrigation works. The supplying of them would set idle hands to work
> in many industries. It would increase employment and purchasing
> power at home, as well as in the countries where the work of develop-
> ment was proceeding. . . . Their development is a question of money
> —and money from outside. . . . There could be no stronger argument
> for a policy of vigorous development in the Dependent Empire than
> the results achieved by such a policy in the Dominions ... it is
> surely not beyond the reach of financial ingenuity by pooling the
> resources of a group of Colonies, or better still, by means of an
> Imperial Development Fund, to extend to the more backward com-
> munities under the British flag the credit which is all they need to
> start them on the path of progress.[4]

And he emphasized the importance of transportation and research,
especially in health and agriculture, both with an eye to the development of primary production in the tropical dependent Empire.

These views were faithfully echoed by L. S. Amery. Indeed, he tells
us[5] that in 1919 Milner would take the Colonial Secretaryship only if he
could have Amery as parliamentary under-secretary. He knew their
views coincided. Thanks to Amery's energy, the Imperial Vision was
kept steadily before the Cabinet, which repeatedly acted in accordance
with it.[6] In 1922, he was arguing for Empire development by means of
outlays on transport and communication. These, he wrote, would
develop Empire natural resources while creating immediate jobs in the
United Kingdom.[7] He became a zealot in the cause of Empire settlement. When introducing his Empire Settlement Bill to the House of
Commons, he explained the Vision in considerable and forceful detail.

> Any permanent scheme for Empire migration and settlement must
> clearly be based on the full cooperation of the Dominions concerned,
> whose need for population to develop their resources, sustain their
> defence, and build up their standard of progress, is at least as great as
> our need for the transfer of surplus population ... the capacity of

---

[4] 'Our Undeveloped Estate', in *Questions of the Hour* (London, 1923), 146–73.
Earlier published in *The Observer*.

[5] L. S. Amery, *My Political Life* (London, 1953), ii. 176.

[6] See, for examples, CAB 23/46, July 9, and October 22, 1923.

[7] CO 532/229, letter, Sir E. Harding to L. S. Amery, October 2, 1922, covering
TP 43, Amery's memorandum on development strategy. For his concern later,
see CAB 23/53, Cabinet 45(26), July 7, 1926, and CAB 23/60, April 17, 1929.

the Dominions to absorb additional industrial and urban population, and, in fact, to deal with any immigration on a really large scale, is strictly conditioned by the opening up of their agricultural resources. The direct settlement of men on the land as primary producers must be the foundation of any broad policy of economic regeneration in the Empire. . . . To attempt to solve unemployment here by taking the unemployed, as such, and dumping them down in the Dominions without regard to the conditions there, without regard to their own fitness, would be a policy cruel to the unemployed themselves and in any case impossible because the Dominions would never consent to it. What we are aiming at is only incidentally the relief of the immediate crisis; our main object is to find a permanent constructive remedy for the enduring problem of the economic situation which the War has left behind it. . . . The transfer of population to the Dominions before the war strengthened the forward impulse of trade at the same time as it eased the pressure on employment. It acted like a great flywheel steadying the whole industrial process. That flywheel has been stopped by the War. I ask the House . . . to give it a new momentum sufficient for the magnitude of the economic task before us. That task, as I conceive it, is essentially the task of securing a right distribution of our population in the Empire. Given adequate resources and a right distribution of population between the areas in which these resources exist, and between primary production and industry, there can be no reason or excuse for permanent under-employment. . . . But when we have three-quarters of our people penned, confined, and congested in this little corner of the Empire, and millions of square miles of the richest lands in the world—boundless plains, forests without end, water and coal power without computation; I wish I could bring before the eyes of Hon. Members the vision of what I have seen—waiting for the homesteads and great cities which they could so easily support, when we have so completely lost the true balance of the economic system that we have over 90 per cent of city workers here, and fewer white agriculturists in the British Empire than there are in France alone, is there any wonder that unemployment is an ever haunting spectre, and that the combined burden of our external responsibilities and of an ever-growing social problem threatens to overwhelm us?

I have commended this Bill to the House as the first step forward on the right road to economic recovery. I would also commend it as a measure of Imperial defence. . . . What would we not have given if only a more far-sighted policy in the past had doubled or trebled, as it easily might, the men and resources they [the Dominions] had contributed to the common cause. . . . Nor should we forget that the dangers of the future may well arise in regions far remote from this old fortress of Empire. If so, it is not by ever-increasing expenditure on armaments here that they can best be avoided, but by building up new centres of British power where the potential menace may be greatest. . . .[8]

The documents show how consistently Amery urged the Vision upon his colleagues in the Government—and later in the Cabinet. The three basic themes—subsidized emigration, capital export to the Empire, and Imperial Preference—were equally important to him, and he worked diligently on all three fronts.

Amery succeeded so well in verbal terms that the Vision became a commonplace in the first and second Baldwin Governments. Baldwin himself was converted to it. Opening the Imperial Economic Conference of 1923, he spoke in Visionary terms—first emphasizing the unemployment, and then calling for a redistribution of population and a growing intra-Imperial trade:

> The economic condition of Europe makes it essential that we should turn our eyes elsewhere. The resources of our Empire are boundless and the need for rapid development is clamant. I trust that we shall not separate until we have agreed upon the first steps to be taken to create in a not too distant future an ample supply of those raw materials on which the trade of the world depends. Population necessarily follows such expansion, and that in turn leads to a general expansion of business from which alone can come an improvement in the material condition of the people.[9]

Thomas Jones reports[10] that Baldwin wrote this passage himself—'in a shy way'. In the first and second MacDonald governments J. H. Thomas was equally inclined to talk like this.

Actions, however, were something else again. There was an enormous gap between Vision and reality, between hope and achievement. We can see this gap most clearly by examining the three components of the Visionary policy: capital export, preference, and emigration.[11]

---

[8] 153 HC Deb 5s cols. 575–591, April 26, 1922.
[9] Cmd. 1988, 8–9.
[10] T. Jones, *Whitehall Diary*, I (London, 1969), entry for September 30, 1923.
[11] Many years ago, Sir Keith Hancock, borrowing S. B. Bruce's rhetoric, described these as 'men, money, and markets' (*Survey of Commonwealth Affairs, II: Problems of Economic Policy* (London, 1940)). What follows is, in a sense, a series of footnotes to Sir Keith's great study. However, my point of view is different: I have tried to see things from the British angle, and to describe the making of economic policy in Great Britain. Hancock tried to deal with the entire Commonwealth. If his work has a major defect, it is its Australo-centricism.

II

During the nineteen-twenties, there was never any thorough-going control of British capital exports. London's capital market was accustomed to manage its own affairs. New issues had been regulated during the War, and for some time thereafter, but these controls were loosened as quickly as possible. From 1919 to 1925, the pound floated, and there was no balance-of-payments case to be made for the regulation of capital exports. If a new loan were transferred abroad, sterling would depreciate, encouraging exports and discouraging imports, thus transferring the real resources which the export of capital funds was meant to effect. In 1924 and 1925, before and after the return to gold, the Government did seriously try to control the export of capital. The Bank of England was regularly consulted about new issues through the decade.[12] It appears that this consultation was used to discriminate in favour of Empire borrowers, though the evidence is far from complete. But during the months of tighter control, in 1924–25, the Bank was actively trying to make the Dominions reduce their borrowings—over Amery's opposition, though apparently with his eventual acquiescence.[13] The 'embargo' was removed on November 9, 1925, and thereafter, Moggridge tells us, 'there is no recorded attempt to block loans'. There was, presumably, some continued *de facto* discrimination in favour of Empire borrowers, and against foreign borrowers: issue houses were less likely to take Empire proposals to the Bank for vetting.

More important was the built-in discrimination of the Colonial Stocks Act, 1900. This statute allowed trustees to hold colonial and dominion government securities; it must have had some effect on the interest which these borrowers were obliged to offer. Treasury officials believed that they saved a full percentage point—that is, 20 to 25 per cent of the interest they would otherwise have had to pay.

But the Colonial Stock Act, like the administrative discrimination in the management of the new issue market, was not really part of the Visionaries' programme. Besides these arrangements, they favoured an active policy of capital export under Government sponsorship. Some was already occurring through the Trade Facilities Acts of 1921, 1922,

---

'Men, money, and markets' made sense of Australia's economic policies during the Bruce-Page era (1923–29). They have less to do with the actual economic policies of the other Dominions. And they are relevant to the United Kingdom only insofar as the Vision, and Australian pressure, were mediated through an economic and political environment where many other circumstances were far more important.

[12] D. E. Moggridge, *The Norman Conquest of 4.86* (Cambridge, forthcoming), ch. IX.

[13] Ibid.

and 1924.[14] These measures could assist Empire borrowers by guaranteeing some developmental loans, without specially favouring them. But, the Visionaries thought, more was needed. The more Britain lent her Empire, the higher her exports and employment would be—a sound insight, which today's macro-economic analysis would support.

The first steps to encourage capital export were taken in connection with Australia's settlement schemes. These are described in the next section. The next was taken in 1923, when the British Government proposed 'cooperation for financial assistance to Imperial development'. This involved a sharing of interest-costs on certain kinds of public-utility projects. The idea was to bring them forward more quickly than would otherwise occur. British emigration and engineering exports would both gain.

Similar things had been seen in Australia before 1921, where the States and the Australian Government had begun to share the interest-costs of soldier-settlement. In Britain, the first formal proposal seems to have come from Amery. Late in 1922 he proposed an Empire Development Bill which would give authority to spend up to £10 million a year for fifteen years on transport, irrigation, power supply, or other similar public works. Early in 1923, Bonar Law asked the Colonial Secretary and the President of the Board of Trade[15] to draft a proposal for financial assistance to accelerate imperial resource-development. The Board of Trade proposed that the Colonial Secretary should be allowed to spend up to £2 million a year to such ends. Amery, at this point First Lord of the Admiralty, strongly supported the proposals, but wanted £5 million.

The eventual proposal was more modest: the United Kingdom would spend up to £1 million per year or £5 million in all on interest charges for Empire public utilities. Britain would pay three-quarters of the interest, for the first five years, on that part of the loan which would be spent in Britain. The idea was proposed to the Dominions in the summer of 1923, formally announced at the seventh session of the 1923 Imperial Economic Conference, and incorporated in the Trade Facilities Act of 1924. Though welcomed,[16] the scheme did not lead to large

[14] 11–12 Geo. V, ch. 65; 13 Geo. V, ch. 44; 15 Geo. V, ch. 8.

[15] Respectively, the Duke of Devonshire and Sir Philip Lloyd-Graeme. Hewins, pointedly ignored, heard of the scheme only much later. See University of Sheffield, Hewins Papers, diary for May 29, 1923.

[16] For the Australian Government's excitement, and for its attempt to dredge up suitable proposals, see Commonwealth Archives Office, CP 317/9: telegrams, Prime Minister of Australia to Premier of Queensland, October 17, 1923, Premier of Tasmania to Prime Minister of Australia, October 30, 1923; CP 290/4/1 Bruce to Earle Page, October 11, 1923, November 2, 1923, November 13, 1923, December 19, 1923.

outlays. Empire governments and companies do not seem to have found it easy to satisfy the two necessary conditions: the United Kingdom must supply the needed capital goods, and the projects must be ones that would otherwise be undertaken later or not at all. By January 28, 1926, only twelve applications had been received, and three were passed. A mere £480,653 had been spent in the United Kingdom under the 'cooperation' arrangements. By then, Whitehall officials believed they had no real future,[17] though Amery did not agree.[18] The scheme expired on schedule in 1927.

Before it left office early in 1924, Baldwin's Government had begun to consider a proposal for the financing of railway extensions in Kenya and Uganda. British Exchequer-advances had paid for the first Kenya railway, to Lake Victoria. The Colonial Government, though prepared to extend the system at its own expense, could not finance the continuation of the main line to Uganda, where the prospects for cotton-growing were already known to be splendid. The matter came before the first Labour cabinet soon after its accession to power. J. H. Thomas, the new Colonial Secretary, supported the measure on Visionary grounds: it would raise cotton production and help East Africa to develop.[19] However, he also noted that it would relieve British unemployment. Other Labour ministers were equally impressed; the unemployment committee endorsed the proposal, and the full Cabinet confirmed this recommendation.[20]

After returning to power late that year, Baldwin was urged by the Balfour Committee on industry and trade to aid transport development in East Africa. The basic proposal had come from the East Africa Commission, a trio of parliamentarians whom Amery had appointed to survey the area.[21] The Commission had recommended that the United Kingdom should guarantee up to £10 million in new loans, and should pay the interest for five years. The Balfour Committee explained to Baldwin that such aid would increase cotton production and raise purchasing power in East Africa, while generating new orders for British engineering firms.[22] Not surprisingly, Amery, now Colonial

[17] CO 532/222, TP 43, TP 13; CAB 24/158, CP 90(23), February 9, 1923; CP 93(23), February 12, 1923; CAB 24/161, CP 369(23); CAB 24/180, CP 260(26).
[18] CAB 23/53, July 7, 1926.
[19] CAB 24/165, CP 183(24).
[20] CAB 24/64, CP 83(24); CAB 23/47, February 8, 1924.
[21] Cmd. 2387. The Chairman was W. Ormsby-Gore. The report dealt with Northern Rhodesia, Nyasaland, Tanganyika, Uganda, and Kenya.
[22] PREMIER 1/75. Later published as Cmd. 2463.

Secretary, agreed, and Cunliffe-Lister, again President of the Board of Trade, took the same line:

> We should speed up, as much as possible, railway construction and other development in the Empire, particularly in Africa. I am convinced that nationally the most remunerative expenditure we can incur is in the development of markets which will be complementary and not competitive. Africa fulfils this condition in a peculiar degree, and is at the same time the great potential source of supply for raw cotton. Substantial loans for Crown colony development supplies a positive and convincing alternative to the persistent demand of the Socialist party for loans to Russia.[23]

The Cabinet agreed to proceed with the guaranteed loan, though it decided not to pay any of the interest. Also, the Colonial Office was asked to prepare proposals for railway construction and other development projects as part of unemployment-programming.[24]

In addition to the development that such assistance might permit, the African colonial administrations were urged throughout the twenties to develop their transport systems from their own resources as rapidly as their finances allowed.[25] Unless the British Exchequer was paying some of the current administrative expenses, a colonial administration could undertake such projects subject to Colonial Office approval but without Treasury scrutiny. So long as the Treasury was kept out of the picture, colonial administrators could make their reputations by successful development. Amery and the Colonial Office officials could work out their Visionary plans for overseas lending, British export of capital goods, and expansion of primary production. They could also spend on medical and agricultural research. Hence the universal desire to avoid the budgetary deficits which would expose the colonial governments to 'Treasury control'. Once a colony had begun to develop along the expected Visionary lines, its exports would rise, and so would its

---

[23] CAB 24/174, CP 366(25). See also CAB 24/274, CP 389(25), and for Amery's view CAB 24/175, CP 434(25).

[24] CAB 23/50, August 7, 1925; CAB 24/176, CP 129(26); Cmd. 2696, Cmd. 3848, Cmd. 3494. By 1929, £8,269,864 had been authorized for East Africa, even though Kenya had decided to use the open market without the guarantee. The statute also guaranteed £4·5 million of Palestinian borrowing for railways, harbours, and other development. Guarantees were needed for Palestine and Tanganyika because both were mandates, a status which until 1929 precluded trustees from purchasing their ordinary securities. Further guarantees were needed in the nineteen-thirties: on £750,000 for Tanganyika in 1931–32, see Cmd. 4032; and on £2 million for Palestine in 1933–34, see Cmd. 4576.

[25] For examples of the attitude to primary exports and transport development in West Africa, see Cmd. 1600, Cmd. 2744.

imports, generating an increase in government revenue both from customs duties and from local taxation. The proceeds could be used for further developmental spending, for interest on the past overseas loans, and for local amenity-spending on such things as native education.

All over British Africa, during the nineteen-twenties, railways and ports were improved in line with this developmental Vision. Further, with respect to cotton-growing, special efforts were being made.

The concern with Empire cotton production was not new. It had various roots—supply and exchange difficulties during the War, concern lest the price of cotton might rise excessively, fear that the American crop, on which Lancashire depended so heavily, might shrink because of the boll weevil, urbanization of the blacks, and soil erosion.[26] The Egyptian crop, which supplied Lancashire with the really fine fibre, had been declining for some time.

Accordingly, in 1920 the Cabinet was urged to use £1 million from its profits on the wartime cotton control scheme for cotton development. This subvention was turned over to a new body, the Empire Cotton Growing Corporation, which was set up on November 1, 1921. In 1922, the Corporation was given the statutory power to collect from British cotton spinners a levy of 6d. per hundred pounds of cotton. The Corporation would not grow cotton itself, but it would give guarantees, conduct research, and spread information.[27]

In Uganda, African peasants had been rapidly expanding their cotton output since before 1914. The Uganda Government had helped by distributing seed and technical advice. Further, in the Anglo-Egyptian Sudan there was already a large cotton-growing project—the Gezira

---

[26] For the views of the Dominions Royal Commission, see Cd. 8462(1917). In 1918, Lord Balfour of Burleigh's Committee on Commercial and Industrial Policy after the War urged that the Government should encourage cotton production, by means of guaranteed purchase prices and/or developmental assistance (Cd. 9035, 19, 48). In 1920, the Empire Cotton Growing Committee spoke of rising prices and 'evidence of a growing world cotton shortage' (Cmd. 523, 52–3). In 1923, the Director of the Empire Cotton Growing Association expressed his concern about boll weevils, black urbanization, and the increase in American consumption. He also worried about the exchange cost of American cotton, given the new war debts (CO 532/263 from Board of Trade, October 1923). See also CAB 24/40, CP 4336, November 30, 1922, where Lloyd-Graeme argues that 'the extension of cotton growing within the Empire is a matter of urgent necessity'.

[27] CAB 24/96, CP 497; CAB 23/23, December 23, 1920; CAB 23/32, December 19, 1922; CAB 24/140, CP 4336; for the measure's parliamentary reception see 156 HC Debs 5s 1922, cols. 1057–59. Introducing the measure, Lt. Col. Hurst explained that it would tend to reduce cotton prices, and would 'bring nearer to realization that long-cherished ideal of a self-sufficing Empire'. The actual initial Treasury subvention was £978,715.

irrigation scheme. Here the entire initiative had lain with the Government, which had undertaken surveys, rearranged land-tenure, prescribed the share-cropping terms on the newly-irrigated lands, financed the irrigation itself, and arranged with a syndicate for ploughing, seed-distribution and marketing.[28] The planning of Gezira began before 1914, when it was decided to irrigate 300,000 acres. The Gezira area was expected to produce as much cotton as the entire Egyptian delta.[29] As the Anglo-Egyptian Sudan was not a British possession, it could not borrow on the favourable terms which were available under the Colonial Stocks Acts. Accordingly, in 1913, the United Kingdom Government had guaranteed a loan of £3 million. In 1919 the guarantee was raised to £6 million. In the season 1921–22 the first of the new irrigated areas yielded a crop. In 1923, a further loan of £3·5 million was guaranteed so that the project could be finished by 1925. In the later twenties Gezira paid off handsomely, both in value and volume: from 1924 until 1927, the quantity of Sudanese cotton export rose from 8400 tons to 28,900 tons, and the value rose from 1·5 million Egyptian pounds to 3·19 million.[30]

Even in 1927, the Sudan still produced only 4 per cent of the cotton which Britain used. It is meaningless to relate other cotton schemes to cotton supplies, because we do not know how much cotton output would have risen in other areas even without special stimulus. Still, we can be sure that Gezira and the other special stimuli must have lowered the price of fine cotton, at least a little. Because the British economy was so large an exporter of cotton cloth, this price mattered a great deal, even though British cotton spinners paid the same price as everyone else. Higher raw-cotton prices meant higher prices for cotton piece goods, and therefore a smaller world sale—a specially serious matter for the British economy, because, compared with other economies, the cotton industry was so large relative to other industries.

In the same way, the other development projects must have lowered some other world primary product prices. However, Britain was in no sense a special beneficiary: all the industrialized countries benefited, because all could buy their imports of primary products at the same prices.[31] The Empire strategy of African economic development was as much in America's and Germany's interest as in Britain's.

The Visionaries did not want to apply the same medicine throughout the dependent Empire. The West Indies were thought to need help, but

---

[28] See Cmd. 2171 for details of the scheme and of the pre-existing tenurial system.
[29] Cmd. 523 (1920).
[30] Cmd. 259,267 (1920), Cmd. 3283 (1928–29).
[31] After deducting transport costs and import duties if any.

not large investments. Their sugar industries were kept alive only by the artificial stimulus of British imperial preferential duties, and they were not rich in the relevant natural resources. Much was hoped from Trinidad oil, but relatively little was realized. In the Far East, private enterprise could be left to deal with tin and with plantation agriculture, while for rubber the problem was not further development but a price-raising restriction of output which could restore the prosperity of the plantations and extract more dollars from the United States.[32]

Before the 1929 election, Amery tried to get Baldwin to accept a programme of Empire development as an election platform. Once again he urged this as an anti-unemployment policy. Baldwin, while wishing to avoid details, replied that he intended to refer in general terms to the importance of the multiplication of markets at home and abroad.[33] J. C. C. Davidson, the Chairman of the Party Organization, pressed Baldwin in identical terms.[34] Amery has recorded his frustration, blaming Baldwin's reticence partly on the evil influence of the Treasury and Winston Churchill and partly on Baldwin's own 'laziness and love of peace'.[35] Though Churchill had been of Amery's mind when Colonial Secretary, as Chancellor of the Exchequer he had resisted development spending at every turn.[36] In doing so he was highly traditional; Sir

[32] On the Stevenson Plan for rubber restriction, which lasted from 1922 to 1928, see Cmd. 1678(1922), and 187 HC Debs 5s 1924–25, 88–90, 104–6. On the relation between rubber restriction and the increasing of Britain's dollar receipts, see CAB 23/50, July 29, 1925. For comment, see: C. R. Whittlesey, 'The Stevenson Plan: Some Conclusions and Observations', *Journal of Political Economy*, 39: 506–25, August 1931; P. Lamartine Yates, *Commodity Control*, (London, 1943); P. T. Bauer, *The Rubber Industry*, (London, 1948); K. E. Knorr, *World Rubber and its Regulation* (Stanford, 1946).

[33] CAB 23/60, April 17, 1929.

[34] Quoted in K. Middlemas and J. Barnes, *Baldwin*, (London, 1969), 514.

[35] Amery, *My Political Life, II*, 356–7, 504–505. Until mid-1925, the Colonial Office looked after Dominion affairs.

[36] See CAB 24/129, CP 3415, and CAB 23/53, July 7, 1926. On Amery's impact, see the comments of Sir R. Furse, his recruiting officer for overseas colonial service: 'To my mind he [Amery] was unquestionably the most effective Secretary of State for the Colonies that I served under between 1910 and 1948 . . . His greatest handicap, and it was serious, was that, for reasons I do not know, he never quite commanded that influence in the Cabinet essential for carrying through all he wanted to do and which greatly needed doing in that vital time' (R. Furse, *Aucuparius*, London 1962, 145–6). Baldwin had certainly not meant to accede to Amery's policies merely by making him Colonial Secretary. In November 1924, Baldwin had explained his motives to Tom Jones as follows: 'I am sending Amery to the Colonial Office. He is a hard worker, keen on the Colonies and on Empire settlement. I am not sure that the Dominions have forgiven Winston the Chanak incident, and I do not want him to go to the Colonial Office' (T. Jones, *Whitehall Diary*, i. 302: diary entry for November 4, 1924).

Michael Hicks Beach had done the same to Joseph Chamberlain,[37] and Philip Snowden would shortly do it to J. H. Thomas. It was also true, however, that by 1929 the unemployment picture, though still serious, was much brighter than in 1922–23. The Government was experimenting with new solutions—derating to encourage business enterprise, small-scale tariff 'safeguarding' to protect threatened jobs, and 'industrial transference' to shift workers from declining trades and regions.

When Labour came back to power in 1929, one of its first acts was to set up an interdepartmental committee of officials to brood about unemployment. J. H. Thomas, the Lord Privy Seal and minister charged with unemployment policy, had been Colonial Secretary in 1924, and was soon to be both Dominions Secretary and Colonial Secretary once again. He approached Empire development with a truly Amery-like zeal, and was at one with his Conservative predecessor in linking unemployment and Empire investment. At the first meeting of the Unemployment Committee, he told the members that questions of colonial development and overseas migration would be considered by a separate Committee—thus underlining the relation between these two subjects and unemployment.[38] He told this separate Committee that

he attached great importance to stimulating development projects such as the production of cotton and other projects within the Empire and other direct ways of providing employment at home.[39]

From these discussions, from staff work during the Baldwin Government's dying months, and from Thomas's concerns, emerged the Colonial Development Act of 1929.[40] It provided small loans and grants to the dependent Empire, under carefully circumscribed conditions, so as to generate jobs in Britain.[41] Aid was to be disbursed by an Advisory

[37] See Robert Kubicek, 'Joseph Chamberlain, the Treasury, and Imperial Development, 1895–1903,' Canadian Historical Association, *Report of Annual Meeting*, 1965, 105–17.
[38] CAB 27/389, DU(29) 1st conclusions, June 11, 1929.
[39] CAB 27/382, ODM(29) 1st conclusions, June 13, 1929.
[40] See Doc. 12.
[41] The precise sum to be spent had been a matter for close discussion. Like all other expenditure programmes, Colonial development had to be fitted into Philip Snowden's budgetary rectitude. Further, there was doubt about the amount that could usefully be spent. The Colonial Office had prepared a list of projects, but many of them had not been costed, nor could their employment effect be traced. Thomas himself remarked that it would be foolish to ask Parliament to spend as much as £3 million until it could be shown that as much as £1 million could be laid out to good effect. See CAB 27/382, ODM(29) 4th conclusions, July 11, 1929.

Committee, which would annually request funds, up to a maximum of £1 million per year.

The Committee quickly made its rules known. It would not consider any economically unsound schemes, anything which was so immediately remunerative that the private sector should undertake it, or anything which colonial governments could or should readily finance on their own. Further, it insisted that 'save in exceptional circumstances all orders for imported material should be placed in the United Kingdom; and that the plant, machinery, materials, etc. be of British origin and manufacture'. By June 1930 it had committed itself to assist schemes costing £6·6 million, to which it would contribute £682,000 in grant and £1·1 million in loan over a period of years. In true Visionary fashion, it concentrated its aid on transport, health, and research. Indeed, many of the projects it aided, like the Zambesi Bridge to Nyasaland, had been in circulation for years, while others, such as research on pineapple canning in Malaya, represented no departure in principle. The Committee argued plausibly that education was not within its purview; schools were not economically productive, at least in the colonial context, and so local budgets should finance them.[42]

The Committee lingered on through the 1930s, a Visionary survival without macro-economic significance, until it was replaced under the much more ambitious Colonial Development and Welfare Act of 1940, a measure which falls outside the scope of this essay. It is easy to make fun of the Committee and its tiny outlays—only £3 million by March 31, 1935, and not much more during the entire decade. Certainly it is hard to see how anybody could grant much 'economically sound' aid to expand the production of primary products during a decade in which the prices of these products had collapsed, and in which everybody was trying to *restrict* output. The Colonial Development Act is significant almost entirely as a *symptom*. It shows how widely accepted were the Visionaries' ideas about the links between unemployment, the expansion of primary production, and the 'appropriate' management of capital-export.

III

Besides fostering the 'correct' movement of capital, the Visionaries of the twenties were keen to make some progress—as they might have said

---

[42] The Colonial Development Advisory Committee reported annually from 1929. Its first report is Cmd. 3540 (1929–30). For accounts of its early proceedings see Cmd. 3628, 3629 (1929–30). Its behaviour has been discussed *inter alia* by George C. Abbott, 'British Colonial Aid Policy during the 1930's', *Canadian Journal of History*, V (1970), 73–89.

—'on the preference front'. In a sense the United Kingdom remained a free-trade country until the Import Duties Act was passed in 1932. Nevertheless, there had always been some customs duties, imposed for revenue purposes and, where necessary, countervailed by excises on domestic production. It was on these 'old' duties, and on the protective 'McKenna' duties which had been imposed in 1915 to save shipping space and foreign exchange, that preferential concessions were introduced in 1919 and extended in 1925 and 1927. The 'key industries' and 'safeguarding' duties also included preferential arrangements.

The Finance Act of 1919 provided that Empire tea, cocoa, coffee, chicory, currants, certain dried and preserved fruits,[43] sugar, glucose, molasses, saccharin, motor spirit and tobacco should pay five-sixths of the full duty. Empire motor cars and parts (excluding tyres), musical instruments and their parts, records, clocks, watches and cinema films, all taxable at 33⅓ per cent under the second Finance Act of 1915, were to pay only two-thirds of the normal rate. Wines were to pay from 60 to 70 per cent of the full rate, depending on type.[44]

These concessions were of value to South Africa with respect to wine, to Australia with respect to wine, currants, dried fruits and sugar, to India with respect to tea and coffee, and to the West Indies, Mauritius, Australia and perhaps Fiji with respect to sugar. As British import exceeded Empire output under all these headings, it is reasonable to suppose that both outputs and prices would rise in the producer countries as a result of these concessions. That is, the Empire producers would get higher prices because the ruling price in the United Kingdom would continue to be the world wholesale price plus the duty on *foreign* goods. Given the level of British government spending, the preferential concessions necessarily involved an increase in some other British tax. Thus the Imperial preferences implied a transfer of resources from British residents to Empire producers. Though spasmodically recognized by free traders,[45] by Visionaries this fact was never admitted—and was perhaps never understood.

Behind the 1919 Finance Act lay three years of discussion. Though in a sense requested by the Dominions, these concessions were not the result of a bargain. Britain received no concessions in return. The Dominions, admittedly, had charged lower rates on British goods for many years—in Canada, since 1897. But Dominion rates were in no

---

[43] The fruits in question had been defined in the 1915 Finance Act no. 2 as: 'figs and fig cakes, plums (commonly called French plums or prunelloes), prunes, all other dried and preserved plums, and raisins'. Finance Act, no. 2 1915, 5–6 Geo V, ch. 89.

[44] Finance Act, 1919, 9–10 Geo V, ch. 32.

[45] For example by Lord Arnold in Doc. 11.

sense dependent upon British rates, nor were they adjusted in response to Britain's 1919 adjustments. Indeed, the main beneficiaries of the Finance Act were the sugar-raising West Indies, India, which still gave no preferential concessions to British goods, South Africa, which never gave many concessions, and Australia, which continued to give less than Canada or New Zealand—the two Dominions that gained nothing from the Finance Act. It is ironical that Canada invented the modern preferential system, and that W. F. Massey, the Prime Minister of New Zealand, made the motion which led directly to the 1919 Act.[46]

The unilateral concession of preferential rates was consistent with a principle which continued to dominate official British thinking about the tariff system until after the Imperial Conference of 1930. No one wanted to make intra-imperial tariffs a matter for bargaining. In part, the officials feared, bargaining would bring ill-feeling. Further, bargaining could not succeed, because the tariff systems of the Empire were so diverse. Finally, to some Empire politicians—especially to Canada's W. L. M. King[47]—bargaining implied interference.[48] If Canada were to

[46] Massey (1856–1925) was prime minister of New Zealand from 1912 to 1925. In 1915–19 he headed a coalition National Government, while at other times he headed a Reform ministry. He represented New Zealand at the Imperial War Cabinets and Conferences, 1921 and 1923.

[47] King (1874–1949) began as an economist (Ph.D. Harvard 1909), became a politician, succeeded Laurier as leader of the Canadian Liberal Party, and ruled as Prime Minister from 1921 to mid-1926, late 1926 to mid-1930, and 1935 to 1948. He represented Canada at the Imperial Conferences of 1923, 1926 and 1937, and at the Imperial Economic Conference of 1923.

[48] At the 1923 Imperial Economic Conference, and before it, King made his feelings clear. In July, Amery had suggested that the United Kingdom might grant concessions which 'might justify a considerable extension of preferences by the Dominions'. King responded that Canada granted preferences because of what she 'conceived to be her own best interests', and said that he had no desire to make the preferences a matter for bargaining. (Public Archives of Canada, W. L. M. King Papers, 70169–70: letter, L. S. Amery to W. L. M. King, July 4, 1923, and 70175–6, Letter, W. L. M. King to L. S. Amery, July 17, 1923.) At the Conference, O. D. Skelton, King's advisor, urged King to abstain from joining in the Australian demand for preferences, and drafted a letter to Lloyd-Graeme which King forwarded not only to the President of the Board of Trade but also to Neville Chamberlain. The letter explained that Canada did not make its preferences to the United Kingdom conditional on British reciprocity, but that, if the United Kingdom should 'make far-reaching changes in its fiscal policy, Canada would naturally expect that, in the establishment of a tariff, full consideration would be given, through preferential duties, to the interests of Canada's producers and to the substantial preferences which Canada accords to British goods'. He went on to state the goods on which Canada would like preferential concessions: wheat, barley, flour, fresh fruits especially apples, cheese, butter, eggs, bacon and ham, canned vegetables, canned salmon, forest products, ferrous and non-ferrous metals, iron, steel, agricultural implements, electrical

ask for tariff concessions from Britain, did that not mean that the reverse could happen ? And would that not endanger Canada's fiscal autonomy ? Nonsensical though this final point now sounds, in the twenties the Dominions' politicians might plausibly have worried about it, though they were less than consistent in advocating it.[49] Britain began to move toward some sort of preferential arrangement early in 1917. The summer before, a Reconstruction Committee had been set up under Lord Balfour of Burleigh. It was subjected to vigorous lobbying by Hewins, and, presumably, by other Tariff Reformers. Expiring with the Asquith government, it was resuscitated under Lloyd George, who was far from committed to Tariff Reform and Imperial Preference. Bonar Law, too, though later seen by Lord Beaverbrook as the white hope of the Empire Free Traders, was equivocal and evasive.[50]

---

apparatus, woodworking machinery, rubber goods, and 'other manufacturing industries'. To show how good Canadian apples were, he sent some to Neville Chamberlain. And later, when he suspected that the United Kingdom might subsidize shipping to the Antipodes, he wrote, 'I sincerely hope that the like would be done for Canada'. King Papers, 803, 377–8: O. D. Skelton to W. L. M King, October 21, 1923; 75, 617–22: letter, W. L. M. King to Sir Philip Lloyd-Graeme, October 23, 1923; King to N. Chamberlain, October 23, 1923; 71, 843: N. Chamberlain to W. L. M. King, October 29, 1923. See also King Papers File 333, 43454 ff, for a background memorandum by Skelton.

[49] The last footnote may seem to contain an inconsistency, though King would have argued that he asked for these things only because *he* was asked to say what Canada might want. More serious are the manœuvres of his High Commissioner, in London, P. C. Larkin (1856–1930)—a tea magnate and confidante of King, whom he subsidized. He supported King's view that tariff bargaining was inexpedient. But he fought to get a British duty on motor lorries so that Canada might enjoy a preferential market. And when Philip Snowden proposed to abolish the McKenna duties on passenger cars, Larkin wrote, 'I would like you to feel assured that I am not sparing any effort diplomatically to have at least the duty on motor cars left and thus continuing to benefit from the preference. The difficulty is that if the Government do not remove these duties the Liberals will vote against them and so out of office they will go'. Later, Larkin wrote again,'I have done everything I feel possible to prevent these duties being removed for not only am I strongly impressed myself as to the injury it might do our large export motor trade but I have had several people in the business waiting on me with whom I have talked it over, but I think the case is perfectly hopeless'. King is known to have been nervous about these representations. But the British civil servants must have concluded simply that the Canadian Prime Minister was a hypocrite. See King Papers; letters, Larkin to King, June 29, 1923, March 5, 1923, May 2, 1924, June 14, 1924.

[50] See M. Beloff, *Imperial Sunset*, (London, 1969), i. 225–6; on Lloyd George and Bonar Law as seen by Beaverbrook, *The Decline and Fall of Lloyd George*, (London, 1963), 16, 29, 212–215, 226–230. Hewins' view at the time is reproduced from his diary in W. A. S. Hewins, *Apologia of an Imperialist*, (London, 1929), ii. 106, 111–12, and on Lloyd George Ibid., ii. 130–132.

In mid-January, Lord Balfour circulated a memorandum on the preference question which infuriated Hewins; he, Balfour of Burleigh, and two others were appointed to draft a preference resolution which was prepared on January 22, 1917, accepted by the full Committee, and passed to the Prime Minister on February 2nd. The resolution said:

We have arrived at the conclusions indicated chiefly on the ground that although to some of us any measures which may act in restraint of trade are distasteful, we think it necessary that for the sake of the Empire a serious effort should now be made to the declared wishes of the Dominions and Colonies . . . and that any abstract opinions which we may hold should not, under the circumstances in which we are placed and with the experience gained during the war, stand in the way of any measures which are seen to be important, having regard to the general interests of the Empire. . . . The Dominions have not asked, and we do not understand them to ask, that duties should be imposed by the United Kingdom for the sake of granting a preference to their products. But we feel that . . . it will be necessary to take into early consideration . . . the desirability of establishing a wider range of Customs duties than exists at present. . . . We do not overlook the practical difficulties involved, but we desire to emphasise the fact that for the purpose of recovering trade lost during the war, of securing new markets, and of consolidating the resources of the British Empire, the development throughout the Empire of a system of mutual tariff preferences is a subject which cannot, in our opinion, any longer be neglected.[51]

Meanwhile, the Dominions had been invited to attend an Imperial War Conference and Cabinet. Preliminary agenda were sent out on January 21st. 'Not intended to be exhaustive', they mentioned 'policy after the war as regards commerce and industries'.[52] Shortly, thereafter, Long told Hewins that the agenda were so constructed as to include a discussion of preference, and that the Dominion Prime Ministers understood this.[53] The Colonial Office officials wanted to know what the Cabinet thought of Balfour's report before informing the Dominions, who, they believed, could be counted on to raise the matter in any event. By February 8th, they were noting, 'It appears to be no longer a secret

---

[51] CAB 24/6, GT 58, February, 2, 1917. Published as Cd. 8482. On the devising of the text and its passage through the Reconstruction Committee, see Hewins, *Apologia*, ii. 106, 115.

[52] CO 886/7, p. 160: telegram, Walter Long to Dominion Governments, January 21, 1917.

[53] Hewins, *Apologia*, ii. 109. The unpublished Hewins diaries (University of Sheffield) cast no new light upon the events of 1916–17.

that Lord Balfour of Burleigh's Committee have passed resolutions in favour of Preference'.[54] And on February 15th, New Zealand cabled that among other subjects 'which have been suggested for discussion', are 'reciprocal preferential trade relations'.[55] Balfour of Burleigh's report of February 2nd was eventually published, and transmitted to the Dominions on March 2, 1917.

Meanwhile, however, the British War Cabinet was getting cold feet. Talking to Lloyd George on April 10th, Hewins got the impression that the Prime Minister was most reluctant to move on the question of preferences. The Prime Minister did agree that if the Imperial War Cabinet should endorse the idea of preferences the British Government would set up machinery to introduce them. But his tone was 'very hesitating and virtually negative', and he emphasized that food taxes must not be suggested. He also talked of preferences 'by tariffs or some other means'.[56]

The Imperial War Cabinet began to sit on March 20th. Though in the end its meetings were carefully organized by Sir Maurice Hankey, at first Lloyd George had summoned the Empire Prime Ministers before he had any idea of what he would discuss with them.[57] Bonar Law, also, had not been anxious to face the gathering. Given both men's evasiveness with respect to the preference question, they must have felt some embarrassment when, on April 24th, Prime Minister Massey of New Zealand proposed the following resolution:

That the time has arrived when all possible encouragement should be given to the development of Imperial resources, and (consistent with the resolutions of the Paris Conference[58]) especially to making the Empire independent of other countries for the food supplies of its population and raw materials for its manufactures. With these objects in view, this Conference expresses itself in favour of:

---

[54] CO 532/104, from miscellaneous offices, February 8, 1917, various minutes.
[55] CO 886/7; telegram, New Zealand Government to Colonial Office, February 15, 1917.
[56] Hewins, *Apologia*, ii. 132. Walter Long, the Colonial Secretary (1916–18), was a Tariff Reformer, and he consulted regularly with Hewins. Long was not a member of the War Cabinet, though he did sit on the Imperial War Cabinet.
[57] Stephen Roskill, *Hankey, Man of Secrets* (London, 1970) i. 348, quoting Hankey's diary for December 26, 1916.
[58] For the Paris resolutions of June 1916 see Cd. 8271. In effect they committed the Allies to take temporary and permanent steps to make themselves independent of enemy countries with respect to raw materials, essential manufactures, and financial, commercial, and maritime organization. They also spoke of cheapening inter-Ally transport, post, telegraph, and other communications.

(1) A system by which each country of the Empire will give Preferences through its Customs to the goods produced or manufactured in any other British country; and

(2) An arrangement by which, in the case of intending Emigrants from the United Kingdom, inducements will be offered to such migrants to settle in countries under the British flag.[59]

The Imperial War Cabinet discussed this motion at two sessions. The proceedings[60] show how uncertain the United Kingdom members were, and how eager the New Zealanders and Canadians appeared. If Australian representatives had been present, they would certainly have added their voices.[61] The final resolution, modified in details but not in essentials, was passed to the Imperial War Conference, where it was quickly passed—and soon published.[62]

On August 14th, Long told the House of Commons that he would chair a Cabinet Committee which would study the best ways of giving effect to the 1917 resolutions. Hewins was asked to help in its work, but at first he refused and threatened to mobilize party forces to turn the Government out. Attaching enormous importance to the Paris resolutions and to the War Conference results, he seems to have believed that because the United Kingdom Government had agreed to them, it was pledged to carry them out—regardless of the political problems they posed, or of the war conditions which had led people to agree to them. On September 6th Bonar Law offered him the colonial under-secretaryship, presumably to involve him in the planning of a preferential system. He thus became a member of Long's Committee—soon to be known as the Committee on Trade Relations of the United Kingdom within the Empire.[63] Deciding to ignore migration, on which another body was brooding, Long's Committee set up a sub-committee under Hewins' chairmanship to consider preferences on articles already dutiable. It also ruled out the possibility of free entry for Empire goods, believing that the Exchequer could not bear the cost. Nevertheless it was able to recommend a generous scale of preferential concessions.[64]

Treasury officials continued to oppose the grant of Imperial Preference, correctly pointing out that it gave 'a partial and irregular advantage to the producing members of the British Empire at the

[59] CAB 23/40, Imperial War Cabinet 11, April 24, 1917.
[60] See Doc. 1.
[61] Prime Minister Hughes had been kept in Australia by political crises.
[62] In Cd. 8566.
[63] Hewins, *Apologia*, ii. 161–4; CO 532/99, from Colonial Office, December 12, 1917.
[64] See Doc. 2.

expense of the consuming member'.[65] The Hewins–Long concessions would have cost Britain 18 per cent of her 1912–13 customs revenue. Unless other taxes could be raised by £6·4 million, government spending would have to fall *pari passu*. But the Dominions were pressing for a discussion of imperial preferences at the coming Imperial War Cabinet and Conference.[66] When the report of his Committee came before the War Cabinet on July 11, 1918, Long urged his colleagues to grant the recommended preferences. He reminded the other ministers that there was no question of imposing new food taxes. But the 'overseas Dominions were wondering whether the United Kingdom might have changed the policy of Imperial Preference agreed to in 1917'.[67] On July 16th and 17th, the War Cabinet did approve the committee's proposals, but nothing was to be done until after the War.[68] Shortly afterward, Bonar Law told the House of Commons that for the postwar period the Imperial Government had adopted the principle of Imperial Preference—'and nothing more'.[69] Hence the public and the Dominions did not know exactly what the form or extent of the preferences might be.

Amery has explained that, after a Parliamentary debate on the preference policy in March 1919, he attended a Treasury conference at which the amount of the rebate was discussed. Hewins was now out of office and out of Parliament. Long had gone to the Admiralty. Though Amery maintained the pressure for the 33⅓ per cent margin which their committee had recommended, he was obliged to admit that only one-sixth could be afforded. He did however convince Austen Chamberlain to grant the one-third margin on the McKenna Duties. He writes, 'Austen laughed at my pertinacity, but gave way as no appreciable loss of revenue was involved—I am not sure that he knew that Canada actually produced motor cars.'[70]

On April 16th the War Cabinet approved the preferential proposals, and Austen Chamberlain announced them to the House on April 30th, when he presented his budget.[71] He estimated that the preferential concessions would cost the Exchequer £3 million if there was no expansion in the import of Empire products. Amery, however, was hoping for exactly this:

[65] CO 532/124, from Treasury, May 1, 1918.
[66] See the Dominions' telegrams in CO 886/7 which are responses to the Colonial Office's agenda-telegram of February 27, 1918.
[67] CAB 23/7, July 11, 1918. Long's arguments are in CAB 24/57, GT 5057. The Committee report is in CAB 24/57, GT 4903.
[68] CAB 23/7, July 16, 17, 18, 1918.
[69] 109 HC Deb 5s 1918, 39, 614–15.
[70] Amery, *My Political Life*, ii. 186.
[71] CAB 23/10, April 16, 1919; 115 HC Deb 5s 1919, 194–99.

All through I think the note to emphasise from our point of view is that the benefit lies, in most cases, not in the financial value of the preference on the existing import from Empire sources, but in the total possibilities, i.e. the measure is not the present United Kingdom consumption of a particular article from the Empire, but its total consumption from all sources. That is the field which the Imperial producer is to be encouraged to conquer.[72]

Of course, this was exactly what the Treasury feared.

Amery's remarks seem overblown in view of the narrow range of goods to which the 1919 concessions applied. But he still hoped for an extension of the system along Tariff Reform lines. Lloyd George, however, was proving stubborn. On August 8th, he explained that the 'Dominion Premiers, during their recent visits, had not evinced any special keenness with respect to Imperial Preference, but they were all very anxious that the commodities of their countries could be brought to our markets without the cost being increased to such an extent as would render them subject to close competition vis-à-vis the USA.'[73] He then returned to his earlier prescription: cheaper and improved shipping.

Though the British Government showed little interest in extending the system, Ministers faced continuing demands for this—not only from the domestic lobby of Tariff Reformers, but from Australia, whose post-war development and resettlement schemes made sense only if the British Government would grant such concessions. The Australians proposed to settle ex-soldiers and new migrants on irrigated lands in the Murray Valley. There they would raise dried fruit, canning fruit, and grapes for wine-growing. The result would be 'closer settlement', an Australian ideal. But the market would be in Britain, and the settlers could neither enjoy a 'white man's standard of living', nor repay the Australian governments for their development outlays, unless preferences were granted. Hence the Australian Prime Minister, W. M. Hughes, a member of the British War Cabinet in 1918, had worked hard to induce the British Government to give more preferences.[74] In autumn 1921, the Australian Dried Fruit Association, faced with an exportable 'surplus', asked its Government to try to get a wider British

[72] CO 532/136, April 29, 1919: letter, Amery to Austen Chamberlain, covering a Colonial Office Memorandum on the effect of preference which had grown out of a series of conferences with the affected trades.

[73] CAB 23/15, August 8, 1919.

[74] See National Library of Australia, Pearce Papers, MS 213, Ser. 12: minutes of meeting of Nationalist Party (Parliamentary), October 6, 1921. Hughes (1864-1952) was Prime Minister from 1915 to 1923. Originally a Labourite, he formed and led a Nationalist coalition during the War. In the process he split the Labour party, most of which stayed out of the Nationalist Party. Hughes

preference. Hughes agreed that this was very important,[75] and on January 28, 1922, he cabled the Colonial Office to request a monstrously increased tax on foreign dried fruits. Hughes wanted the British to impose a duty of $1\frac{1}{2}d$. per pound on foreign currants, and $2d$. per pound on raisins and all other dried fruits. Justifying his request, he spoke of Australia's unlimited powers to produce dried fruit, and the importance of the industry with respect to 'the settlement of British ex-soldiers [and] of effective migration'.[76] The Colonial Office staff was not impressed. It noted that as the present duty on currants was only $2s$. per hundredweight, and on other dried fruits only $10s$. $6d$. per hundredweight, while dried apricots and peaches paid no duty, Hughes was asking an increase in the preferential margin from $1s$. $8d$. and $1s$. $9d$. per hundredweight to $14s$. $1d$. and $18s$. $8d$.[77] The Board of Trade also opposed the request, saying that because less than 10 per cent of British dried fruit came from Australia, the suggestion would imply a very large increase in food duties. The Treasury was equally hostile; Otto Niemeyer wrote that Parliament would never accept such a proposal, and that it would be many years before emigrants could hope to augment the Australian fruit supply sufficiently to eliminate the price-raising effect of the higher tariff on foreign fruit. He also feared that if Britain granted so large a percentage margin of preference in this one case, other Empire Governments would make similar demands.[78] Hence on March 18th Geoffrey Whiskard wrote a memorandum for Churchill, now Colonial Secretary, suggesting:

> unless you are prepared to take the matter of dried fruits preference to the Cabinet, I should recommend a reply to the effect that . . . the proposal is not practicable for the reasons given.[79]

Such a reply was cabled on March 24th.

---

attended the Imperial War Cabinet in 1918, and stayed on as a member of the British War Cabinet. He also attended the Imperial Conference of 1921. In the nineteen-thirties he held office in the United Australia government of J. A. Lyons.

[75] Conference of Commonwealth and State Ministers, Melbourne, October–November 1921: *Report*.

[76] CO 118/218: telegram, Prime Minister of Australia to Colonial Office, January 28, 1922.

[77] Ibid., minutes on Hughes' cable.

[78] CO 418/225 containing CO 11120/22 and CO 11659/22. Niemeyer's letter is dated March 10, 1922.

[79] Ibid. Whiskard was a senior civil servant first in the Colonial Office and then in the Dominions Office. In the mid-thirties he was High Commissioner in Australia.

In the Coalition and Conservative governments of 1922–24, the Colonial Secretaries were free-traders—first Churchill and then the Duke of Devonshire. After Lloyd George's fall, Bonar Law pledged his Party to make no change in the fiscal system without another election. The anti-preferential forces were strong. Still, in 1923 Lloyd-Graeme was President of the Board of Trade, and Amery was at the Admiralty. This balance of forces helps to explain the confusion with respect to the preparations for the 1923 Imperial Economic Conference, and it has much to do with Amery's extraordinary pre-conference lobbying.

When the Dominions first received draft agenda on November 29, 1922, there was no mention of tariffs or preferences. But the agenda-drafting committee had not meant to exclude them.[80] And the Viceroy of India was told that some governments would doubtless bring up these subjects.

Amery was working vigorously to ensure exactly this. Late in 1922, he wrote to the Prime Minister of Canada: 'There will still be room at the forthcoming Conference to consider possible extensions in detail of Empire preference and there may be particular things in which Canada is specially interested where we might be able to meet her, without creating serious parliamentary difficulties.'[81] In June 1923, he asked the Canadian High Commissioner, 'Why don't you ask for a preference on your flour and other manufactured articles?'[82]

The Australians, meanwhile, had seized the opportunity to raise the question of preferences once more. We do not know if Amery prompted Prime Minister Hughes, but we have every reason to believe that the Australian leader would have needed no prompting. On February 2nd he cabled: 'If you want us to buy more British goods there is only one way in which it can be done—Britain must buy more Australian products ... what is really wanted is action by Britain.' On February 24th, his successor repeated the demand: 'Commonwealth's position such that it will have to press some further preferences in return for substantial preference granted British goods.'[83] But Prime

---

[80] CAB 24/159, CP 158(23); CO 532/214, November 25, 1922. The telegram was prepared on a week's notice by Devonshire, Amery, Lloyd-Graeme, and officials.

[81] King Papers: Letter, Amery to W. L. M. King, December 27, 1922.

[82] King Papers: letter P. C. Larkin to W. L. M. King, June 29, 1923. Larkin remarks, 'I am quite sure that other members of the Cabinet do not see eye to eye with him ... it might be, therefore, that Amery wants to use you to force the Government's hands ...'.

[83] CAB 24/159, CP 158(23): telegrams, Prime Ministers of Australia to Colonial Office, February 2, and February 24, 1923.

Minister Bruce[84] received a dusty answer from the United Kingdom:

> I announced before the election that this Parliament would not make any fundamental changes in the fiscal system of this Country ... hence when discussing any proposals put forward in regard to preference our attitude would necessarily be governed by this pledge. This will not however prevent you from raising the subject but I am sure you will agree that a broad policy of economic cooperation such as we hope to realise must include much that is not fiscal. ...[85]

Bruce responded:

> These pledges would not debar you from assenting to some of proposals my government would submit. They would not involve any fundamental change in your fiscal system or in your maximum tariff rate. For example, where preference at present exists in favour of the Dominions, such preference could be increased ...[86]

The Australian pressure ensured Imperial Preferences a place on the final Conference agenda.[87] It also led the Board of Trade officials to consider the possibilities for some extensions of the preferential system. They recommended free entry for Empire dried fruits, a higher preference on Empire wine, and an increase in the preference on canned fruits. They also suggested that the preferential concessions could be stabilized for ten years, though they thought that Bonar Law's pledge, and the cables to Australia, precluded the imposition of any new taxes for the sake of giving preference. 'If any proposal for new duties can be entertained, there is a good deal to be said for a duty on foreign canned fish', and perhaps, but much more controversially, on apples. Canada would benefit from both, and South Africa from the former.[88]

This memorandum provoked a rejoinder from Amery. In June, he urged Lloyd-Graeme to suggest a comprehensive scheme with a 50 per

[84] S. M. Bruce (1883–1967) succeeded Hughes on February 9, 1923. He headed a coalition of Nationalist and Country party members until 1929. In the thirties he was Australian resident minister in London, and High Commissioner, 1932–45. He represented Australia at the Imperial and Economic Conferences of 1923, 1926 and 1932.

[85] Commonwealth Archives Office, CP 103/3, vol. 2: telegram, Prime Minister of the United Kingdom to Prime Minister of Australia, February 28, 1923.

[86] CO 532/231, February 2, 1923: telegram, Governor General of Australia to Colonial Office, March 5, 1923.

[87] As cabled to the Dominions on March 14, 1923. See King Papers, 79523–4: telegram, Colonial Secretary to Canadian Government, March 14, 1923.

[88] CO 532/222, from Board of Trade, January 4, 1923 et seq: undated memorandum by Board of Trade, clearly prepared after February 28, 1923.

cent preference all round. He expected and hoped that the coming Conference would produce 'A Treaty or Agreement'. *Inter alia* he urged that the preference on sugar should be doubled at once. Sir Gilbert Grindle, a senior official, minuted: 'I agree. It is the form of preference which is most likely to attain its objects. But it was impossible to overcome the obstructive tactics of the Treasury on this question of preference.'[89]

Early in August, the Cabinet considered the offers it might make to the Dominions. As Lloyd-Graeme has since explained, the Government's objective was to 'develop Imperial resources by an extension of preferences and by financial cooperation between different parts of the Empire and the mother country; to increase the opportunities of Empire settlement. . . . All these matters were interdependent. . . .'[90] But in fact the Cabinet was not prepared to offer very much. It felt constrained by Bonar Law's pledge, and by the effect of preferences on customs revenues. It also worried about new taxes on the food of the Lower Orders. Hence, it agreed, the United Kingdom ministers could propose a new duty of 5s. per hundredweight on foreign preserved apples, pears, pineapples, peaches, apricots and nectarines. They could, if requested by the Dominions, offer a new duty of 10s. per hundredweight on foreign canned salmon, lobster and crayfish. They could offer to stabilize the existing sugar-preference for ten years. And they could offer to raise the preference on all non-Indian Empire-grown tobacco from one-sixth to one-quarter of the normal duty. Up to stated limits, they could acquiesce in Dominion pressure with respect to dried fruits, hops and 'luxury' fruits. *But* they should refuse to consider any change with respect to fruit pulp, wines and spirits, raw apples, tin-plate, or containers.[91] These were the concessions recommended by the Cabinet's Documents Committee. They were much less generous than those which Amery demanded—and somewhat smaller than the Board of Trade had suggested in a memorandum. Further, they were to fit within an overall control: any new food duties should be so balanced by reductions elsewhere as not to increase food taxes in the aggregate.

The course of the Conference cannot be traced here. At first the Australians expressed regret at the smallness of the British offers. Then Chamberlain made a crucial concession: the British proposals, he said, were not the last word, and the United Kingdom would consider any

---

[89] CO 532/261, from Board of Trade, June 20, 1923, covering letter, L. S. Amery to Sir Philip Lloyd-Graeme.

[90] Lord Swinton, *I Remember*, 31.

[91] CAB 23/46, August 2, 1923; CAB 24/161; CP 360(23), August 1923; CO 532/261, from Board of Trade, June 27, 1923.

suggestions from the Dominions.[92] The Dominion suggestions rapidly became demands, and the British Cabinet accepted some though not all.[93] In the end, it had agreed to new duties on foreign apples, canned fish, canned and dried fruit, and fruit juices, increased preferential concessions on such articles as tobacco, wines and dried fruits, and the stabilization of the sugar preferential margin.

Meanwhile, Stanley Baldwin decided, for reasons that remain obscure, to call an election, hoping to obtain a general mandate for protection.[94] This was clearly needed if any really significant preferences could ever be granted the Dominions. And Baldwin explicitly cast his proposal in the context of Empire development. But his party lost the election. And the new Labour Government was unwilling to introduce the new food taxes, or grant the increased preferences, which Baldwin had promised in 1923. Indeed, it abolished the McKenna Duties, and the preferences that went with them.[95]

As the 1923 election seemed to have been fought and lost on the issue of food taxes, in the 1924 campaign Baldwin pledged himself to impose no such taxes, and to abstain from any major change in the fiscal system. In the euphoria of late 1923 he had asked Lord Milner to form a Tariff

---

[92] CAB 32/26: Stenograpic Notes from Imperial Conference, 1923: 5th meeting.

[93] CAB 23/46, October 29, 1923. For some Australian demands, see CO 532/263, from Board of Trade, November 3, 1923, covering a memorandum from the Australian delegation.

[94] For discussion of the background to this decision, see Middlemas and Barnes, *Baldwin*, Chapter 10. They suggest that Baldwin was eager for the sort of development which actually occurred at the Conference. If so, his views must have changed and developed rapidly during the summer of 1923. In May, he had told Austen Chamberlain that he had appointed McKenna to the Chancellorship without discovering or knowing McKenna's views on preferences or safeguarding (University of Birmingham, Austen Chamberlain Papers, AC 35/2/11b: memorandum of a conversation with Stanley Baldwin, on or just before May 27, 1923). On June 25th, at Hewins' request, Baldwin talked with the eminent Tariff Reformer, who had been excluded from all preparations: at S. B. Bruce's request, Hewins was trying to mobilize support for an advance on the preference front, but his Empire Development Union was underfinanced, and politicians were wary of him. Baldwin told Hewins that he had not yet thought of any policy for the coming Conference, and asked Hewins for a memorandum on the whole field of the Conference. Hewins prepared such a document, but did not send it to Baldwin until the Conference was about to meet, and did not see Baldwin again until October 4th, when Baldwin told Hewins that he 'was prepared to go all the way on preference'. Hewins' diary-entries strongly suggest that Baldwin made his own decision, and then began, after October 22nd, to consult Hewins about details. See University of Sheffield, Hewins Papers, diary entries for June 5, July 19, October 12, 18 and 22, 1923.

[95] For the Labour attitude to preferences, see Doc. 11.

Advisory Committee, and to draft a scheme for general protection.[96] Yet, on returning to power he was unwilling to act on this or any other such proposals. To Amery's fury, he installed a free-trader, Churchill, as Chancellor of the Exchequer. And his Government resisted efforts to expand the preferential system.

In the 1925 Finance Act, the Baldwin Government did make those adjustments from the 1923 package which did not involve new taxation. Empire currants and dried fruits were to come in without duty. Heavier preferential concessions were granted on wines, tobacco and sugar. The sugar preferences were guaranteed for ten years. And the McKenna Duties and preferences were restored on the 1919 basis. In the 1926 Finance Act, all preferential concessions were guaranteed for ten years, and motor trucks were brought within the protective and preferential net of the McKenna Duties. The next year the same was done for motor tyres, and the wine duties were rearranged to give more preference. But in 1929 the tea duty was repealed—and the tea preference went with it. It was re-imposed, on a preferential basis, only in 1932,[97] when special concessions were also granted to Colonial but not Dominion sugar.

Besides the small concessions of the 1925, 1926 and 1927 Finance Acts, Baldwin tried to honour the pledge of 1923 by setting up the Imperial Economic Committee and the Empire Marketing Board. The former had been proposed at the 1923 Conference, but was strongly opposed by Canada, whose Government congenitally disliked any attempt to create permanent imperial machinery. The first MacDonald Government considered the possibility of a committee too; after deciding that it did not want one, it consulted the Canadians, but nothing was done until early 1925, when, after complex negotiations with Canada, the Baldwin Government decided to set up an *ad hoc* body 'to consider the possibility of improving the methods of preparing for market and marketing within the United Kingdom the food products of the overseas parts of the Empire, with a view to increasing the consumption of such products in the United Kingdom, and to promote the interests both of producers and consumers'. The Committee was also authorized to suggest ways by which the United Kingdom might spend £1 million per year on Empire marketing projects. This was roughly the

---

[96] For the report, see Doc. 10.

[97] Finance Acts, 1925 (15–16 Geo V, 1925, ch. 36), 1926 (16–17 Geo V, ch. 22), 1927 (17–18 Geo V, ch. 10), 1929 (19–20 Geo V, ch. 21), 1932 (22–23, Geo V, 1931–32, ch. 25). The 1932 act imposed a duty of 4*d*. per lb. on foreign tea, and 2*d*. per lb. on Empire tea. It was a revenue-restoring measure which the Depression was thought to require.

value of the preferences which Baldwin had promised in 1923, but which he did not now feel able to grant.[98]

On July 30, 1925, the Imperial Economic Committee suggested that the £1 million should be turned over to a Board, which could spend freely on research, and on the promotion of Empire goods, thus creating a 'non-tariff preference'. Amery strongly favoured this idea, but Churchill opposed it just as strongly. The result was deadlock until February 1926, when the Cabinet, after referring the matter to a cabinet committee and to a group of officials, decided that 'in view of the paramount importance of fulfilling the pledges given to the Dominions it was necessary to make provision in the Estimates for some substantial expenditure in connection with the Empire marketing scheme'.[99] The exact amount, after negotiation between Churchill and Amery, was later set at £500,000 for 1926 and £1,000,000 for 1927, as the Cabinet committee had suggested.[100]

In fact the Empire Marketing Board never received or spent anything like one million pounds a year. Its publicity campaigns were widely noticed, and its research-grants may have done something to improve the production and transport of Empire foodstuffs. But the Canadians continued to dislike it. Further, after 1932 the United Kingdom ministers became disenchanted. Why should the Exchequer provide funds in lieu of preferences, after the preferences had in fact been granted? In 1933, the inter-governmental *ad hoc* Committee on Economic Consultation and Cooperation suggested the Board be wound up. It vanished on September 30, 1933, though some of its functions were transferred to the Imperial Economic Committee—a

---

[98] For the negotiations with Canada, see CO 884/11. For the decision to make a grant for Empire marketing in lieu of the preferences, see CAB 23/49, December 17, 1924. For the confusion and unease which this proposal occasioned in the Canadian Government, see King Papers, letters, Larkin to King and King to Larkin, December 18 and 26, 1924. The decision to refer the spending of the grant to the Imperial Economic Committee was taken on or shortly before December 13, 1924. The Colonial Office officials had been strongly opposed to the 1923 proposals for a permanent committee. Sir Edward Harding had described it as 'a convenient waste basket for schemes of no particular interest' (CO 532/262, from Board of Trade, July 10, 1923: letter, Sir E. Harding to J. Llewellyn Smith, July 17, 1923). For the Labour decision to have no Committee, see CAB 23/47, February 18, 1924. For the beginning of the Imperial Economic Committee's work, see Cmd. 2493 (1925).

[99] CAB 23/52, February 11, 1926.

[100] The Australians, when they learned of the amounts, accused the United Kingdom of breaking faith. Amery worried about the Australian attitude at the forthcoming 1926 Imperial Conference, but he was unable to extract more from his colleagues. See CAB 24/179, CP 112(26), March 15, 1926. For the Cabinet committee, see CAB 24/178, CP 60(26), February 22, 1926.

body which, after many changes of name, has lingered dimly into the nineteen-seventies.[101] It has produced hundreds of reports on the production, transport and marketing of primary products. Scholars have often found them useful. I doubt whether anyone else has.

It is hard not to laugh at these pathetic efforts to create 'non-tariff preferences' for Empire goods. Their roots are obvious. In the later twenties, advertising was making a really big splash on the British scene. One can see why politicians might think it could make the British housewife prefer Australian butter to Danish. As for the financing of research, this was hallowed by the whole Visionary tradition. Information-gathering and publication fitted nicely into the *laissez-faire* view: businessmen should first be given the facts and then be left to maximize profits. I see no reason to believe that the British were plotting an evil recentralization of the Empire, as the Canadian and South African politicians suspected. But these Committees and Boards satisfied various desires—the wish to be visibly active, the longing for consultation, and the urge to do something—anything—in a political environment which precluded general protective tariffs and preferences.

Like the Empire Marketing Board and the Imperial Economic Committee, free trade survived the 1929 change of government. But the Dominions were growing more and more importunate. In Canada, Prime Minister King was pursuing a policy of unilateral preferential tariff-reduction in the hope that he would thereby induce the British Government to grant more, and more helpful, concessions. Canada's 'Dunning Tariff' of 1930 was an earnest of the hopes.[102] But in Australia, Prime Minister Scullin's new Labour government was moving rapidly toward a protectionism even more intense than that of Prime Minister Bruce. When R. B. Bennett's Conservative party drove King from office in mid-1930, largely on a protectionist platform, it was entirely predictable that, when a new Imperial Conference assembled in London on October 1, 1930, the British Government would face a renewed demand for preferential concessions.

Robert Skidelsky has described the paralysis of wit and will which afflicted the second MacDonald Government.[103] This paralysis was

---

[101] On Canadian officials' dislike of the E.M.B., see Bennett Papers, 108, 172 and 114, 370–114, 377: background papers for the 1930 Imperial Conference. For the 1933 recommendations, see Cmd. 4335 and DO 35/203/8178/61.

[102] King kept Baldwin and Amery informed about his intentions. After the event he expressed his hopes. See King Papers: letters, Amery to King and vice versa, April 1, 1930, May 12, 1930, May 5, 1930, June 7, 1930; letter, O. D. Skelton to King, May 6th, 1930; letter, King to Baldwin, June 5, 1930; letters, King to Ramsay MacDonald, August 25, 1930 and December 3, 1930.

[103] Robert Skidelsky, *Politicians and the Slump* (London, 1967).

much in evidence with respect to the 1930 Conference. Fiscal policy was run by Philip Snowden, a doctrinaire free-trader who vigorously defended his policies.[104] When Bennett demanded that the United Kingdom accept the principle of preference and when the other Dominions demanded an extension of the preferential system, the Cabinet could say nothing but 'no'. To the despair of J. H. Thomas, an experienced negotiator who understood the importance of making some sort of concession, Snowden was not even willing to promise to continue the existing preferences for a few years.[105]

On October 9th, the Cabinet agreed that there would be preferences as long as there were duties, but that there could be no new taxes on food and raw materials. On October 27th, MacDonald asked the Cabinet's permission to promise that the present preferences would be retained for a fixed period. Four days later, the Cabinet, having read a desperate memorandum from Thomas,[106] decided to announce that the Government had no intention of abolishing the existing duties and preferences on tobacco, wines, and spirits; further, that there was no likelihood of abolishing the duties or preferences on dried fruits, sugar, and other taxed commodities for the next two or three years—except for the McKenna Duties, on which no such undertaking could be given. Snowden, however, began to have scruples. How could the Government bind Parliament in this way? The suggestion was constitutionally unsound! Other ministers pleaded with Snowden. W. Graham, the President of the Board of Trade, said that he 'quite understood the Chancellor's position, but if he maintained it we should have nothing to offer to the Dominions. He could not agree with the Chancellor that breakdown was of no importance. It would play into the hands of the Tariff Reformers'. Arthur Henderson, the Foreign Secretary, asked 'what was the difficulty, given the present financial situation, in saying that we should allow the duties to remain for two or three years?' Snowden said it was a 'surrender of principle'.[107] It was agreed that Snowden would go away and draft a statement which he could live with. In the end, the United Kingdom ministers proposed that the conferees

---

[104] See Viscount Snowden, *Autobiography* (London, 1934). II. 868–71. Henry James Scullin (1876–1953) led the Australian Labour Party from 1928 to 1935. He was Prime Minister from 1929 to 1931. R. B. Bennett (1870–1947) led the Canadian Conservative Party from 1927 to 1938, and was Prime Minister from 1930 to 1935. He retired to England in 1938 and was created a Viscount in 1941.

[105] James Henry Thomas (1874–1949), union leader, was Secretary of State for the Colonies in 1924 and 1931, 1935–6; Secretary of State for the Dominions, 1930–35. Attended Imperial Conference 1930 and Ottawa Conference 1932.

[106] CAB 24/216, CP 366(30), October 27, 1930. See Doc. 14.

[107] CAB 23/65, Cabinet 65(30). See also October 9, 24 and 28, 1930.

should pledge themselves not to change preferential margins for three years, or until the next Imperial Conference.[108]

For a while, Ramsay MacDonald believed that the Dominion Prime Ministers might be induced to accept this declaration—though they pointed out that the full statement committed them to maintain existing preferences, while the United Kingdom would give nothing in return. The next day, MacDonald agreed that the 'binding of preferences' clause should be a unilateral declaration by the United Kingdom. And the next day it was agreed that the United Kingdom should make one declaration and the Dominions another—a General Resolution which Bennett had prepared.[109]

The conferees agreed to reconvene a year hence at Ottawa—though to what purpose was far from clear.[110] Thereafter, though many Labour ministers were moving toward protectionism, the Government as a whole did remarkably little to prepare for this coming second round. In the end, because a suitable date could not be found, the Ottawa meetings were deferred until July 1932. But by then, new powers ruled in Whitehall and the world had changed.

Surveying the history of imperial preferences from 1917 to 1931, we can understand the frustration which Amery and Hewins expressed in their memoirs. Nevertheless, we must laugh at the disproportion between the Visionaries' ends and their means. It was simply grotesque to believe that Britain could be revivified and the Empire transformed by any tariff concessions of the sorts which were politically possible in those years. It was the electorate which defeated Tariff Reform, then as before 1914. Further, it was naïve to believe, as Amery clearly believed, that the United Kingdom could extract meaningful concessions from the Dominions merely by adhering to the 'principle' of preference. India and the West Indies gained the most from the preferential arrangements of 1919. Australia and South Africa gained a little. Canada and New Zealand gained nothing. But in the later twenties, South Africa, though conceding wider preferential margins on some goods, was moving away from the preferential principle as rapidly as it dared. So was Australia,

---

[108] CAB 24/216, CP 377(30), November 11, 1930.

[109] CAB 32/79: PM(30) 23, 24, 26: minutes of meetings of heads of delegations November 11, 12 and 13, 1930. Conference proceedings were published in part in Cmd. 3717 and Cmd. 3718. The British declaration was: 'His Majesty's Government in the United Kingdom have declared that the existing preferential margins . . . will not be reduced for a period of three years or pending the outcome of the next Imperial Conference, subject to the rights of the United Kingdom Parliament to fix the budget from year to year.' In the Bennett Papers (100, 323) the Canadian Prime Minister's copy is annotated: 'This may be a concession won by R.B.'

[110] See the note to Bennett, in Documents Section, Item 15.

where, though preferential margins did not always shrink, the tariff level was rising so rapidly as to exclude more and more British manufactures—even though they faced lower duties than foreign goods. Only Canada was prepared to make unilateral concessions. But there is no reason to think that the British concessions of 1919, 1923, or 1926 had anything to do with these. Mackenzie King really did believe in low tariffs—so long as the lowering did not cause anybody to vote against him. And to win votes at home, he was concerned to demonstrate by his tariff policy his espousal of Empire solidarity.

These facts were not amenable to adjustment—either by British tariff arrangements, or by the more subtle mechanisms of Round Table opinion-moulding.[111] In Ottawa, at least, King and his advisers were well aware of these manœuvreings, and profoundly distrusted them.

Similarly, during the twenties the history of imperial capital movements must have been a frustrating one. As we saw in Chapter 1, during this decade Britain in fact did lend the Empire a great deal. But little of this flowed from the schemes which the Imperial Visionaries were able to promote. Further, at all times there was a ludicrous imbalance between the means they proposed and the needs they perceived. It is approximately true that Treasury opposition prevented them from spending more. But they would never have spent enough significantly to affect the pace of Empire development, or the level of British economic activity. They simply had no idea of the sums required. During his years as Colonial Secretary, Amery did a great deal to develop scientific and technical services for the colonies. But he did little for project-making—perhaps because he was never able to finance some of the projects already in existence, and of whose soundness he was convinced. Indeed, it was only in connection with Empire Settlement that he and the other Visionaries really thought in appropriately large terms. And it was only under the Empire Settlement Act that really large sums were borrowed, and really large things were achieved. We must now consider its origins.[112]

IV

When in 1922 Amery moved the second reading of the Empire Settlement Bill, he traced its origin to the reports of two *ad hoc* bodies: The Dominions Royal Commission, and Lord Tennyson's Committee

[111] See Carroll Quigley, 'The Round Table Groups in Canada, 1908–38,' *Canadian Historical Review*, XLIII (1965), 204ff.

[112] A fuller account of the Empire Settlement Act appears in the author's *Expansion and Protectiveness: Making Imperial Economic Policy in the Nineteen-Twenties and Nineteen-Thirties* (forthcoming).

which had considered the emigration of ex-servicemen. Both had reported in 1917. He also noted the preliminary work which since late that year had been done by a special committee—first called the Government Emigration Committee, and then renamed the Overseas Settlement Committee.[113] Understandably, he did not trace the strange permutations by which a concern to control and limit emigration had become a scheme to encourage it. And he did not discuss the connections between the evolution of the Bill and the emerging unemployment problem.[114]

The post-war settlement schemes originated in the wartime concern with soldier resettlement, and in the desire to retain blood stock in the Empire after the War. Late in 1915, the Royal Colonial Institute sent Sir H. Rider Haggard, the Chairman of the Dominions Royal Commission, on an Empire tour to discover what the Dominions might do for British ex-servicemen. The Colonial Office expected that the tour would not be productive, and made very sure that no one would think Haggard a government emissary. In fact, Haggard did extract pledges from all the Dominions, and his visit seems to have caused a flurry in Australia, where serious planning for post-war development really dates from his visit.

At this point, early in 1916, the United Kingdom Government had not decided whether it really wanted Dominion land for its ex-soldiers.[115] Haggard's success had forced Whitehall's hand. Meanwhile, the Board of Agriculture and Fisheries was worried about the possibility of a labour-shortage in post-war agriculture. Fearing that the Dominions might outbid Great Britain for agricultural labour, Lord Selborne proposed to Bonar Law, the Colonial Secretary, that the United Kingdom should confer with the Dominions on the subject.[116] On the Reconstruction Committee, Lord Balfour of Burleigh was painfully

---

[113] 153 HC Deb 5s, col. 575. April 26, 1922. Amery was chairman of the Oversea Settlement Committee almost from its inception. It contained lay persons and officials.

[114] He explained that he was 'not recommending . . . Empire settlement as a panacea for the immediate crisis of unemployment . . . To attempt to solve unemployment here by taking the unemployed, as such, and dumping them down in the Dominions . . . would be . . . cruel . . . and in any case impossible because the Dominions would never consent to it'. Though accurately describing the situation, and his own beliefs, this statement does not correctly represent the process by which the Government was brought to accept the principle of emigration-aid.

[115] CO 532/84, M.O., May 1, 1916: minute by T. C. Macnaghten, the official most concerned with settlement matters, and later attached to the Overseas Settlement Committee.

[116] CO 532/88, M.O., February 23, 1916: Board of Agriculture and Fisheries to Colonial Office, May 8, 1916.

asking for guidance. Should the Government encourage post-war emigration, or discourage it, and how might it effect the desired policy?[117] Therefore, in August, the Colonial Office began to prepare a proposal for a central authority to 'formulate plans and coordinate efforts' in ex-servicemen's emigration. The Dominions were asked to name representatives.[118] Their response was lukewarm and long-delayed, and no such body was ever set up. But as a proposal it re-appeared in a new guise when, in 1918, an Emigration Bill was introduced.

Meanwhile, the Colonial Office had set up a consultative committee under Lord Tennyson's chairmanship. It resembled the 'central authority' in that it contained Dominion representatives. It was unable to decide whether Britain should encourage or discourage emigration after the War, but it did recommend free passages to Empire destinations for ex-servicemen. And it thought the United Kingdom might well finance overseas land-settlement schemes.[119]

At the same time, the Dominions Royal Commission issued its final report. Like the Tennyson Committee, it did not know what post-war migration policy should be. But it was worried about some pre-war abuses—the 'booming' of passages to places in which the migrant could not hope for a good life. Hence it recommended a central migration authority, with power to regulate passage brokers, agents and propaganda.[120]

Additional steam was provided by the Imperial War Cabinet and Conference of 1917, which, as we saw, had resolved that there should be arrangements to induce migrants to settle under the British flag. This part of Mr Massey's resolution was not debated at all.

Not surprisingly, the Colonial Office decided to splice these recommendations together.[121] By mid-July 1917 it had begun to draft an Emigration Bill. The bill would establish a Central Migration Authority with very wide powers over propaganda and recruitment, but without explicit powers to prohibit migration or subsidize it. Nevertheless, as Hewins explained in the House, the Bill was meant to give power to

[117] CO 532/89, M.O., August 11, 1916: letter, Reconstruction Committee to Colonial Office, August 11, 1916.

[118] CO 532/89, M.O., August 5, 1916: dispatch, Secretary of State for the Colonies to Governors General, September 21, 1916.

[119] Cd. 8672, 1917–18. Advance copies reached the Colonial Office in July 1917.

[120] Cd. 8462. The Commission had arisen from recommendations of the 1911 Imperial Conference. Appointed in 1912, it was especially concerned with natural resources.

[121] CO 532/106, July 16, 1917.

'direct' migration and to 'assist' it. Colonial Office officials thought that the Bill was meant to discourage emigration.[122] This was believed to be Bonar Law's intention, and it was certainly Walter Long's.

The Bill had a difficult time in the House, where it stuck in Standing Committee B and died with the death of the first Lloyd George Government. It was also given a scathing examination by the Dominion Prime Ministers at the Imperial War Conference and Cabinet of 1918. The Dominions were annoyed to find that their representatives were expected to serve on a central control body which would have executive authority in the United Kingdom.[123] They were furious to discover that their own propaganda was to be screened. And they believed, in spite of Long's disclaimer, that the Bill was meant to restrict emigration, not merely to influence its destination.

Meanwhile, Long was obliged to proceed without the Bill. On November 16, 1918, he set up a three-man departmental committee to prepare the migration-information which the demobilized would shortly demand. When the unexpected parliamentary dissolution killed the Emigration Bill, he set up a non-statutory emigration committee. Containing a shipowner, a lady, several independent members, and departmental representatives but no Dominion ones, the committee was to keep ex-servicemen informed and to work on the Emigration Bill. The vice-chairman and administrative officer was to be T. C. Macnaghten, who had worked in the Colonial Office for six years on migration questions. First called the Government Emigration Committee, after some confusion it became the Overseas Settlement Committee in April 1919. At the same time the Emigrants Information Office, which had lurked dimly in the Colonial Office for many years, was transformed into the Overseas Settlement Office. As the Emigration Bill was never re-introduced, these *ad hoc* arrangements became permanent, launching the Empire Settlement Committee on a long career of administration—and of lobbying.

In December 1918, Long asked the Committee to tell him what the Government's emigration policy should be. They were to report by the end of January 1919.[124] The suggestions, developed at first under Hewins' chairmanship and, after January 14th, under Amery's, were remarkably modest. The Committee was not prepared to recommend any general aid to emigration. But it did propose financial aid for the emigration of women and children. Its members believed that children would root more easily in overseas soil, and that the War had increased

---

[122] CO 532/114, April 30, 1918: minute by T. C. Macnaghten.
[123] See Cd. 9173, 1918.
[124] CO 532/118, December 20, 1918: Letter, H. Lambert to Secretary of Government Emigration Committee, December 20, 1918.

the pre-existing imbalance between the sexes. Men were dispropor-
tionately plentiful in the Dominions, and women in the United Kingdom. The Committee also recommended free passages for ex-servicemen. In so doing, it was concerned with fairness, not with the economic
situation.

Neither the Committee nor the Cabinet, which accepted this recommendation on March 31st, knew how many ex-servicemen might want
to go, or how much their emigration would cost.[125] Later, when Amery
announced the policy in the House,[126] he carefully explained that the
Dominions would have to approve any migrants under the scheme. In
the end they approved less than one-third of the applicants. Yet
£2,700,000 was spent in three years. And 82,196 people emigrated by
the end of 1922.[127]

The Government did nothing about female and child migration. Of
course, the Poor Law authorities did not abandon their long-standing
practice of exporting child paupers. Dr Barnardo's Homes maintained
their arrangements for shipping children to Canada. In Western
Australia there was a boys' farm-school. These private and local
arrangements continued. Further, the Committee extracted £250,000
from the National Relief Fund, to help with the emigration of persons
who had suffered from the war but who did not qualify for the ex-
service scheme.[128] By the end of 1919, the Committee was exporting
civilians and reorganizing the private societies for female emigration,
though it was using private funds to do so.

During 1919 and 1920, the Government was unable to make up its
mind with respect to emigration policy. Would the United Kingdom
have a shortage of labour, or a surplus? The opposing views are shown
very clearly in the proceedings of a Cabinet conference on unemployment and the state of trade.[129] The Overseas Settlement Committee
had resolved, in July 1919, that there should be a general scheme for
overseas settlement, and that the costs should be shared by the
Dominions.[130] But the Treasury would give them no funds to finance
the emigration of women and children. Milner and Amery had begun to
meet regularly with the Dominion representatives, for discussions of
migration problems and planning. Some sessions were devoted to the
revised Emigration Bill, now called the Empire Settlement Bill, which

[125] CAB 23/9, March 31, 1919.
[126] 114 HC Deb 5s 1919, col. 1857–8.
[127] Including dependants.
[128] CO 532/150, October 20, 1919: minutes of 28th meeting, Overseas Settlement Committee, August 19, 1919.
[129] See Doc. 4.
[130] CO 532/150, October 20, 1919: minutes of 27th meeting, July 24, 1919.

the Colonial Office still hoped it might be allowed to re-introduce. Others were given over to more general discussions. Canada made pessimistic noises about the Dominion's absorptive capacity. Australians pointed out that they could accept many migrants only if the United Kingdom would lend them the money for railway development. On August 7, 1919, the New South Wales representative suggested that the United Kingdom should contribute to a joint shared-passage scheme. Amery was sceptical, and 'saw difficulties'. Later he was to feel differently.[131]

Meanwhile, it had become necessary to extend the free-passage scheme for ex-servicemen. Commending this extension on October 15, 1920, Milner reminded his colleagues that the money spent on migration relieved the housing problem and unemployment in the United Kingdom.[132] Housing was dear to Lloyd Goerge's heart. And the unemployment note would be heard again.

Further, there was increasing unease about the question of a Dominion contribution. For many years the Australians and New Zealanders had been subsidizing their immigrants. Though there is no proof, British officials appear to have believed that, if the free passage scheme were continued much longer, or extended, the Dominions would stop doing so. The Treasury was criticizing the ballooning outlays on emigration. Whitehall was dissatisfied about the arrangements which the Dominions, especially Australia, were making for the settlement of British soldiers. In November, Amery told Senator Millen, the Australian Minister of Repatriation, that if the schemes were to be continued or extended, the Dominions would have to contribute.[133] When Milner informed the Dominions that the ex-servicemen's programme would continue until the end of 1921, he cabled a similar warning to Australia and New Zealand—though not to the other Dominions.[134]

It was largely on the recommendation of the Cabinet's Unemployment Committee that this extension was allowed. Amery and the Overseas Settlement Committee had lobbied vigorously to this end. Appointed on August 13, 1920, to consider unemployment problems in the winter of 1920–21, the Committee had no powers to discuss a

[131] CO 532/150, October 20, 1919: minutes of meetings of High Commissioners and Agents General.
[132] CO 532/158, October 15, 1920.
[133] CO 532/168, January 6, 1920: memorandum on a Colonial Office Conference, November 10, 1920.
[134] CO 532/167: telegrams, Secretary of State for the Colonies to the Governors-General of Australia and New Zealand and to the Governors of the Australian states.

longer-run policy with respect to emigration or anything else. But it did recommend that the Overseas Settlement Committee should be allowed to spend between £75,000 and £150,000 on the emigration of necessitous civilians during the winter. Its members also thought that the Colonial Office should consult with the Dominions, and then 'formulate a scheme for assisted emigration on a large scale, for submission to the Cabinet'. On December 6, 1920, the Cabinet concurred. The Committee was given £100,000 to spend in the first months of 1921. The Colonial Office began to arrange a conference.[135]

Telegrams went to the Dominions late in December. In a general way, their Governments were ready to take advantage of this initiative. New Zealand had just decided to accept more migrants, and had liberalized her system of 'nomination'; Australia had arranged to coordinate the migration efforts of its various Governments, and had sent its Minister of Repatriation to London to arrange for a much-expanded flow—hopefully, 100,000 per year. Even Canada was sounding hopeful. Though eager for quality rather than quantity, the Canadian Prime Minister hoped to attract more settlers whose ideas of government were consistent with Canadian—that is, British—ideas.[136]

On the other hand, the Dominions were having trouble with the settlement of their own soldiers. Some of them, especially Australia, could arrange more settlement schemes only if they could borrow massively. Partly for political reasons, partly because of their own ideas about 'appropriate' development, their leaders would never assist all sorts of immigration. Farm workers, women and children would always be given a better deal; others might be assisted only if 'nominated' by resident friends, relatives, or employers, of if 'requisitioned' by a local government. Further, South Africa could not be expected to cooperate. These attitudes and habits, firmly established by the end of 1920, were well known to the Colonial Office when, in December 1920 and January 1921, it began to prepare an Empire settlement scheme.

In 1916–17, few of these developments had been foreseen or recommended. Nevertheless, by the end of 1920 a great deal had changed. For the first time in many decades, the United Kingdom Government was

[135] CAB 23/22, Cabinet 48(20), August 13, 1920; CAB 27/114/1: conclusions of Cabinet Committee on Unemployment, 6th meeting, October 15, 1920; CAB 23/23, Cabinet 66(20), December 6, 1920; CO 532/158, December 21, 1920: telegrams, Secretary of State for the Colonies to Dominion Governors-General, December 21, 1920.

[136] Sir Robert Borden, *Memoirs* (Toronto, 1937) ii. 1037–8, reporting his farewell address to the Canadian Conservative Caucus, June 30, 1920. Borden (1854–1937) led the Canadian Conservatives from 1901 to 1920, and was prime minister from 1911 to 1920. He attended the Imperial War Cabinets and Conferences in 1917 and 1918.

subsidizing emigration—aiding not merely ex-servicemen, and not merely the Poor Law children whom the Guardians had been exporting for generations, but ordinary citizens. The management of migration was now a live issue. Interested persons were now installed in the Colonial Office and the Government. Whatever might be done about financial aid or the details of intra-Imperial cooperation, it was inconceivable that things could revert to the pre-war situation of unconcern. By January 1921, migration was definitely—and permanently—on the Imperial agenda.

The year 1921 saw vigorous lobbying by Amery and the Overseas Settlement Committee, renewed Treasury opposition, and continued Government indecision with respect to emigration policy. Before the Dominions representatives assembled late in January, the Chancellor of the Exchequer authorized Amery to offer to spend up to £2 million annually on Empire settlement. Amery did so, proposing to spend £1 million on passage-assistance and £1 million on land-settlement schemes. The Dominions would share on an equal basis. Land-settlement had been adumbrated by Lord Tennyson's Committee in 1917, and was always a live issue among the more romantic of England's country gentry. But it was placed before the Conference largely to accommodate a specific proposal which Western Australia had made late the preceding year. Amery was already keen to spend on this scheme. Canada and New Zealand had no specific ideas, but the Australian representative, Senator Millen, offered a new device. Australia would spend £20 million in five years, if the United Kingdom would pay half the interest for five years. Enormous areas could then be opened for settlement.[137] The conferees welcomed the British offer and agreed to join in the financing of migration.

There followed a series of wrangles with the Treasury. Amery was keen to begin immediately upon Western Australian settlement, and he saw no reason to object to Senator Millen's interest-sharing device. The Treasury found constitutional objections: it feared the implications of an Imperial contribution to the interest-obligations of a self-governing

---

[137] No such proposal had previously been seen in London. It stalks the subsequent papers as 'Senator Millen's Scheme'. It seems to have originated at the Australian Premiers' Conference of January 1919, when the Queensland Treasurer, Mr Theodore, asked the Australian Government to extend such assistance to the States, which were spending heavily on soldier settlement. Theodore's final proposal was identical in form with 'Senator Millen's Scheme'. See Australia, *Parliamentary Papers*, Session 1917–18–19, Vol. IV: 'Report of the Resolutions, Proceedings and Debates of the Conference of Commonwealth and State Ministers ... Melbourne', (No. 142 of 1919). On group settlement in Western Australia, see I. L. Hunt, 'Group Settlement in Western Australia', *University Studies in Western Australian History*, October 1958.

Dominion. It also argued that funds were not available, and that all relevant funds had already been allocated. Finally, it insisted on May 17th that nothing could be done until after the Imperial Conference, already scheduled for the summer of 1921.

No one had originally intended that the 1921 Imperial Conference should discuss migration. It appeared on the agenda only through the persistence of Amery and the Overseas Settlement Office. Indeed, it was added only after the preliminary agenda had been circulated. When he distributed the results of the February conference to the Dominions, Churchill, now Colonial Secretary, urged them to bring specific proposals to the Imperial Conference. He reminded them of his hopes for a 'carefully considered scheme of Empire settlement'. But by May 6th, Amery was still urging the Cabinet to endorse the February conference conclusion: that its recommendations should form the basis of discussions at the summer Imperial Conference. Only on June 16th was Amery actually authorized to begin negotiations.

The summer Conference approved the idea of cooperation for Empire settlement. But its endorsement did not move matters forward. Asked how many settlers they might take if the February terms were offered, the Dominion Prime Ministers were cautious: they could take only 1600 to 2300 men per year.[138] The Overseas Settlement Office concluded that it was not enough to offer a £300 advance to each settler, and urged the Government to over-ride the Treasury's objections and accept the basis of Senator Millen's scheme. That is, funds should be advanced to the Dominion Governments themselves, or the United Kingdom should agree to pay some of the interest on any settlement-loans they might float. These urgings did not convince the Cabinet, which still had no definite policy, and which did not seem to be enunciating any.

The Overseas Settlement Office continued its pressure by requesting a great deal of money for the 1922-23 fiscal year. It wanted £750,000 for free passages, £1,000,000 for cooperation with the Dominions along the lines of the February conference, £200,000 for paying interest on Dominion borrowings, and £40,000 for the Western Australian scheme, which would settle 200 men of the officer class upon newly-cleared dairy-holdings. This request had to pass through the Colonial Office, where Sir Edward Harding minuted critically upon it. Churchill reserved his opinion 'until the general policy of His Majesty's Government has been more precisely defined'.

All were waiting upon the new Unemployment Committee of Cabinet. Its chairman, Sir Alfred Mond, the Minister of Health, strongly

---

[138] CO 536/198, M.O., July 18, 1921: Amery's notes of the discussion of the settlement sub-committee at the Imperial Conference.

favoured assisted migration and land settlement as *permanent* solutions for the unemployment problem. That is, he did not regard emigration as a palliative, because he was convinced that unemployment was 'likely to go on for years rather than months'. He strongly urged Amery to raise the whole question of Empire settlement with his Committee. And he told the Cabinet, on October 7th, that his Committee was not overlooking the migration problem. Following a vigorous mobilizing of opinion by the Overseas Settlement Committee, he was able to claim support from the Ministries of Health and Labour, the Board of Trade, and Churchill at the Colonial Office. On October 13th, the Committee recommended that the Overseas Settlement Office should be given £300,000 to continue the emigration of civilians. The Chancellor had already said that he favoured this outlay, and that he would look into the Treasury obstruction which the Colonial Office officials reported.

In November the Australians provided a new push. Though there is no evidence that Amery had arranged it in collusion with Prime Minister Hughes, such a stimulus is at least highly likely. On November 24th, Hughes cabled to propose formally the Millen Scheme, now grown to £50 million. On November 30th, the Overseas Settlement Committee approved Hughes' request, and recommended a short Bill which would allow them to spend £4 to £5 million a year. Urging this scheme on Churchill, Amery emphasized its double-barrelled effect: it would reduce unemployment both directly and indirectly, because it would create work in Britain's machinery industry.

On December 7th, an Interdepartmental Committee of officials began to draft a Bill which would give effect to the decisions of the February conference, while allowing interest-sharing. This Bill, which eventually became the Empire Settlement Act, was totally different from the various drafts of Emigration and Empire Settlement Bills which had been in circulation since 1917. It was concerned with aid, not with regulation. It explicitly allowed for interest-sharing, and for a maximum outlay of £5 million per year. But Cabinet approval had yet to be obtained. The Cabinet was waiting to receive the Geddes Report on Expenditure, and would take no action on Empire Settlement for the time being. Meanwhile, Hughes had not been answered, and the Committee was revising its draft—removing the explicit reference to interest-sharing, while hoping that Amery would tell the Cabinet of it. Only on February 24, 1922, did the Cabinet consider the new Bill.

The Cabinet does not seem to have disputed the principle of the Bill, but the Chancellor violently disputed the amount of spending, and the principle of interest-sharing. Amery and Churchill had to settle for less money than they had first hoped to get, agreeing on £1·5 million for the first year and £3 million for each of the next fourteen years. The members of the Cabinet were not told that £1·5 million was £490,000 less than the Overseas Settlement Office had already requested for 1922–23. No wonder the Treasury accepted the figures! Even Prime Minister Hughes acquiesced. On March 24th, he cabled plaintively, asking what had happened to his proposal of November 24th. Could answer not be vouchsafed soon? On April 3rd, he was informed that there would not be enough money to handle his proposal of November 24th, unless the United Kingdom were to contribute only one-third of the interest—not the half he had requested. Would that do? Hughes replied that it would do splendidly.

In this whole saga the Australians play an oddly prominent role. At critical points it is their intervention and their suggestions which move the project forward and modify its nature. Consider land-settlement. The Tennyson Committee report, and the predilections of the British governing elite, ensured that it would have had a place in any scheme of migration-aid. But without Australian pressure, its place would almost certainly have been smaller. Further, the idea of interest-sharing was an Australian invention, which the British Treasury was extremely reluctant to accept. In subsequent arrangements under the Empire Settlement Act it played a very large role—especially but not exclusively in the Australian schemes. It even spread to other Visionary projects. In particular, the scheme for Financial Cooperation in Empire Development, which we have already mentioned, was obviously modelled on it.

Amery's role is also immense. No wonder he thought that the Empire Settlement Act was the major work of his years as Colonial Undersecretary.[139] Before he joined the Government, no one was pushing forward on the Empire settlement front, and the Government had been given no coherent reason for spending on emigration, or even for planning it. Hewins and Long, because they wanted an essentially irresponsible 'control', probably did more harm than good. Further, they offered no coherent ideology into which Empire settlement could be fitted. Amery supplied this lack, in a fashion particularly apposite to an under-employed economy. Admittedly, many of his themes could be found in the Report of the Dominions Royal Commission. But no one seems to have noticed them there. In any event, the Committee had not urged His Majesty's Government to do anything much. Amery harnessed the vision to a programme.

Nevertheless, the ideology of Empire settlement, and the Australian pressure, would probably not have yielded an Act if the British Government had not been worried about unemployment, which at critical points advanced the Cause. Much of Amery's support came from

[139] Amery, *My Political Life*, ii. 182

Ministers who were departmentally concerned with the unemployment problem. A good deal of mileage could be gained—and was gained—by comparing emigration spending with the dole. The former was once and for all; the latter was permanent. The Poor Law Guardians had long recognized the force of this argument. Though evidence is hard to find, it must have helped to drag the Bill from under the shadow of the Geddes Axe.

Once the Act had been passed, things moved swiftly. The Overseas Settlement Department began to negotiate with the Dominions, working both on passage-assistance and on settlement schemes. Agreements were quickly signed, but disillusionment quickly set in: the Dominions were much less forthcoming than the Whitehall activists had hoped. By year-end, some officials looked toward the coming Imperial Economic Conference. Surely if the Prime Ministers could be gathered and harangued. . . . But the Conference itself did not pay much attention to settlement as such. In offering 'financial cooperation' and increased preferences, the United Kingdom Government certainly hoped to induce the Dominions to cooperate more fully. But only the Australians seem to have used the Conference venue to discuss migration seriously.[140] And even they made no concrete proposals. These came only in the spring of 1924, when William Lunn, Labour's Colonial Undersecretary, was chatting with visiting Australian politicians. From these conversations eventually emerged an extraordinary scheme—the 'thirty-four-million-pound agreement'.

The Agreement was hard to prepare. Treasury officials and Philip Snowden were inclined to oppose it; Otto Niemeyer and other Treasury knights did not believe that emigration would help Britain to digest her unemployed, while Snowden thought it a waste of money. Australia did not help matters; to Whitehall her original proposals seemed unreasonable, and they were escalated several times in the course of 1924. After the Baldwin government returned to power, Australia made further demands, and the Treasury eventually gave up, allowing Amery to settle on whatever terms he wished. At long last, signatures were exchanged in April 1925.

It was hoped that the Agreement would settle 450,000 new migrants over ten years. The United Kingdom would contribute £130,000 for every £750,000 that the Australian Government could raise and re-lend to the States for development: the acquisition, resumption and clearing

---

[140] See Commonwealth Archives Office, External Affairs File I/3/2, telegram, n.d., Australian High Commissioner in London to Prime Minister of Australia, Melbourne, suggesting that the Australian delegation bring information on development proposals for discussion at the Imperial Economic Conference.

of land suitable for farms, advances to settlers, actual settlement of persons on farms, railways, tramways, roads, bridges, irrigation, hydro-electric works, and 'similar enterprises tending to assist in the development of rural areas'. For every £130,000 contributed, 10,000 migrants were to be accepted within ten years. Besides the £14 million already arranged under agreements of 1922–24, the new plan provided an extra £20 million—hence the £34 million total. The Treasury officials had originally insisted on some link between money and new farms. They feared that the Australians would simply use the money for public works, not for settlement. Prime Minister Bruce was equally insistent. Hence there was a clause by which *land* settlement schemes would involve a definite commitment to establish one new farm for every £1000 advanced on them.[141] On its advances to the States, under the Agreement, the Australian Government agreed to demand only 1 per cent interest for the first five years.

Amery was most concerned that the Agreement's capital should not be frittered away on small projects which would be invisible at Westminster. When he visited Australia to confer with Bruce and with the Australian Migration Commission, he explained that he wanted something big. He asked the Commission to prepare a comprehensive plan, covering a period of seven or eight years—something he could present to Parliament and explain to the Cabinet. The expenditure-implications, he said, should be made clear. If possible the outlays should rise a little from year to year.[142] The Commission did agree to produce a five-year plan. But the worsening economic situation, and the growing Australian doubts about land settlement and development generally, seem to have overcome this resolution. Relatively little was actually borrowed under the Agreement, and one cannot discover its effect on migration, because at the same time the British and Australian Governments were directly assisting migrants by paying some of their steamship fares.

Nothing so dramatic was arranged with the other Dominions. True, New Zealand and Canada entered into a series of passage agreements; some land settlement schemes were arranged in Canada; a few settlers were sent to Rhodesia. The Overseas Settlement Department made arrangements with a private association in South Africa, and with women's and children's emigration societies everywhere. It even began to run hostels and training farms. The Department could not manage to spend its £3 million per year. It had arranged some ten settlement schemes. And it had assisted the departure of 249,000 persons—55 per

---

[141] For Bruce's reasons, see National Library of Australia, Sir George Pearce Papers, MS 23, ser. 15: 'Minutes of a Conference', November 3, 1927 *et seq.*
[142] Ibid.

cent of all the migrants who left the United Kingdom for the Empire during 1922–27.[143]

Nevertheless, more was expected. Unemployment, though falling, remained high. The preferential system could not be extended. Domestic protection, though spreading slowly under the 'safeguarding' legislation, could do little for the old staple export industries, especially coal and textiles. The pound was stabilized, over-valued, but fiercely defended. Only emigration remained.

In June 1928, the Cabinet received the report of its Industrial Transference Board.[144] The Board found a concentrated surplus of 200,000 men, mainly miners. It saw little hope but emigration—not in spectacular waves, but through long-continued flow both inside the Empire Settlement framework and outside it. Besides recommending that the Dominions should change their attitude, the Board suggested that ordinary third-class passages should be subsidized. Thus people could move cheaply but without the formalities which the Empire Settlement Act required.

This report was referred to a Cabinet Unemployment-Policy Committee. Over Churchill's strenuous objections, the Committee endorsed Amery's suggestion that there should be a general subsidization of third-class passages. But Churchill, who wanted to subsidize only the necessitous, had the last word: 'The Chancellor of the Exchequer informed the Committee that it would be necessary, if new taxation was to be avoided, that the expenditure necessary on the Committee's recommendations should be met out of savings, administrative economies, and the postponement of expenditure throughout the public service.'[145]

The Cabinet endorsed the Committee's recommendations,[146] but Britain could not act without each Dominion's consent. Amery rightly feared that the Dominions might suspect the United Kingdom of dumping her unemployed on them. Canada agreed to permit a £10 third-class fare. In 1929, 33,833 people—half of all United Kingdom migrants—went to Canada at this fare. But the cheap fares were not extended to the other Dominions. As they were already beginning to

---

[143] The 'net balance outward of migrants' was 449,000. See CAB 32/82, EE(30)14: 'Imperial Conference 1930: Overseas Settlement'.

[144] CAB 24/196, CP 206(28), June 29, 1928. The members were Sir Warren Fisher, Sir John Cadman, and Sir David Shackleton. Warren Fisher returned to this theme in November, in the report of the Interdepartmental Unemployment Committee (CAB 24/198, CP 325(28), November 2, 1928).

[145] CAB 27/374, UP(28)3d conclusions.

[146] CAB 23/58, July 23, 1928.

shut down their assisted-passage schemes, they would certainly not have welcomed such general subsidization.

Meanwhile, by early 1928 other and much more grandiose proposals had come into circulation.[147] Might the Prince of Wales lead a mass of settlers to establish a new Canadian province in the Peace River district of the north-west? What of a great 'Pioneer Settlement Scheme', financed by land bonds? In Canada, Lord Lovat, the British Colonial Under-Secretary, was travelling to spread the gospel with respect to the latter. In Whitehall, Thomas Jones, the Assistant Cabinet Secretary, was working hard on the former.[148]

Unfortunately, nobody in Canada was prepared to take such designs seriously. The agricultural provinces were opposed, because their leaders believed—correctly—that more agricultural settlement meant lower agricultural prices. The Dominion Cabinet was sceptical of the financial aspects. Prime Minister King distrusted Whitehall's motives. The British Conservative Government, he believed, connived with the Canadian Conservatives to present impossible immigration proposals. The purpose was to embarrass him in his own Parliament.[149] No welcome could be expected from the Canadian Government.

In fact, emigration was already falling away. The peak year had been 1926. Even the £10 fare did not arrest the downward trend in 1929. In Australia and New Zealand, economic conditions were known to be bad, and the Governments now took a dim view of immigration. The New Zealand Government began to restrict its assistance in 1927 and became more rigorous in each succeeding year. In 1926–27, New Zealand assisted 11,239 migrants under the Empire Settlement Act. In 1929–30 she aided 1790, and in 1931–32, 290.[150] Australia received 31,260 assisted migrants in 1926, 12,943 in 1929 and 2683 in 1930. In December 1929, the new Australian Labour Government, which in opposition had never welcomed the Bruce-Page Government's migra-

---

[147] See K. Feiling, *The Life of Neville Chamberlain* (London, 1946), 162, who says they first arose in 1927.

[148] For the Lovat Scheme, see King Papers, letter, Lord Lovat to W. L. M. King, September 3, 1928, with accompanying memorandum. For the Prince of Wales scheme, see Jones, *Whitehall Diary*, II. (1969), 169.

[149] On the Canadian background, see King Papers: cable, Robert Forke to W. L. M. King, 1928; letter, Robert Forke to W. L. M. King, October 30, 1928; letters, Burgon Bickersteth to W. L. M. King and reply July 3, 1928 and July 13, 1928; Vol. 80 File 625, Memorandum by W. L. M. King on discussion with Sir William Clark, November 15, 1928, and on subsequent Cabinet discussion. King's immigration policy is surveyed in H. Blair Neatby: *William Lyon Mackenzie King: The Lonely Heights, 1922–1932* (Toronto, 1958), 240–1, 249. Robert Forke, a prairie Progressive, was King's Immigration Minister.

[150] From New Zealand Department of Immigration, *Reports*. (In New Zealand, *Appendices to Journals of House of Representatives*.)

tion plans, began to negotiate a reduction in the flow of assisted migrants. In February 1930 it imposed the most stringent restraints.[151]

Against this gloomy background, the second MacDonald Government at first treasured the same hopes that Baldwin and Amery had nourished in 1928. In August 1929 J. H. Thomas went off to Canada on a migration mission.[152] Before his arrival, Prime Minister King had asked his Minister of Immigration to prepare a quenching memorandum. To King's delight, Burgon Bickersteth had already warned Thomas that Canada would not be able to accept any large number of migrants.[153] In Whitehall, the Overseas Settlement Committee was encouraging Thomas to believe that there were good prospects for agricultural migrants in Canada.[154] But even so, it emphasized that one must go carefully. It reported the prairie opposition to State-aided migration, and the widespread fear that Britain intended to shift her unemployed to the Dominion's shoulders.[155]

These cautions should have warned Thomas that not much could be achieved. Indeed, he and others seem to have reached this conclusion before he sailed: trade quickly joined migration among the objects of the trip. In Canada, he won few concessions with respect to the former and made little headway with respect to the latter.

On coming to power in mid-1930, R. B. Bennett stopped all migration-assistance.[156] The Labour Government was doing the same thing in Australia. Unfortunately, the Labour faithful in Britain did not know how unresponsive the Dominions were becoming. Late in 1930, George Lansbury was still arguing for a massive settlement scheme. He thought that hundreds of thousands of coal miners should be moved to Australia and settled as wheat farmers.[157] By this time, however, it had long been clear to the responsible Departments that no such thing could be attempted. The Government had asked the Economic Advisory

[151] Australia, *Parliamentary Papers*, 1929, Vol. II; Development and Migration Commission, *Second Report*, 1320–1.

[152] His trip is described from newspaper reports in Skidelsky, *Politicians*, 102–3.

[153] King Papers, letters, King to Robert Forke, August 1, 1929, Burgon Bickersteth to King, July 14, 1929 and King to Burgon Bickersteth, July 30, 1929. Bickersteth, the warden of the men's union at the University of Toronto, visited his home in England almost every summer. He was well connected on both sides of the Atlantic, and regularly used his visits to discuss migration with Whitehall officials.

[154] CAB 27/382, ODM(29)5.

[155] CAB 27/382, ODM(29)15.

[156] DO 35/118/8010/7: dispatch, R. H. Hadow to Dominions Office, n.d.

[157] CAB 24/215, CP 390(30): 'Unemployment policy: Note by George Lansbury.'

Council to report on migration policy.[158] Pending this report, the Departments were required to brief the Government for the 1930 Imperial Conference. They wrote that the Dominions would not be receptive to any proposals, and that the most important thing was to retain the fifty-fifty sharing of migration aid.[159] This provision of the Empire Settlement Act had so far protected the Treasury against 'extravagant demands'; it must not be surrendered now.

The Cabinet approved these recommendations.[160] And little more was heard of Empire Settlement until after 1945. In the late thirties there were further reports[161] and investigations. The Act was renewed with a few modifications in 1937. But under depression conditions the subject could hardly remain alive.

By 1936, the Australians were again making familiar noises about men, money and markets. Canada, asking for tariff concessions, was also using the old argument. But nobody took such noises seriously. They were properly regarded as the thoughtless responses of such long-lived politicians as Earle Page. In Britain, Milner was dead and Amery out of office. Cunliffe-Lister had turned his attention to other matters: first to the restoration of colonial budgetary balance, and then to the air force. Baldwin, Neville Chamberlain, Thomas and Walter Elliot were happily installing the tariffs which most Conservatives of the nineteen-twenties had wanted but which Churchill and the electorate had denied them.

What is one to make of these migration programmes? Certainly they helped many thousands of people to leave Britain—almost entirely for Canada, Australia and New Zealand. The Soldier Settlement Scheme accounted for 86,000 including families, before it was wound up in May 1934.[162] Under the Empire Settlement Act, 332,000 received assistance between 1922 and 1929, while 13,400 more were aided in 1930–31. 58,000 people travelled to Canada on the subsidized £10 fare. Compared with total net migration from Britain during the twenties, these are large figures. Unfortunately we do not know how many of the assisted would have emigrated in any event. Australia and New Zealand would certainly have spent heavily to subsidize passages. Many would have gone to these countries, and to Canada, without any government aid. However, many of these would probably have settled in the United States or South America. Thus the Act did tend to retain the white

[158] The report was published as Cmd. 4075 (1931–32).
[159] CAB 32/176, IEC(30)107, a brief agreed by officials of the Dominions Office, the Treasury, and the Ministry of Labour.
[160] CAB 23/65, October 15, 1930.
[161] For example, Cmd. 4689, 1933–34.
[162] Amery, *My Political Life*, ii. 185.

migrants within the Empire, and it must have raised British emigration. But we cannot measure either effect.

In other directions, the Act's success was certainly modest. The Visionaries had hoped to redistribute population in several senses. Women were to go to the Dominions and find husbands; children were to go overseas and become happy farmers; urban workers were to be re-trained and settle on the Dominions' boundless acres. All these things did happen to some extent. The Act's statistics reveal significant move-ments of women and children. But almost everywhere the land-settlement projects were grotesque failures. In Australia their dissection has become an academic industry.[163] In Canada, some approved pro-jects were never even begun. In both countries, few of the new agri-cultural labourers and farmers remained on the land. Like the female domestics whom the politicians cherished, they quickly moved to other work. In any event, the vast majority of subsidized migrants were not destined for agriculture at all. In spite of the Visionaries' hopes, the chief beneficiaries of the assisted-passage agreements were 'nominated' and 'requisitioned' workers for whom urban work was always the prospect.

Though the Visionaries and the Dominions' own politicians deplored the drift to the cities, we, with the benefit of hindsight, should be glad that the migrants did not settle on the land. Agricultural prices were already falling in the late twenties, and were shortly to fall farther. Mechanization was already reducing the need for farm labour, and average farm sizes were rising throughout the Empire. It was in con-struction work, and in cities, that labour was needed. So long as reason-ably full employment could be maintained, migrants would do better in cities, and they ought to have been going there. The Act and the other programmes were successful, in spite of their promoters' inten-tions, in so far as they speeded the urbanization of the Empire.

Admittedly, there were problems in the Empire's cities. Poor relief was ill-organized and ill-financed. The Dominions' economies were cyclically unstable. Their prospects depend heavily upon investment activity and primary-product prices. Both were variable. Hence unem-ployment was endemic, and sometimes serious. Besides, cities were more likely to attract the urban socialists of Britain. The homesteading farmer could not become unemployed. He created traffic for the over-expanded railway systems. He was less likely to be radicalized by the

---

[163] See Kathleen Jupp, 'Factors affecting the Structure of the Australian Population with special reference to the Period 1921–33', unpublished M.A. thesis, Australian National University. For this reference I am indebted to Professor Appleyard of the University of Western Australia.

activities of leftist agitators. So Empire politicians thought. Unfortunately, the experiences of the thirties showed that there were worse things than unemployment. A price-collapse would pauperize the cash-crop farmer just as efficiently as unemployment would pauperize the construction worker. When destitute, farmers became as radical as city dwellers.

Consciously or unconsciously, the politicians of the twenties had wanted land-settlement because they hoped it would bring social peace and stability. It could have done so only if it had been designed to produce subsistence farmers who grew their own food and did not depend on the market. But the settlement-schemes were not intended to produce subsistence farming, and nobody meant them to do so. Prime Minister Bruce had made the point in 1923: the men would come, and the capital would flow, only if the markets existed. Unhappily for the farmer-settlers of the twenties, the markets were feeble. And both farmers and markets soon dribbled away.

3

Ottawa and After:
British Protectionism and the Empire
in the Nineteen-thirties

I

It is impossible to examine British imperial economic policy in the
nineteen-thirties without concentrating upon the Ottawa Conference.
Admittedly other things were happening as well. The British Government was concerned to develop preferential arrangements within the
dependent colonial Empire. Leading politicians and officials worked
hard on colonial 'restoration' by constructing cartels: Britain connived
with the Netherlands and other countries to organize the world markets
for tin and rubber, while trying to devise some suitable agreements for
wheat and sugar. The Treasury and the Board of Trade were trying to
manage British capital-export. Nevertheless, the Ottawa Conference,
to which this chapter is largely devoted, preoccupied the attention of
ministers and officials throughout the decade. The following three
sections trace the preliminaries, the negotiations and the Agreements
themselves, and some of the more important effects.[1] The final section
treats some other policies.

II

Only after the National Government came to power did the United
Kingdom seriously begin to prepare for the Ottawa Conference. After
the deadlock of 1930, Cabinet opposition to tariffs and preferences had
not diminished, though protectionist sentiment was growing. The
Preparatory Cabinet Committee met only a few times, and was able to
decide only one thing: to offer the Dominions some sort of 'wheat

---

[1] A fuller account, with more extensive documentation, is in Drummond,
Expansion and Protectiveness, Chs. 3, 4.

quota'.[2] The Board of Trade began to prepare 'schedules'—lists of commodities on which Dominion concessions would be helpful. The idea was to draw up one for each Dominion, one for Southern Rhodesia, and one for India. However, things went slowly, and the important policy questions were never settled. If the Ottawa Conference had met in the summer or autumn of 1931, as originally intended, it would have been no more fruitful than the 1930 Conference. However, because the various governments found that they could not agree upon any date in 1931, the meeting was deferred until summer 1932. Though not the result of British Government policy or pressure, this delay gave the new National Government time to conduct a most elaborate set of pre-conference manœuvres. Also, in Australia they found a new and more cooperative Government. The Scullin administration was gone, and in its place was a 'United Australia Government' which contained many familiar faces from the Bruce-Page era.[3]

Preparations began in November 1931. Thomas, who at that time hoped to tour the Dominions for pre-conference discussions, asked his colleagues to decide several matters of strategy and tactics. A Cabinet Committee was set up, and quickly decided, at Chamberlain's insistence but over Thomas' opposition, to abandon the old principle of unilateral preferential concessions: at Ottawa, Britain would offer to barter advantages.[4] This new idea was in accord with the old Tariff Reform principle: customs duties should be used as bargaining counters. The 'schedules' would be sent out to the various Empire Governments as soon as British industrialists had screened them.[5] The British Government would receive Dominion requests in advance of the Conference. However, offers and requests would not be matched until the Conference actually met. The preliminary interchanges were meant to explore the terrain, and perhaps to help Governments take some decisions with respect to 'possible' and 'impossible' bargains. Further, though committed to the idea of bilateral bargaining, the British

---

[2] For the meetings, see DO 35/243/8835. The 'wheat quota' involved a commitment that British millers would obtain a certain minimum percentage of their wheat from the Dominions. No price-guarantee was intended.

[3] The new Prime Minister was J. A. Lyons (1879–1939), who left the Labour Party in January 1931 and aligned himself with the Nationalists to form the United Australia Party. He was Prime Minister from November 1931 to April 1939. Because the Country Party was not at first attached to his Government, Earle Page did not join it until 1934. But S. B. Bruce was a leading member from the beginning.

[4] For the proceedings of the Committee, see CAB 27/473, OC(31), 1 through 11 conclusions, November 16, 1931 to July 6, 1932.

[5] For Thomas' comments on the schedules, see CAB 27/473, OC(31)2; the schedules themselves are in CAB 27/243, OC(31) 6 through 11.

politicians and officials wanted to generalize concessions as far as possible. They wanted 'most-favoured-Imperial-nation' rates which would be lower than their general tariff rates. Finally, they hoped that the Dominions would extend as many concessions as possible to the Indians and to the rest of the dependent Empire. Cunliffe-Lister, now Colonial Secretary, was prepared to negotiate on the colonies' behalf. In the months before the Conference, his staff prepared lists of colonial goods on which particular Dominions might be asked for concessions. Britain was not very much interested in the bargains which the various Dominions might strike among themselves, though there was some concern that in the Australasian market Canada might win concessions for her manufactures at British expense.

On December 10th, the Dominion Governments were told that the 'schedules' would soon be sent. In January 1932 they were dispatched. These immense and detailed documents must have given the Dominion officials some pause. Though no tariff rates or margins were specified, the schedules would have to be explored item-by-item. And the Empire bureaucracies were ill-equipped for this task.

In Australia, the Cabinet responded by setting up a sub-committee, which senior officials regularly attended. The senior British trade commissioner and senior representative were also present much of the time. This group began to devise a 'formula' for preferential margins which could be applied to the Australian tariff in whole or in part. It also devised a more favourable 'sub-formula'. However, though the new Australian Government was publicly committed to tariff-reduction, they felt obliged to reserve many items for later examination: some had already been referred to the Tariff Board, while others raised awkward questions for local employers and unions.

In Canada, the British High Commissioner was welcomed at a Cabinet meeting, where he presented the 'schedule' and discussed its contents. Prime Minister Bennett assured him that the document would be examined carefully. But nothing more was heard of it until the conference actually began. At the time the High Commissioner, Sir William Clark, suspected that Bennett was deliberately evading the issue. The documents now reveal that the problem was largely one of staff work. Bennett had asked the Canadian Manufacturers' Association to list all the goods 'of a class or kind not made in Canada'. Only on such goods was he prepared to make tariff-cuts. The list was very late in coming, and it reached him in an unusable form—9553 items listed helter-skelter.[6] His own staff seems never to have been asked to examine the British schedule of 269 items, though it did prepare its own 'class

[6] For Bennett's attitude to the list, see Documents Section, Items 17, 19, 23.

or kind' list—of 7000 items! Hence Bennett's increasing tendency, as the Conference drew near, to see it in flatulent terms: it should, he told Sir William Clark, confine itself to 'principles'; the awkward bargains should be struck later, or not formalized at all.[7]

Long before the Canadian officials' committees had begun to function, the Australian ministers had set up their Cabinet sub-committee and had begun serious discussions with the British representatives. They had also briefed their London representatives with respect to the concessions they wanted from Britain. Bennett never managed to achieve this. The Canadian delays certainly reflect errors of judgement and defects in administration, both in Cabinet and in bureaucracy. They do not, however, appear to reflect any strategy with respect to the Conference itself. The documents show that Bennett wanted a successful meeting as much as the British did.

Both New Zealand and South Africa made efforts to discuss matters with British officials. However, the South African ministers were reluctant to do much until they could actually confront their British opposite numbers. The New Zealanders began earnestly, but ministers' attention was diverted by the serious internal financial crisis.[8]

Hoping to speed the Dominions in their preparatory work, and to get more out of them at the coming Conference, the United Kingdom Cabinet gave careful attention to the preferential clauses in the Import Duties Bill, which it introduced early in 1932. Should there be free entry for Empire goods in the hope of a satisfactory *quid pro quo*? No preferential concessions for the present, pending the results of the conference? Or some other arrangement? Neville Chamberlain consulted Bennett in Canada and Thomas at Geneva, who in turn consulted the Dominions' representatives at the League. In its first draft, the Bill had granted no preferences for the time being. But Chamberlain believed this provision would be 'disastrous', and Bennett agreed. Hence the final formulary: the dependent Empire was granted permanent free entry, but the Dominions were granted free entry only until November 15, 1932.[9] If the results at Ottawa were unsatisfactory, many of their imports would pay a duty of 10 per cent.

---

[7] DO 114/42, pp. 125–6: telegram, Sir William Clark to Dominions Office, March 26, 1932.

[8] The same thing had happened to some extent in Australia, where the New South Wales Government default exercised the attention of senior ministers at an inconvenient moment for the Anglo-Australian discussions.

[9] Derek Aldcroft, *The Interwar Economy: Britain, 1919–1939* (London, 1970), 285–6, 293–4, wrongly states that the Act granted permanent free entry; hence it is also wrong to believe that its terms hampered the British negotiators at Ottawa. The documents suggest the reverse. For the views placed before

The Act does not seem to have accelerated matters in any Dominion. Hence, perhaps, the extraordinary 'hurry-up' telegram which the Dominions Office dispatched, following a meeting of ministers, on May 9th.[10] It reminded the Dominion Governments that the new preferences were temporary, asked them to speed their negotiations, and warned them not to ask for new duties or concessions unless they were willing to make really great concessions themselves. In New Zealand and Australia, the telegram caused fury, and a serious setback to the local talks; in Canada, Bennett was annoyed but did nothing.[11]

Further problems were arising about the agenda. As convener of the Conference, Canada was supposed to prepare this document. In London everyone expected that past practice would be followed. A draft would be cabled to the other Governments, who would comment and suggest additions and deletions, so that the final agenda would be agreed. But Bennett was preparing the agenda himself—very slowly. Only on May 24th—two months before the Conference was to open—were preliminary agenda at last vouchsafed.[12] To the British officials and ministers, the contents were as alarming as the delay. First of all, the Canadians proposed to lumber the Conference with all sorts of trivia—the stuffing with which, in the past, the Imperial Government had padded the economic agenda of Imperial Conferences which were really not supposed to do anything much. The Canadians also had ignored the question of 'machinery for economic cooperation', to which Britain attached much importance. Further, they had specifically mentioned the problem of trade with Russia. Finally, they showed an obsessive though vague interest in monetary questions. As their second main item they listed 'consideration of desirability and feasibility of taking steps to restore and stabilize general price level and to stabilize exchange including consideration of monetary standards'. The Canadians

---

Cabinet, see CAB 24/227, CP 49(32), January 28, 1932, CP 31(32), January 18, 1932. For the Geneva conversations, see Bennett Papers, 113, 568–75: memorandum by Canadian participants.

[10] See Doc. 18.

[11] DO 114/42, p.187, 188: telegrams, New Zealand Government to Dominions Office, May 19, and June 21, 1932; DO 35/241/8831J/47: dispatch, United Kingdom Senior Trade Commissioner in New Zealand to Department of Overseas Trade, May 30, 1932; DO 114/42, pp. 169–71: telegrams, Australian Government to Dominions office, May 17, 1932 and United Kingdom Representative in Australia to Dominions Office, May 24, 1932; DO 35/420/8831H/90: dispatch, United Kingdom Representative in Australia to Dominions Office, June 1, 1932; DO 114/42, pp. 138–9: letter, Sir William Clark to Sir Edward Harding, May 11, 1932.

[12] DO 114/42, p. 87: telegram, Canadian Government to Dominions Office, May 24, 1932.

and Australians were known to want a British boycott of Russian wheat and timber, currently coming to Britain in large quantity. But Britain could not accede without serious financial problems: she had exported machinery to the USSR on short-term credit which only the proceeds of the wheat and timber sales could repay. As for monetary matters, Chamberlain and the Treasury feared the 'naïve' monetary expansionist views that they knew to be widespread in Canada, Australia, and New Zealand. Like many economists of the period, they did not think that the Empire could 'reflate' itself to prosperity simply by monetary expansion. Having just escaped from the rigidities of the gold standard, they were not prepared to stabilize their own exchange rate, even though they knew that a falling and fluctuating pound caused trouble in their trade relations with the two 'gold bloc' Dominions, South Africa and Canada. By admitting that Russia should be discussed at Ottawa, they got the Canadians to omit the country's name. However, on the monetary clause they were obliged to accept:

> Consideration of existing interrelationships of various currencies and monetary standards of the Empire, and of the desirability and feasibility of taking steps to restore and stabilise the general price level and to stabilise exchanges.[13]

In this form the agenda were finally settled on July 7th, and published on July 12th—eight days before the Conference's opening, just before the sailing of the British delegation, and long after the Antipodean Prime Ministers had left for Ottawa.

The agenda-discussions had put the United Kingdom delegates on notice that money and Russia would be important matters at the Conference. However, the Government did not discuss the question of monetary policy. On Russia, it considered the possibility of a new Anglo-Soviet trade agreement. The Cabinet's Ottawa Committee and its Trade-with-Russia Committee had recommended that the old agreement should be denounced, and that after the Ottawa Conference a new agreement should be prepared. However, their idea was to increase Russia's purchases of British goods, not to reduce Britain's purchases from the USSR. The Cabinet took no decision with respect to Soviet trade before the British delegation sailed.[14]

The Government had also been put on notice that Australia and New Zealand would demand concessions on meat and dairy produce—

---

[13] DO 114/42, telegram, Canadian Government to Dominions Office, July 3, 1932.
[14] CAB 24/230, CP 169(32), May 30, 1932; CAB 23/71, June 1, 1932, June 8, 1932(2); CAB 23/72, August 4, 1932, August 27, 1932.

higher duties and quantitative restrictions on foreign goods.[15] Both Governments pressed the United Kingdom officials and ministers to give some clue as to their intentions. From Melbourne, Sir Henry Gullett[16] repeatedly urged the British trade commissioner to extract some commitment from the United Kingdom Government. Thomas' position was that because discussions had not advanced equally with all Dominions nothing could yet be said about meat—or about the other concessions for which the Australians has asked.[17]

There could be no word on meat because the United Kingdom Cabinet had not decided what to do about it—or about any other matter which might arise at the Conference. A wheat quota would be offered. But the Dominions were known not to want this. As for the other issues, the delegates sailed off for Quebec with an open brief[18]—as Chamberlain and Thomas both wished.[19] They were reminded of the Cabinet's agreement to differ about the tariffs. And that was all. On July 8th, the committee of officials had prepared a long list of 'questions suggested for consideration'.[20] Their list shows on how many basic questions no decision had yet been taken. What was the national policy toward the price level? Tariff structure? Artificial fostering of Dominion manufacturing? Agriculture at home and overseas? On July 12th, nobody knew.[21] Policy would emerge *de facto*, in the pressure-cooker of an Ottawa August.[22]

---

[15] On April 7th, New Zealand asked for preferences on meat, butter, cheese, wool, eggs, processed milk, and fresh fruit. DO 35/241/8831J/10: memorandum by Sir H. Wilson. On March 10th, Australian representatives in London broached the question of a foreign-meat quota. On April 13th, they proposed a meat duty and spoke favourably of a quota. On June 15th, they again stressed the importance of some concession on meat. DO 114/42, pp. 153–176 ff: notes of second and third meetings with the representatives of Australia; letter, F. L. MacDougall to J. H. Thomas, June 15, 1932.

[16] Sir Henry Gullett (1878–1940) was Australian minister for trade and customs 1928–29 and 1932–33; in 1934–37 he was minister for the negotiation of trade treaties. In this capacity he visited London several times. In 1939–40 he was Australian minister for external affairs and information.

[17] DO 35/240/8831H/110: dispatch, R. Dalton to Department of Overseas Trade, June 20, 1932; DO 114/42, pp. 179–80: letter, J. H. Thomas to F. L. MacDougall, June 17, 1932.

[18] CAB 32/72, July 12, 1932. The delegates were Baldwin, Chamberlain, Thomas, Hailsham, Cunliffe-Lister, Gilmour, and Runciman. A large secretariat accompanied them.

[19] CAB 27/473, OC(31), 9th conclusions, June 9, 1932.

[20] CAB 32/105, O(B)(32) 136. See Doc. 22.

[21] In December 1931, the Cabinet Committee had rejected the idea of new livestock-products duties, while recommending new or increased duties on foreign butter, cheese, honey, raw apples, raw pears, oranges, grapes, other raw fruit, canned fruit, canned fish and dried fruit. But the Cabinet had never

III

The British ministers[23] did not go to Ottawa in a protectionist mood. They wanted to create jobs for British workers; to this end, they hoped to reduce Dominion and Indian duties, in exchange for the maintenance of duty-free entry under the Import Duties Act. They also hoped for some improvement with respect to some less obvious trade barriers. Canada, in particular, had ingeniously developed arbitrary practices which created enormous uncertainty with respect to duties. The customs law gave so much discretion to officials, and provided so generously for the representation of Canadian manufacturers, that both British exporter and Canadian importer often got a nasty shock when the British goods were already landed in a Canadian port.[24] The delegates hoped that they would be able to reduce or eliminate various special levies—the Australian 'primage', and the Canadian and South African 'exchange-dumping' duties. The former was an emergency revenue device; the latter were meant to offsct the depreciation of sterling *vis-à-vis* the South African pound and the Canadian dollar. Finally, they hoped that the Conference would contribute to a general lowering of world tariffs. Some of the British delegates were prepared, or eager, to raise Britain's own food duties. They must have recognized that the Dominions and India would not be able to widen preferential margins only by reducing the preferential rates; sometimes the rates on foreign goods were bound to rise. But for some of them, especially Walter Runciman,[25] the only logical basis for the entire operation was in tariff-reduction. Others, especially J. H. Thomas, possibly hoped that the clever British delegates would out-manœuvre the opposite side.

In their hearts the delegates must have known that their hopes would be disappointed. Their overseas representatives and home advisers had

---

approved these recommendations, which were in any event less extensive in coverage and rate than what the Australasians were already demanding. See CAB 24/225: CP 324(31), and CAB 23/69, December 16, 1931.

[22] Fortunately, in 1932 much less steamy than usual.

[23] And their very large staff of senior civil servants.

[24] Some of the trouble centered on the provision by which lower duties were levied on goods 'of a class or kind not made in Canada'. If a Canadian manufacturer represented that he did produce a good—or even *could* produce it—the customs officials automatically and immediately raised the duty. Also, the law allowed them to fix completely arbitrary valuations on imported goods. Hence, ad valorem duties could be sharply raised in dollar terms, even though the percentage rates were not raised.

[25] Walter Runciman, first Viscount Runciman (1870–1939) was a Liberal free-trader. He held office in the pre-war Liberal government, and was President of the Board of Trade in 1914–16 and 1931–37. In 1938–39, as Lord President of the Council, he led the mission to Czechoslovakia.

told them repeatedly that Canadian and Australian sentiment was strongly protectionist—in the former country because the steel and cotton manufacturers had the Prime Minister's ear, and in the latter because the Government, though formally committed to tariff-reduction, would not dare destroy jobs. South Africa was uninterested, and New Zealand a small and near-bankrupt market whose tariffs were already relatively low. India could not afford much tariff-reduction. No Conference was needed to expand the preferential arrangements in the colonial Empire. Most important, none of the delegates had the slightest experience in tariff-bargaining. Not since the mid-nineteenth century had the United Kingdom undertaken any such negotiations.

Yet the Conference could not be avoided. British public opinion, stirred by some newspapers' unrealistic 'Empire Free Trade' slogans and by the ministers' own public statements, hoped for great things. In some Dominions, especially in Canada, hopes ran equally high. Most of the Conservative Party was emotionally committed to the idea of Empire Development. Tariff Reformers, like Chamberlain and Cunliffe-Lister, were bound to regard the Conference as a chance to attain the ends which they had sought for thirty years. Anyway, with luck something useful might be made to happen.

In so gloomy and inherently hopeless a negotiation, it is hardly surprising that one new idea—Bennett's 'domestic competition' formula—appealed strongly to the delegates, who would have to salvage something from their weeks at Ottawa. However small the immediate benefits might be, the Agreements could then be praised for their long-run implications—a restraint on 'uneconomic' Empire manufacturing, and a gradual fall in Dominion tariffs.

'Domestic competition' was not invented at the Conference. In the preliminary talks, the Australians had emphasized the role that their Tariff Board might play in gradually reducing their protective tariffs. Bennett had begun to speak of broad principles—in particular, that of admitting British goods on terms which would just offset their presumed competitive edge. Both lines of thought should have had an immense appeal to lovers of 'scientific tariff-making'. Both were consistent with the proposition, which everybody accepted, that the Dominions could not be asked to sacrifice their secondary industry so as to create jobs in the United Kingdom. Both ideas were transmitted to London, but neither idea seems to have been noticed there. Until they reached Ottawa, and discovered how little the Dominions would offer by way of immediate tariff-cuts, no British ministers ever discussed them.

The Conference opened on July 20th, with a rousing but empty speech from Bennett.[26] The next day, the heads of delegations met to

[26] Printed in Cmd. 4175.

set up five committees which would carry forward the common work of the Conference. It was already clear that the most important work, the tariff-bargaining, would be conducted on a bilateral basis, though the Dominions would coordinate their demands with respect to foodstuffs and raw materials.

Of the five committees, only that on monetary and financial questions had any importance. Though it took no binding decisions, and produced a vacuous report, Chamberlain used it as a forum for expounding his solution to the problem of low prices. The right course was for the *producers* to raise prices by controlling output. Britain could and would keep credit cheap, but British monetary policy could not raise prices by itself, especially where a product had a world market.[27] Further, for the time being there could be no question of stabilizing exchange rates: the world monetary system was still disturbed by the disorders which had forced Britain to leave the gold standard in 1931. To the delegation's relief, the other conferees accepted this British lead.[28]

We can now see how unfortunate Chamberlain's position was. The Ottawa Conference should have been working on exchange rates, not tariffs. By devaluing their own currencies *vis-à-vis* sterling, the Dominions and India would have raised the domestic-currency receipts of their primary producers. Demanding more goods, these producers would have generated more demand for local factories to satisfy. Given the probable demands for their exports, and their own response to higher prices in terms of local currency, they would have produced more and earned more sterling, thus lightening the burden of their external sterling debts and raising their own real incomes. British exporters, though hindered by the devaluation, would have gained something from the higher real incomes of the Empire primary producers. It is a great pity that Chamberlain did not say, 'We think that you should all devalue your currencies *vis-à-vis* sterling and then fix them to sterling as some of you have already done. This devaluation will help you but it will hurt our export trade. Please, therefore, reduce your duties on our manufactures, at least a little.'

---

[27] Chamberlain's statement is printed in Cmd. 4175, pp. 166–72.

[28] See 'appreciation' cabled to Ramsay MacDonald on August 3. CAB 24/232, CP 277(32). MacDonald, like Runciman, had long opposed the Conservatives' agricultural protectionism, and had disliked the protectionist suggestions of December 1931 (see above, note 21). The 10 per cent general tariff, and the continued free entry for meat and wheat, had been suggested by Runciman to prevent a Conservative three-decker tariff. See the account of the talks between Runciman and Chamberlain in University of Newcastle-upon-Tyne, Walter Runciman papers, Box 3, file 'Cabinet Colleagues': letters, Runciman to Mac-Donald and vice versa, December 21 and 28, 1931.

No one knows what would have happened if he had done so. As Australia and New Zealand had already devalued, they might have been willing to repeat and extend the process. India, fixated on the rupee cost of servicing its sterling debt, might have clung to the old rupee-sterling exchange rate. But the British Cabinet, not New Delhi, had decided in September 1931 to maintain this rate. Bennett, we know, wanted a stable exchange rate between the Canadian dollar and sterling, primarily because floating rates could weaken the protective force of Canadian tariffs.[29] He certainly used clandestine devices to preserve the fiction that Canada was still on the gold standard at the old parity. But his advisers were telling him that Canada should consider devaluation, and that Empire countries should stabilize their currencies *vis-à-vis* the pound, while the pound floated *vis-à-vis* the dollar.[30] South Africa was still clinging to its old gold parity. But late in 1932, she reduced the gold content of her pound. Hence it is at least conceivable that the Dominions would have welcomed a genuine British initiative with respect to exchange rates.

Yet, one suspects that none of the Governments possessed the sophistication to see what devaluation could do. Most professional opinion, and most economists, still thought it was evil to manipulate the currency in this way. Certainly Chamberlain and his party could much more easily imagine Empire economic integration and reconstruction through tariffs. Monetary devices came from cranks, carping Liberals, and out-of-office Tories like Amery. Yet it is true that a monetary conference would have done more to raise Empire employment and re-integrate Empire commerce than any tariff conference could possibly have done.

Nevertheless, it was tariffs with which the Conference was chiefly concerned. On July 23rd, the British discovered that the initial Dominion offers did not amount to much.[31] Thereafter, the British would be obliged not only to resist the more outrageous of the Dominions' demands, but to fight for some increase in the Dominions' offers. But from this meeting, the delegates extracted some comfort. Frederick Field, the Senior Trade Commissioner in Canada,[32] suggested that 'there would be better prospects of success if gradual reduction

---

[29] Bennett Papers, 115, 243–4.
[30] Bennett Papers, 112, 587–92.
[31] CAB 32/105, O(B)(32) 141: notes of discussion with ministers and officials, July 23, 1932.
[32] Frederick Field (1884–1960), edited the *Monetary Times* of Toronto from 1906 to 1917. He was United Kingdom Trade Commissioner in Toronto from 1918 to 1924, and Senior Trade Commissioner in Canada from 1924 to 1948.

were agreed upon'.[33] To Chamberlain this was 'a new point, at least new to me'.[34]

As we have seen, this idea was not really new; Bennett had put it to Field and to Sir William Clark[35] before the Conference. But the idea seems to have grown in Chamberlain's mind after he heard it. Its development may have been encouraged by contact with the Indian delegation, because the Indian protective tariff was already framed upon appropriate lines. The simple suggestion quickly became a scheme for 'competitive' customs-duties. The Dominions would agree to protect only plausible industries. They were to submit their duties to impartial Tariff Boards, which would decide how much protection the domestic industries really needed. The Dominions would agree to impose only such 'scientific' tariffs on British goods, which would then enter their territories with the status of 'domestic competitors'.

On July 25th–26th, the British delegates agreed to seek this status for their exports.[36] They were successful with respect to Canada, Australia, and New Zealand, but not with the South Africans, who would not accept the principle.[37] The New Zealanders agreed to set up an *ad hoc* Tariff Tribunal. The Canadians promised to constitute the Tariff Board for which their statutes already provided. Everyone promised to protect only plausible industries, and not to impose prohibitive duties.

Later the 'domestic competition clauses' were to cause immense trouble, especially with Australia. Partly the problem was faulty drafting—in particular, vague terminology which could mean anything or nothing. But basically the difficulty was with the concept itself. 'Domestic competition' rested on a fallacy—the idea that all British producers operated at a single relatively low-cost level, while in each Dominion all producers of the same good operated at a single but higher-cost level. In fact, different firms had different costs, and within a firm or an industry, unit-costs depended upon the scale of the plant and the size of current output. Further, a higher price would always

---

[33] CAB 32/105, O(B)(32) 141.

[34] Feiling, *Chamberlain*, 212, reporting Chamberlain's diary entry for July 23, 1932. See also Middlemas and Barnes, *Baldwin*, 676.

[35] Sir William Clark (1876–1952) was the first United Kingdom High Commissioner in Canada (1928–34). He had entered the service of the Board of Trade in 1899 and had been Comptroller-General of the Department of Overseas Trade from 1917 to 1928. Later (1934–39) he was United Kingdom High Commissioner in South Africa.

[36] CAB 32/101, O(UK)(32), 15th meeting, July 26, 1932.

[37] The relevant clauses in the trade agreements are as follows: Canadian Articles 10–15, Australian Articles 10–13, New Zealand Articles 7–9 (Doc. 28).

attract a larger output from any particular 'set' of plant and equipment. Hence there could be no one 'competitive' tariff. The higher a Dominion's duty on a British commodity, the more of the goods the Dominion would produce, and the more men would work at its production. Logically, therefore, one could fix the 'competitive' tariff only after someone—Tariff Board or Government—had fixed the output and employment at which the industry was to operate, both in the relevant Dominion and in the United Kingdom. One may talk evasively about 'reasonable chance' and 'efficient production' but one cannot avoid this fact. Hence one cannot expect a Government in a world of unemployment to honour a pledge which relates to 'domestic competition' unless the implied tariff level leaves industrial employment as high as before. In effect, this means that Tariff Boards will cut tariffs only when it can be shown that local firms are 'profiteering'—that at their present actual outputs their profits are 'excessive' relative to their capital. Only in such cases might Boards and Governments lower duties without expecting any extra unemployment.[38]

Besides the meaningless concession of 'domestic competition', the British managed to improve the initial offers of Australia, New Zealand and Canada. In so doing, they encountered many obstacles, not the least of which was Bennett's ill mannered deviousness.[39] The final Agreements committed the Dominions and India to adjust rates and margins on many goods. The delegates knew they were still not getting much. On August 7th, Baldwin had circulated a memorandum in which he thought the concessions amounted to an extra £12·5 million in exports.[40] To this must be added the Canadian concessions which Baldwin had omitted, and various other later adjustments. We have no evidence that the delegates ever added things up in this way, but if they had, they would have got a total of £18 million—4·5 per cent of Britain's total exports in 1931, and 10·5 per cent of her exports to the Empire.

These figures should not be taken very seriously. In most instances we do not know how the officials and ministers did their sums, and we certainly do know that they could not have got the right answer at the time, because hindsight is needed to assess the Agreements' impact. To each Empire country, British exports were determined by several things—habit, trade connections, consumer preferences, the composition of local output and demand, the price of sterling, domestic prices, and trade barriers, including exchange controls, quota restrictions, and

---

[38] In fact, even then there may be some displacement of labour.

[39] For a recent and well-documented but incomplete account, see Middlemas and Barnes, *Baldwin*, 673–83. For Bennett's strategy, see Docs. 25, 26, 27.

[40] CAB 32/103, O(UK)(32), 25, August 7, 1932.

tariffs. We could in principle carry out an econometric analysis of intra-Empire trade so as to analyse the separate effects of these independent variables. This would be complicated. Fortunately, there is a simpler approach which, though crude, cannot mislead us very much.

We saw in Chapter 1 that in the interwar period there were certain patterns in British overseas trade. We can guess the *maximum* trade-diverting effect of the Ottawa Agreements by examining the change in the percentage of Empire imports which were drawn from the United Kingdom. The result is an over-estimate because it attributes trade shifts to the Agreements, even when we know that to some extent they had different causes—most importantly, the depreciation of sterling relative to the American dollar and the franc. This does not matter so long as we clearly understand the implication: the Ottawa Agreements did not do as much for the British export trade as the following figures suggest.

Our earlier description showed that in the interwar period the Empire drew a declining proportion of its imports from the United Kingdom. However, in 1932–35 the proportion was higher by about 3 per cent than we might have expected in the light of the continuously declining trend. These three percentage points imply an extra £13 million of British exports in 1933, rising to £28 million in 1937. These figures are 3·5 per cent and 5·4 per cent of British exports in those two years. They are also 5·4 per cent and 6·6 per cent of Empire imports from foreign countries.[41]

To win these insignificant gains, the British delegates agreed to impose new or higher duties on wheat, flat white maize, husked rice, butter, cheese, eggs, condensed milk, milk powder, apples, pears, bananas, oranges, grapefruit, grapes, peaches, nectarines, plums, preserved and dried fruit including canned fruit, honey, linseed, cod liver, castor, coconut, groundnut, rape and sesamum oils, chilled and frozen salmon, unwrought copper, and magnesium chloride. They managed to defeat the Australian demand for a meat duty, but they did agree to impose quotas on foreign meat.[42] They also bound themselves

---

[41] For a different and conceptually more sophisticated approach see G. D. MacDougall, 'British and American Exports: a Study suggested by the Theory of Comparative Costs', *Economic Journal*, LXI (1961).

[42] Australia and New Zealand were to control their own meat shipments during 1933, but were to be free from control until the middle of 1935. Canada was guaranteed free and unrestricted entry for up to 2·5 million cwt. of bacon. South Africa was promised that Whitehall would use its good offices with the meat companies to make sure that facilities would be provided for the chilled-beef trade which the South African Government hoped to encourage. All the Dominions were guaranteed free entry for their meat until August 1937. No duty

not to reduce certain preferential margins and certain duties on foreign goods during the five-year term of the Agreement, and for three years they promised to put no duty or quota-control on Empire eggs, poultry, butter, cheese, or other milk products. Finally, they promised Canada that if Russian goods were being offered on terms which undermined the Agreement, the United Kingdom would take action.[43]

Throughout the 1920s, Britain had drawn a remarkably stable percentage of her imports from the Empire. In 1932, this percentage rose sharply, and continued to rise thereafter. Some part of this trade diversion must be attributed to the Agreements. If we project the 1922–30 percentage through the thirties, and calculate 'hypothetical' British imports from the Empire by applying this percentage to Britain's actual total import, we find that the hypothetical purchases are less than the actual by £46 million in 1933 and by £98 million in 1937. These numbers represent 11·4 per cent and 16·5 per cent of British imports from foreign countries in these years, and they are 7·2 per cent and 10·3 per cent of total British imports. They roughly indicate the *maximum* amount by which the Agreements might have affected Britain's import trade.

In fact the Agreement did not prevent foreign countries from increasing their sales both to the United Kingdom and to the Empire. These rose rapidly in 1933–37. Only in 1932–33 was there an actual decrease in foreign sales to Britain and the Empire, whose total imports were falling, but whose imports from foreigners fell much more than one would have expected in light of the patterns in other years before or after 1932–33. Applying these patterns to 1932–33, and attributing everything to the Agreements, we get an 'impact effect' of £12 million— £5 million less in sales to the United Kingdom, and £7 million less to the Empire.

Relative to world trade and output these figures are infinitesimal— even at the depth of the Depression. Nevertheless, the Agreements were serious for some suppliers in some foreign countries. Foreign wheat farmers ought to have known they had nothing to fear. Because the Empire produced more wheat than it consumed, competition would

---

was imposed on foreign meat, but Britain agreed to control imports of foreign chilled and frozen beef, and frozen mutton and lamb. Chilled beef shipments were not to rise above the 1931–32 level, the 'Ottawa year'. Imports of frozen beef, mutton, and lamb, were to be rapidly reduced to 65 per cent of this level. Finally, the Dominions were guaranteed a rising share of British meat-imports.

[43] Canadian Agreement, Article 21. The goods on which margins and foreign duties were stabilized are in the Schedules to the several agreements, as summarized in Doc. 28.

ensure that the Agreements would have no effect on world wheat markets. Britain would take more of her wheat from the Empire, and the Empire would have less wheat to place on foreign markets, where foreign wheat would then replace Empire wheat. The same was true of the foreign lead, zinc, and copper producers, at least in the short run. But for foreign livestock industries the threat was real. The Australians and the New Zealanders were determined to capture the British market from the Argentines and the Danes. Britain had introduced quotas and raised duties to help them do this. Some foreign Governments proved eager for new trade treaties which would guarantee their goods against further protective action.

IV

So far as British domestic policy was concerned, the main legacies of Ottawa related to meat and butter.[44] The actual outcome reflected the British delegation's determination, having conceded a wheat duty and a higher butter duty, to avoid a meat duty. The arrangements had a make-shift look. They did not satisfy Australia's pre-Conference hopes, nor New Zealand's. Nor did they coincide with the wishes of Sir John Gilmour, the British Minister of Agriculture. Perhaps his total silence at the Conference is explained by the earlier and total defeat of his policy—a general duty on foodstuffs, with a preferential but positive levy on Dominion goods.[45] The Cabinet had in fact rejected this policy long before the Conference met, and Gilmour seems to have had nothing else to suggest. In the spring of 1932 his Ministry was prepared to consider a restrictive quota for foreign bacon and perhaps another for butter. But it seems to have done no work on the general question of quotas, in spite of the clear Australian warning with respect to them. In a sense, however, the Agreements did represent a victory for his departmental point of view. The British delegation had explicitly stated that the interest of Britain's own farmers must come before the Dominions'. The Dominions had agreed to regulate their meat-exports during 1933. Afterwards, the officials could contemplate the happy possibility of price-raising quotas on foreign goods—especially the lamb and mutton whose price-situation was most painfully worrying them in 1932. They had also won more protection against foreign dairy products

---

[44] The development of British agricultural policy is discussed and documented more fully in relation to the Ottawa Agreements in Drummond, *Expansion and Protectiveness*, ch. 5.

[45] For the report of Gilmour's Agricultural Policy Committee, CAB 24/227, CP 21(32). Gilmour's own recommendations are in CAB 27/465, APC(31) 2, 3.

—though not against Dominion goods, at least until the expiry of the 'Schedule A reservation' in 1935.[46]

A duty would have been better for Britain than a quota. Hence the dispassionate observer must praise the new cheese and butter levies while deploring the meat quotas. Because Britain was the world's only large importer of meat and dairy products, in the short run any such duty would have been 'shifted backward' to the producers: foreigners would have paid the duty. Chamberlain, we know, would have liked a meat tariff. At the Conference he was prepared to accept it. But he also advocated quotas. In opposition, as chairman of the Conservative Party, he had set the party Research Department to work on a detailed quota scheme.[47] In the delegates' meetings, and before the monetary committee of the Conference, he had strongly pushed for production controls as price-raising devices. Like almost everyone else, he believed that price increases were both necessary and sufficient conditions for the restoration of prosperity. At the 1933 World Economic Conference, he would shortly exhort foreign nations in similar terms.

It was shortly to appear that the meat arrangements were booby-trapped in various ways. They involved civil servants and ministers in constant wrangles with the Dominions. Some of the trouble arose over interpretation. Canada, for instance, maintained that because the Anglo-Canadian Agreement did not *specifically* reserve Britain's right to regulate Canadian livestock shipments after July 1, 1934, it guaranteed Canada free and unrestricted entry until August 1937. Australia bleated constantly about the meaning of 'expanding share'. But most of the trouble arose over the Agreements' implications for domestic protectionism. The Agreements had been made for precisely the wrong term, and with no idea of future price-movements. Accordingly, by the autumn of 1932, when meat and butter prices had begun an alarming downward slide, Britain found that she could neither tax Dominion produce nor impose quotas upon it. During 1933–34, the price situation became more and more critical, especially for British dairy farmers and fat-stock raisers. By this time a further element of rigidity and friction had entered the system: under Runciman's leadership and pressed by his strong advocacy, the United Kingdom had signed trade agreements with Argentina, Denmark, Norway, Sweden, and several smaller states.

Before the Conference, Argentina had been willing to grant Britain tariff-preference in exchange for assurance about Britain's purchases of

---

[46] See Doc. 28, Schedule 1 (originally Schedule A, in the Canadian, Australian, New Zealand, and South African Agreements).

[47] K. Feiling, *Chamberlain*, 181.

Argentine chilled beef. After she learned the terms of the Agreements, which were aimed directly at her beef and lamb shipments, she was naturally not prepared to do so. But she badly wanted some guarantee that nothing more would be done to her. The British negotiators were also eager for a settlement: Argentine exchange control was hurting the British exporter, and inconveniencing the British capitalists who could not readily convert their Argentine currency into sterling. In exchange for commitments on duties and exchange, in 1933 Britain agreed not to increase any new meat or wheat duties until November 1936. She also promised to impose no quota-controls on Argentine wheat, maize, wool, and various other products. With respect to meat quotas, she retained the right to impose unilateral cuts on chilled-meat shipments, but only by 10 per cent of the 1931–32 shipments. Any further cuts in chilled beef imports, and any cuts in frozen beef, mutton or lamb beyond the 35 per cent 'Ottawa cuts', would be allowed only if Britain also cut shipments from the Dominions.[48]

In the same months of 1933, the British officials were devising trade agreements for Denmark and Northern Europe. Here the problem was not beef or lamb, but bacon, ham, and butter. In the course of 1933 the United Kingdom promised not to increase her duties on foreign butter, eggs, or cream, and she guaranteed free though not unrestricted entry for bacon and ham. Quotas were allowed, but only insofar as they were needed 'to ensure effective operation of a scheme or schemes for the regulation of the marketing of domestic supplies of these products'.[49] And minimum butter and bacon quotas were guaranteed.

The Dominions, though informed about these negotiations rather late in the day, were certainly not consulted.[50] Later they argued that the agreements, especially the Anglo-Argentine one, betrayed the 'Ottawa Spirit'. These criticisms were ill-founded. The Dominions were still allowed to capture a rising share of the British market for meat and dairy products; in 1933–34 they proceeded with great vigour to do so. Australasian butter flowed to London in rapidly rising quantities, as the farmers of the Antipodes tried to produce themselves out of their troubles. Chilled beef began for the first time to arrive from Australia: technical progress had suddenly made such shipments possible, and the Australian meat trade was replacing low-value frozen beef with high-

---

[48] Cmd. 4310, 4492, 4494: Anglo-Argentine Convention relating to Trade and Commerce, May 1, 1933, and Supplementary Convention, September 26, 1933.

[49] All the agreements ran for three years. See Cmd. 4323, 4424, 4421.

[50] DO 114/50, pp. 178–9: letters, J. H. Thomas to S. B. Bruce and Sir Thomas Wilford, April 11, 1933. Bruce and Wilford were the Australian and New Zealand High Commissioners in London.

value chilled beef as rapidly as it could. Fortunately, at the Australians' insistence[51] the British had inserted in the Anglo-Argentine Trade Agreement a saving clause about 'experimental' shipments. Because of it, this new chilled meat trade could grow without forcing the British to relax their control of Argentine chilled-beef shipments—so long as the Argentines did not notice. But by the end of 1934 it was already clear that Australian chilled beef was no longer 'experimental'; the trade was regular, large, and growing. Accordingly the Argentines protested. After a long and disingenuous delaying action, late in 1935 the British allowed the Argentines to export 100 per cent of their 1931–32 shipments—not the 90 per cent to which they had been confined almost as soon as the ink was dry on the Anglo-Argentine Agreement.

Meanwhile, by early 1934 Whitehall was growing disenchanted with quotas. Chamberlain had long preferred supplier-regulation. But the existing arrangements were different: several times a year, the British Government had to negotiate with the Dominions and with various foreign countries to fix the next period's meat allowables. The Government's economic advisers soon noticed[52] that quotas raised the prices the British paid for their imported meat and butter, but gave the Exchequer no revenue. Further, the advisers later argued, quotas were hard on the balance of payments, because Britain had to pay more for every pound of meat or butter she imported.[53]

Meanwhile, Britain was successfully subsidizing her wheat farmers by means of a 'levy-subsidy'. Thanks to the Wheat Act of 1932, British millers paid a levy on every bushel of grain they milled, and the proceeds went to British wheat-farmers as deficiency-payments. The system could in principle be applied to every foodstuff where British consumption was far larger than British production. Why should it not be applied to meat and butter?

[51] DO 35/295/9307/20: letter, S. B. Bruce to J. H. Thomas, April 12, 1933.

[52] See CAB 58/20, EAC(E1)104, and CAB 24/251, CP 272(34), for advice garnered during 1934.

[53] The balance-of-payments argument was almost certainly wrong. It would have been right only if the British demand for the relevant foodstuffs had been price-inelastic over the price-range in question. But it is hard to believe that the demand for these semi-luxury foodstuffs with many substitutes could be price-inelastic. Further, even if the foreigners had got more sterling by selling less butter and meat, under the regime of floating sterling which continued from September 1931 to late 1936 the conversion of this sterling would have tended to depreciate sterling relative to foreign currencies, and this depreciation would have tended to encourage British exports. The final effect on the balance of payments would be anybody's guess—and did not matter anyway, because the pound was floating.

Late in 1933 Walter Elliot,[54] energetic Minister of Agriculture and Fisheries, first proposed the extension of the levy-subsidy.[55] At first, nobody agreed with Elliot. Most obviously, levy-subsidies could be introduced only if the Dominions and Argentina would agree with respect to meat levies, and if Denmark and the Dominions would agree with respect to butter levies. Chamberlain remained addicted for some time to supply-regulation—hopeless though it was. Thomas was struck by the negotiating problems which levy-subsidies posed.[56] However, between December 1933 and June 1934 several weighty ministers came to think much better of Elliot's idea. The reasons are hard to trace, but seem to have been connected with Elliot's demonstration that there was no other politically feasible way to raise prices sufficiently. On June 13th, the Cabinet's Produce Markets Supply Committee endorsed levy-subsidies in principle.[57]

The Cabinet had already introduced a temporary repayable subsidy to milk marketing boards.[58] If levy-subsidies could eventually be imposed, prices would then be higher, and the boards would be able to repay the Exchequer when the advances became due on April 1, 1936. In July, the Cabinet decided to pay a temporary grant to fat-stock producers: the subsidy would end on March 31, 1935, by which time, the Government hoped, the Dominions and Argentina would have agreed to a meat levy. The alternative would be 'drastic quantitative restriction'. In a White Paper,[59] in conferences with the Dominions' High Commissioners, and in the careful management of communications with the Dominion Governments, Thomas and the Dominions Office did everything possible to publicize the British Government's determination. Unfortunately for the British, both levy and quota excited the most violent passions overseas—especially in Australia and New Zealand. The farmers of both countries believed that they had a limitless right to sell all they could produce, at 'fair prices'. Politicians encouraged them. The local political environment, though partly of the politicians' own making, impeded compromise, either on quota or on levy. Further, especially in Australia, some politicians seem genuinely to have believed that they had a right to the British market. In the long negotiations which ensued, Sir Henry Gullett repeatedly demanded that

---

[54] Walter Elliot (1888–1958) was Minister of Agriculture and Fisheries in 1932–36, and Secretary of State for Scotland in 1936–38.

[55] CAB 27/560, PMS (33) 1st meeting, December 1, 1933.

[56] For correspondence, see Docs. 31, 32.

[57] CAB 27/560, PMS(33) 7th meeting, June 13, 1934. See also PMS(33) 11, 12, 13.

[58] Cmd. 4519, February 22, 1934.

[59] Cmd. 4651, July 1934: 'The Livestock Situation'.

the British should impose whatever restriction of foreign supplies was necessary to allow Australia to sell all it wanted without quota-control or duty. Neither he nor the New Zealanders seem to have seen the implication of the fact that meat and butter were produced in Britain too. But the New Zealanders were at least willing to make ingenious proposals—for example, in 1933, a customs union with Britain,[60] and in 1937, a bilateral balancing arrangement.[61] The Australians simply demanded, screamed, and obstructed.[62]

From mid-1934 until late 1936, the meat negotiations dragged on.[63] The Dominion Governments and the Argentine could prevent the imposition of any new duties, simply by waiting and arguing. The Argentine Government certainly did this on purpose, and almost certainly the Dominions did likewise. Meanwhile, quota-control continued, and the 'temporary' milk and beef subsidies were repeatedly extended.

Though the overseas Governments would have opposed the schemes in any event, the arithmetic of levy-subsidies prolonged the negotiations and made them more complex. Since the schemes were supposed to be self-funding, the 'right' duty emerged arithmetically from import, domestic production, and the desired domestic producers' price. Only when Chamberlain agreed, on May 4, 1936, that he would permanently subsidize the British beef industry regardless of the yield from any beef duty, was it possible to settle on a scale of beef duties which the Australians and the Argentines could both accept.[64] After further complex negotiations with South Africa and Canada, late in 1936 the Government was able to introduce a Beef and Veal Import Duties Bill. Its expected revenue was far less than the £5 million of Exchequer subsidies to which Chamberlain had agreed.

With respect to beef the levy-subsidy idea died in May 1936. For butter and other commodities it was still alive in principle. Walter Elliot, and W. S. Morrison, his successor in the Ministry of Agriculture, continued to support it vigorously. But its days were numbered.

In the course of the Anglo-New Zealand trade negotiations of 1937, various ministers came to realize that Britain would get nothing out of New Zealand's Walter Nash with respect to manufactures if she offered nothing with respect to butter. In Wellington, the new Labour Govern-

[60] See Doc. 29.
[61] Suggested by Walter Nash, (1882–1968) New Zealand's Labour Finance Minister (1935–1949) and Prime Minister 1957–60.
[62] Their 1936 'trade diversion scheme', though used with vigour in the meat negotiations, does not seem to have originated in them.
[63] See Docs. 33, 34.
[64] CAB 27/619, TAC(36) 3rd meeting, May 4, 1936.

ment was proposing to industrialize New Zealand; the British, for the first time, had cause to worry about access to this reviving market. What would Britain say about butter?

Malcolm MacDonald[65] and Oliver Stanley[66] both opposed any change in the existing arrangements—free and unrestricted entry for Dominion butter. They pointed out that the Dominion Governments knew it was their citizens who would pay the levy through lower producer-prices. Further, the Empire Governments would have to make concessions if the United Kingdom was to conclude a trade agreement with the USA. A new butter duty would infuriate the Australians, whose consent would be essential for Britain to meet the Americans on such products as dried and canned fruits. With Chamberlain's agreement, and over Morrison's[67] protests, it was agreed that the dairy industry should be aided with price-insurance and direct Exchequer subsidies, not levy-subsidies.[68]

When this decision was made public[69] it occasioned a storm of protest from the National Farmers Union, whose leaders professed to believe that the Government was committed to levy subsidies. The Cabinet asked its Agricultural Policy Committee to consider the whole question in principle—for the first time since June 1934.

The Committee's discussions were long and frank. Chamberlain was now more impressed by the negotiatory disadvantages of levy-subsidies than by their revenue conveniences. Further, he now espoused the traditional Treasury view: 'the idea of assigning revenues derived from particular sources to particular objects could not survive critical examination'—especially at a time when defence outlays were rapidly rising. Oliver Stanley was forthright:

> At the present time levy-subsidies were not a practical alternative. Politically speaking, with butter at its present price, it was out of the question to go to the House of Commons and propose a duty on butter. The conditions in 1934, when prices were low, were very different. From the point of view of one who had to negotiate trade

[65] Malcolm MacDonald (b. 1901) was *inter alia* Dominions Secretary 1935–38 and Colonial Secretary 1935 and 1938–40. Later he had a distinguished career in Commonwealth diplomacy.

[66] Oliver Stanley (1896–1950) held various Government and Cabinet offices in the period 1931–45. He was President of the Board of Trade from 1937 to 1940.

[67] William Shepherd Morrison, first Viscount Dunrossil (1893–1961), held various minor offices in 1931–36 and was Minister of Agriculture and Food in 1936–39. Thereafter he held other Cabinet and Government posts.

[68] CAB 27/632, AP(37) 1st meeting, July 13, 1937, and 2nd meeting, July 19, 1937, CAB 23/88, Cabinet 32(37).

[69] Cmd. 5533: 'Milk Policy'.

agreements, levy-subsidies provided greater difficulties than any other form of protection. Our foreign and Dominion competitors understood the working of tariffs, and knew that quantitative regulation would sometimes benefit them, as well as ourselves, but they had no use for levy-subsidies. They did not see why they should have to pay a direct subsidy to their British competitor. The only way of inducing them to do so was for us to pay a heavy price in other directions. These considerations applied with great force in the case of New Zealand, where the Government now bought all the butter from their farmers and were responsible for selling it. The levy would come direct out of the New Zealand treasury ... a levy-subsidy ... would remain the most onerous form of agricultural assistance, that is, the one for which we should have to pay the highest price in trade agreements, both foreign and Dominion.[70]

Even at this bitter end, Morrison spoke vehemently in favour of levy-subsidies. But 'the Committee agreed with the Prime Minister' and on November 17, 1937 the full Cabinet confirmed this verdict.[71]

From this abandonment Oliver Stanley hoped to extract some advantage, primarily in respect of Australia and Canada. Canada wanted compensation before agreeing to facilitate Britain's trade negotiations with the USA. Hence the Cabinet decided that 'the occasion of the announcement of the decision in regard to levy-subsidy should be used to put forward (in a way most advantageous to us in our trade negotiations) an offer on our part to abandon the right to levy any duty on the agricultural products in question during the next three years.'[72]

The next day the Dominions were told what God and Oliver Stanley had wrought. Telegrams confirmed the British decision not to impose any 'immediate' quota or duty on butter.[73] In November, Britain offered to make a binding commitment at least until August 20, 1940.[74] In wiring Canada, the Dominions Office suggested that this offer might facilitate revision of the February 1937 Anglo-Canadian Trade Agreement for the sake of rapprochment with the USA. To New Zealand, it suggested that the New Zealand Government might now be able to

---

[70] CAB 27/632, AP(37) 4th meeting, November 11, 1937.
[71] CAB 23/90, Cabinet 42(37), November 17, 1937: 'In present circumstances the principle of applying a levy-subsidy policy in the cases of meat and livestock, bacon, milk, and other dairy products should be definitely abandoned.'
[72] Ibid.
[73] DO 114/77, p. 21, Dominions Office to the several Dominion Governments, July 9, 1937.
[74] DO 114/77, p. 22: Telegrams, Dominions Office to the several Dominions Governments, November 25, 1937.

proceed with the schedules of tariff requests which the United Kingdom had submitted earlier in 1937, at the Imperial Conference. Wiring its own High Commissioners, the Office pointed out, 'the grant of free entry . . . is not a matter of right, but is a concession in return for which we expect some counterbalancing compensation'.[75] The High Commissioners in Canada and Australia were specially urged to stress this fact in their dealings with Ottawa and Canberra.[76]

By the end of 1937, the British Government had come to decide that the right way to protect its farmers was by deficiency payments, supported in some instances[77] by relatively mild quantitative controls. This decision had evolved more or less accidentally, almost entirely through the commitments which the Government had made at Ottawa in 1932. At that time, nobody had foreseen how extensive a protective system the Government might eventually want to set up. Hence the Agreements limited the Government's protective powers in several respects. The 1933 treaties with foreign countries, which grew directly from the Ottawa terms, imposed further limits. The Government therefore backed into a system of 'temporary' deficiency payments which eventually became permanent.

Given the desire to protect British farmers, and the extent of the protection which was wanted, it can be shown that deficiency payments were the least wasteful way to do the job. Tariffs, whether or not of levy-subsidy form, would have been better than quotas, but deficiency payments were better than either—so long as the Exchequer would impose enough general taxes.

After the Ottawa Conference, and after the initial infatuation with levy-subsidies, ministers gradually came to realize as the years passed that the country could 'afford' the deficiency payments. They did not reject the alternatives as a result of analysing social costs and benefits. Nevertheless, their political and prudential calculations led them to the right conclusions—at long last. The Ottawa Agreements deserve credit for creating the environment in which this evolution was possible and necessary. Without them, we can be certain that after 1933 the National Government would have imposed much higher food duties, much stricter quota controls, or both. The result would have been a reduction in the rate at which British living standards improved in the nineteen-thirties—and perhaps later.

---

[75] For an earlier discussion that settled this point in principle, see Doc. 35.

[76] DO 114/77, p. 24: telegrams, Dominions Office to High Commissioners, November 25, 1937.

[77] Beef, mutton, lamb, bacon.

V

By 1939, the Ottawa pattern had been modified in various ways. As the Americans had become more interested in tariff-reducing trade bargains, in 1938 Britain was able to negotiate an Anglo-American trade agreement—thanks to the acquiescence of Canada and Australia, both of whom had allowed the British to make concessions at the expense of the preferential tariffs and margins which the Dominions had been guaranteed at Ottawa.[78] Canada had also concluded a trade agreement with the USA. As we saw above, Britain had signed agreements with Argentina and several small foreign states.

Though the Anglo-Australian and Anglo-New Zealand Ottawa Agreements had been prolonged after their putative expiry in 1937, elaborate negotiation had centred upon this prolongation: in the event, the United Kingdom ceased to insist upon the 'domestic competition' clauses in the Anglo-Australian Agreement, and it conceded that the New Zealand Government could become more protectionist so long as it did not discriminate against British goods. With Canada, a new agreement had replaced the Ottawa document early in 1937. It did not contain the 'domestic competition' clauses, which Mackenzie King regarded as 'capitulatory'. Thus the 'chief gain' of the Ottawa Agreements had vanished in eight years.

During their life, these clauses had been honoured in the breach. The Australian Government had never tried to enforce them in the sense that the British understood, or as their own negotiators had intended. New Zealand's ad hoc enquiry had functioned, but the Government had not accepted all of its suggestions. In Canada, Bennett had eventually set up his Tariff Board, and had tried to cooperate, but the Board's proceedings were so slow that it produced very few recommendations during the life of his Government.

In the course of the decade, Empire trade negotiations were insensibly assimilated to external trade bargaining in general. There continued to be many informal intra-imperial contacts, and much information passed from one Empire Government to another. The links between civil servants and between politicians in the various Empire countries were undoubtedly closer than the contacts between British and foreign functionaries. This fact gave a different texture to the ceaseless intra-imperial commercial discussions but did not change their essential nature. As Mackenzie King had foreseen in the twenties, bilateral tariff bargaining meant imperial fragmentation. Because Britain herself became ever more protectionist, both in agriculture and manufactures, her imperial tariff commitments became ever more embarrassing. So

[78] For the correspondence after the 1937 Imperial Conference, see DO 114/93.

did the trade patterns which she had inherited from the decades of free trade and economic expansion. The Empire countries, meanwhile, were following their own increasingly diverse paths.

Three decades ago, Sir Keith Hancock argued that in the movement from the Ottawa Agreements to the tripartite trade agreements of 1938 we can see a movement away from imperial self-sufficiency: a recognition that world prosperity depended upon multilateral trade not upon Empire trade alone. This was a reasonable conclusion in 1940. Today it is harder to accept.

First of all, the documents show that the most important participants had always realized what Sir Keith thinks they discovered only in 1937–38. Bennett wanted a trade agreement with the USA as early as 1933. Australia approached the American Government in 1933–34. In 1932, Runciman consciously planned to use the Ottawa commitments as a launching pad for a massive programme of trade-bargaining with foreign countries. Secondly, the British never expected much trade from the Anglo-American Agreement of 1938. It was signed for political reasons, in the hope that it would help to improve relations between the two countries. Thirdly, we now know enough about macro-economics to realize that a general fall in tariff-barriers is neither a necessary nor a sufficient condition for prosperity either in one country or in the world at large. The rhetoric of tariff-bargaining had always been confused. The tariff-reducing incantations of Cordell Hull or Mackenzie King are no sounder than the tariff-raising apologies of R. B. Bennett or Neville Chamberlain. None conveys a correct understanding of economic processes.

VI

With respect to the dependent Empire, during the thirties British Governments followed a reasonably consistent policy of 'restoration', conceived largely though not entirely in budgetary terms. The Depression pushed many colonial budgets into deficit; it was inconceivable that the British Exchequer should indefinitely pay the ordinary running expenses of Colonial Governments. The many commodity-control programmes were undertaken largely with restoration in view. If production-control could restore tin, rubber, sugar, jute, tea and coffee producers to prosperity, they would import more, and customs receipts would rise. It might even be possible to levy heavier direct taxes. Or so administrators hoped, both in Whitehall and in the relevant colonies.

Besides arranging the commodity-control programmes, the Colonial Office maintained free entry for colonial goods in the British market, and tried to extract more tariff-concessions for the Colonies in the markets of the Dominions. These efforts, pursued vigorously and with some success at Ottawa, were continued intermittently through the rest of the decade. Primary products were the significant gainers.

Further, as talents and funds permitted, development projects were gradually resumed. Finance came from local revenues, borrowing, and the Colonial Development Fund, whose shadowy life continued until 1940, when it gave way to the more ambitious Colonial Development and Welfare arrangements.

Production-control was part of the general policy which Chamberlain had enunciated in 1932–33. Prosperity, he thought, would come through higher prices. It was also consistent with the financial interest of shareholders who owned British plantations. Also, by ensuring the financial stability of plantation companies it may have helped protect other financial institutions who held shares in these companies. Production-control, in other words, reflected the British tendency to see 'recovery' and 'stability' in terms of financial security for shareholders and financial institutions.

We cannot pause to trace these agreements in detail. There were two sorts. Britain herself promoted international schemes for agricultural products and tin. Large corporations organized international cartels to control production, marketing, and prices for copper, zinc, diamonds, and oil. The cartels were largely American-based and were often unstable. Britain did not create them, though British-owned firms took part, usually with government approval. But the British Government could not have broken them in its own consumers' interest, even if it had wished to do so.

The cartels and the commodity schemes were trying to raise their members' revenues and profits by increasing prices. The usual method was output-restriction. The agricultural products came partly from British-owned and foreign-owned plantations, and partly from native production. British, American and Dominion firms produced the relevant minerals—largely in southern Africa, but also in Malaya and in the Middle East. These firms, and the plantations, employed small numbers of whites, in supervisory and skilled jobs, and large numbers of non-whites, in the lower sorts of work.

How did the agreements affect the colonial and semi-colonial areas where the goods were actually produced? The present-day reader is almost bound to assume, without thinking, that they were part of colonial 'exploitation'—arrangements by which rich countries became richer at the expense of poor countries. However, he should remember that some rich countries owned the firms which benefited from the cartels, and that the citizens of rich countries consumed most of the artificially-priced outputs. To a large extent, therefore, these arrangements allowed the shareholders in some rich countries to exploit consumers in all rich countries. For any country, the desirable situation was simple: its firms should produce all the cartelized commodity, but its citizens should use none of it. Then all the gains from the price-rising would be at the expense of other rich countries. But the more of the product a rich country consumed, or the less it produced, the greater the likelihood that the cartel would, on balance, cost it something—even though its *shareholders* might be better off, its *consumers* would be worse off.

Britain consumed primary products but her own soil did not yield the relevant minerals and tropical foodstuffs. Though she could not break the oil and copper cartels, she could and did look with favour upon the efforts of British-owned firms to enter the cartelized industries —in the Persian Gulf, Northern Rhodesia, and elsewhere. The more oil and copper these firms could produce, the bigger would be the profits accruing to British shareholders. And the larger would be the offset to place against the inevitable sacrifices of British consumers. The stronger sterling would be. The more jobs there would be for well-educated British young men, and the busier would be the underemployed City of London. There would be more machinery-orders, and more profits, in a decade when both were scarce.

Government did not have to encourage the movement of British capital into oil and copper during the interwar period. The high rates of cartel profits, and the relatively low production costs in the Middle East and Rhodesia, would have been enough. The Government did try to keep Empire oil for Empire companies. Unfortunately, there was little oil in the Empire proper. The real prospects were in client states, where British control was incomplete, and in mandatory territories, where the Government was not allowed to exclude foreign interests. Thus in Iraq, French and American firms owned much of the Iraq Petroleum Company. In Kuwait and the Shaikhdoms, which produced little oil before 1939, British capital was weak or absent. Only in Iran, increasingly independent, did British interests control oil production. In oil, therefore, the British Empire did not mean British capitalism. As for copper, the Zambian deposits were developed by British, South African and American interests; British shareholders were almost certainly a minority. In short, for oil and copper the profits of British direct investment were a useful offset, but a very incomplete one, to the exploitation of British users by rich-country owners.

With respect to tin and agricultural goods the problem was different. There had been British direct investment in tin, tea and rubber for many decades. Both large and small interests depended on regular dividends. Britain drank a lot of tea and used a fair amount of rubber. But other countries used more of both. Prices had collapsed; to raise them would hurt British users, but would extract large sums from foreigners. If native producers were given adequate production quotas, even they would gain.

In the short run the rubber-restriction scheme certainly helped the British economy in all relevant ways. It raised foreign-exchange receipts and maintained dividends at small cost to British users. For tea the case is more obscure, because Britain drank so much of the tea which British-owned plantations produced. In the longer run, even rubber-restriction may have been harmful, because it certainly speeded the development of synthetic-rubber production, and it also led to American plantations in non-cartelized countries.

Between Britain, Europe and America, the cartels and schemes transferred real income; these transfers reflected consumption patterns and patterns of ownership. Within countries, too, there were transfers, as high prices helped shareholders but hurt consumers. All this is clear. But it does not follow that the rich countries, in exploiting one another, were also exploiting the colonials. Indeed, in so far as local citizens produced some of the controlled goods, worked for the cartelized foreign-owned firms, or enjoyed free public services which the firms' taxes financed, the cartels did the reverse.

Unfortunately, local producers did not always get a 'fair share' of allowable production. Professor Peter Bauer has argued persuasively that in the rubber-control they certainly got less than their productive potential would have suggested. The control probably raised their total receipts because of its price-effect, but gave them less of the total gain because it allocated too much of total production to the foreign-owned and British-owned plantations. Perhaps the same thing happened in other control schemes where local interests conflicted with overseas interests.

Nor did the cartels always get their local inputs at 'fair' prices, or pay 'sufficiently heavy' local taxes and royalties.

In British colonies, forced labour was illegal. But colonial Governments usually collected a native head-tax which forced people to seek wage-work, at least for some months. Generally speaking, the plantation and mining companies could get enough native labour at the prices they were prepared to pay. But this supply of labour was conditioned by the tax system; we cannot be sure how much would have come forth if colonial Governments had taxed the natives less heavily.

Further, especially in Africa, many mineral claims were held on terms which generated little tax or royalty revenue. It is tempting to say that colonial Governments should have charged rents and royalties which were sufficiently high to eliminate the 'excess profits' of the expatriate firms. They would then have had more to spend on health, welfare, development, and luxurious living for local potentates. By profits-taxation they could have attained the same end. Some people believe, as a matter of faith, that expatriate administrators would have refused to act in this way. Until somebody studies the budget-making process in the relevant colonies and dependencies, nobody can say whether this belief is true. In any event, if the local Government collects the 'excess profits' for which the cartel is partly responsible, the locals are gaining because somebody is successfully manipulating the market—not just because their own local resources are especially rich. If we say that the indigenous citizens have a right to whatever revenue the cartel can extract from the citizens of the rich countries, we are really saying that poor citizens should be allowed to manipulate markets to their own advantage. Though many would find this morally sensible, others would think it deplorable. Since the profits are the result of the cartel, we cannot say what fair rent or royalty would be in the absence of the cartel. This question is especially important for copper and oil, though it also arises for tin.

The British authorities were happy to see British-owned companies in the oil fields and mining areas of the Empire. Yet the British market put little money into these activities during the thirties. The Government itself held shares in Anglo-Iranian—and therefore indirectly in Iraq Petroleum. On the open market, between the end of 1931 and the end of 1938, £8·3 million was raised for oil, and £58·8 million for mines —including gold mines. These capital issues were very small relative to total new issues during the period, which totalled £1084·3 million. Certainly they were too small to affect British output, income, or wealth at the time—though they held hope for the future. Even if mines and oil wells had returned 50 per cent in 1938, the capital flows of 1931–38 would have accounted for less than 0·7 per cent of British national product. If we make more reasonable assumptions about rates of return, their contribution pales into insignificance. In the late thirties, Britain was increasingly prosperous. But oil, copper, and gold were not the basis of this prosperity.

VII

In the sphere of finance we might detect a genuine 'imperial initiative' during the nineteen-thirties. In one aspect—control of the new issue market—the facts are reasonably clear. In the other—the emergence of the Sterling Area—the research remains to be done.

We saw in the last chapter that before 1931 the United Kingdom Government made only imperfect and spasmodic efforts to regulate the new issue market. However, after Britain left the Gold Standard things were very different. Thereafter, with varying degrees of rigour, the Bank of England and the Treasury controlled the volume of borrowing and the identities of borrowers. The results were striking: foreign loans accounted for a far smaller proportion of the new issues in the thirties than in the twenties, and Empire borrowings were six times as large as foreign borrowings,[79] though still much lower than in the twenties. The discrimination in favour of the Empire, though informal and non-statutory, was perfectly deliberate.[80]

As for the Sterling Area, it emerged quickly after the floating of the pound in 1931. Most Empire Governments[81] and some foreign ones proceeded to stabilize their currencies *vis-à-vis* sterling. They were, on the whole, countries which had long held their official and unofficial foreign-exchange reserves in the form of sterling claims. However, at present we do not know how much initiative the United Kingdom Government may have taken in the formation of the Area. We do know that in 1931 the Indian rupee was pegged to sterling at British Cabinet insistence. We also know that in 1923 the Imperial Economic Conference had recommended that Empire Governments and central banks should hold sterling reserves so as to stabilize their currencies with respect to sterling. However, that recommendation was made in the context of the fluctuating exchange rates which existed between 1919 and 1925. We have no reason to believe that any Empire Government *deliberately* took any such action after 1923. Certainly they and their banks held large reserves in London. But it seems that Empire Governments, banks and currency boards held sterling reserves—instead of gold or dollars—because sterling was convenient and because on sterling reserves one earned a good rate of interest. The Sterling Area 'surfaced', so to speak, when the British Government broke the link between gold and sterling, thus forcing other Governments to decide what to do about their own exchange rates. But its basic constituents had been present for a long time.

There was a connection between the Sterling Area and the control of capital issues. By 1932, the Treasury and the Bank of England were convinced that Britain could not afford to lend overseas on the scale of the twenties. In London's capital market, room was to be made for the British Government, and for home buyers, by means of new-issue

---

[79] Figures as before relate to new public and private issues, excluding United Kingdom government issues, refunding issues, bonuses, bills, and issues made by private companies. Originally compiled by Midland Bank, and reproduced in Balogh, *Studies*, Tables XLVIA, B.

[80] See Hancock, *Survey*, Vol. II, Part I, 184 and DO 35/254/9099/182.

[81] Only Canada did not belong to the Sterling Area.

control. Empire borrowers were much more likely to keep their borrow-ings on deposit in London, and to spend them on British-made goods. Hence Empire borrowings were less of a threat to the exchange rate (in 1931–36) or to British gold and dollar reserves (after 1936). Apart from any feelings of Empire solidarity, therefore, it was sensible to favour Empire borrowers, giving them first claim on the very small 'pool of funds' which overseas borrowers might properly claim.

In the dogmata of imperialism as enunciated by Marx, Lenin and Hobson, Governments encourage capital export and capitalists are eager to cooperate. Unfortunately for these dogmatists, the experience of the thirties does not fit their theories. Physical investment was deficient all over the world; hence, basically, the unemployment and stagnation of the decade. But we have no reason to believe that British capitalists were especially eager to lend abroad. Domestic opportunities were in fact far more attractive than overseas projects, except in gold-mining and in a few specialized non-ferrous metals. Overseas Govern-ments and utilities were, on the whole, not very credit-worthy, and the market knew this. During the thirties, British capitalists were turning their attention inward. It should not be thought that the Treasury controls prevented a great surge of overseas investment which would otherwise have taken place. The controls seem to have been prudential, rather than crucial.

VIII

In the thirties the West Indies posed a special problem for London. From 1930 to 1937, discussion centred upon international control plans —to end 'overproduction'. By 1940, the West Indies Royal Commis-sion, while proposing some changes in sugar preferences and controls, hoped for industrial development. It also wanted a Welfare Fund. In Whitehall these suggestions, merged with others, produced the Col-onial Development and Welfare Act. Though this statute had many origins, one was the long and unsuccessful attempt to restore West Indian prosperity simply by manipulating the sugar market.[82]

---

[82] On the 1930 situation and Snowden's committee, CAB 23/63, March 12, 1930, CAB 24 /210, CP 90(30), CAB 32/76, IEC(30)105. On the sugar preferences of 1932, 264 HC Deb 5s, 1435–37. For Australian reactions, DO 35/222/8848/18, 19, 23, 24. See also Commonwealth Archives Office CP 272/3. On the Chad-bourne Scheme and sugar policy in the mid-thirties, Cmd. 4964 and CAB 24/267, CP 12(37), CAB 24/269, CP 102(37), 126(37). On subsistence agriculture, the West Indies Royal Commission, and the Colonial Development and Welfare Act, Cmd. 6174, 6175 (1940).

4

Indian Tariffs, Cottons, and Japanese Competition, 1919-1939

By now the reader must suspect that the author is unhealthily obsessed with the White Dominions. Unfortunately for the present-day theorist of Empire, the structure of this essay is a faithful reflection of politicians' obsessions during the nineteen-twenties and thirties. It was the Dominions which mattered most: they had the markets; they welcomed the settlers and the capital. Funds moved reluctantly toward the rest of the Empire, and settlers went in small numbers, drawn only by natural resources and by government service. In economic affairs it was Dominion questions, not Indian or colonial ones, which came before the Cabinet frequently, and which preoccupied committees of senior ministers. These are the facts—the conclusions to which the documents force us.

Besides reflecting the documents, the scope of this introduction also indicates something of imperial economic historiography. A great deal is known about Britain and the White Dominions, because a lot of work has been done on them. But many other parts of the Empire have yet to be seriously studied. Extremely interesting work has been done on particular topics, especially on primary production—rubber, cocoa, copper, oil. Where a single primary product dominated a colonial economy, as in Northern Rhodesia, we know a good deal about the total economic history of the colony during the interwar period. Other topics, such as the Kenya land question or the native-labour problem in tropical Africa, have been canvassed in some detail. However, much of this work must be done again, now that primary documents can be studied for the first time. It is all too easy for the external observer to assume that he knows why something was done, simply from the act itself and from its effects.

Some writing has also been done by students of economic development. It is good to find economists who do not think that the world began with independence or at Che Guevara's death. But much of this work is polemical, overtly or covertly.[1] As economic historiography it is usually disappointing. An introductory 'scene-setting' chapter, in a book which is really about something else, can hardly do justice to the complex reality of a past economic system—especially when there is so little decent monographic literature for the synthesizer to absorb. The economic historiography of India is particularly depressing. For good reason it has been largely devoted to anti-British polemic. Monographs exist, but their coverage is limited, and for our period the scholarly literature is slight. Nevertheless, some things are clear from readily available statistics. In the twenties and thirties India became steadily more protectionist. She also experienced a good deal of industrial growth—especially but not exclusively in the factory textile industries. From some angles the British-controlled administration can now be seen to have actively fostered this industrialization—chiefly through customs duties and purchasing policies. These developments had implications for the trading economy of the British Isles. Hence they impinged upon the British Cabinet, and were matters on which the United Kingdom Government had to make decisions. Indian tariff policy was especially relevant for the British textile industry, and in turn the position of the Indian industry depended not just upon the British but upon the competitive thrust from Japan. British and Indian producers alike felt the force of this advance; to some extent the British and Indian Governments cooperated to deal with it. Hence the present chapter, though focused on India, touches on some other matters—in particular, British quota-restrictions on Japanese textiles in the dependent colonial Empire.

Everyone vaguely knows that India was the most important of Lancashire's export markets before World War I. A large part of the industry specialized in supplying the sub-continent. Further, this market had become more and more important, as protective tariffs had closed more and more of the old markets in Europe and the Dominions. In Chapter 1 we saw how unimportant the Indian market was to the British economy as a whole: about 10 per cent of British exports went there, and the proportion fell steadily between 1921 and 1939. But the Indian market remained very important to a Lancashire industry which was trying simultaneously to shrink and to readjust itself to changed world conditions. For this reason, British Governments regardless of party were extremely interested in the level and structure of the Indian cotton-textile tariff.

---

[1] For example, see Michael Kidron, *Foreign Investments in India* (London, 1965), Pt. I, 3–26.

Indian economic historians have often asserted that the evil British prevented India from protecting her cotton textile industry, thereby preventing Indian industrialization and exploiting the Indian consumer. In fact, Indian factories began to spin and weave cotton in the 1850s. Thereafter the industry grew rapidly, even developing large export markets in the East. Nevertheless, it is true that until World War I, Indian tariffs were kept at 'revenue' levels and were almost entirely countervailed by a domestic cotton excise. Before the War, the general rate was 5 per cent, and the domestic excise 3½ per cent. British goods paid the same rates as foreign goods: the Indian tariff system did not grant preferences or in any way discriminate in favour of British exporters.

Partly because of these free-trade arrangements, and partly because of specialization by textile types, in 1913–14 India produced 10,908 million yards of factory cottons, imported 3199 million yards, and exported 89 million yards. By value, 90 per cent of the imports came from Britain, and 1·8 per cent from Japan.[2] Naturally Lancashire protested whenever a new cotton duty was proposed. However, the free-trade arrangement was not maintained just to benefit Manchester. Britain's Indian administrators seem genuinely to have believed that free trade and countervailing excises were in the interest of the Indian masses who wore the textiles. In many British eyes, protectionism would have been a vicious form of class legislation, because it would have aided the relatively prosperous factory owners of India, and hurt the much poorer and more numerous Indian consumers.

Whatever the merits of India's free-trade fiscal policy, it did not survive the War. In 1916 the general tariff was raised from 5 to 7½ per cent, and the list of exemptions was shortened, as was the free list. The Indian Government, faced with rising war outlays and few alternative taxes, was raising customs duties for the sake of revenue. The countervailing excise remained at 3½ per cent. Thus the margin of protection was widened—and further increased in 1921, when the general rate was raised to 11 per cent. In 1922 there were further increases, especially affecting 'luxury' articles, iron, steel, and railway materials, though the textiles rate remained at 11 per cent.

Behind this barrier—a revenue tariff in name, but heavily protective in effect—the Indian textile industry rapidly expanded, helped now and then by the organized boycotts of British goods and Gandhi's cottage-industry campaigns. Indian factory output rose from £256 million

---

[2] Here, and elsewhere in the chapter, trade and production statistics come from *Statistical Abstracts for British India*, Cmds. 725 (1920), 3291(1929), 6079(1939). In the Indian market, factory cottons coexisted with Indian homespuns, which competition had never eliminated.

in 1913–14 to £374 million in 1921–22, while British imports fell —in value terms from 597 million rupees to 474 million. Thereafter, Britain never recovered the Indian textile market she had had in 1913. As the years passed, British textiles paid ever-higher duties at the Indian frontier, while British sales fell and Indian factory-output rose.

This is an extraordinary development in the economic relations between an imperial power and its principal dependency. One is not surprised that nationalists and ideologues have suppressed it. How did it occur? The proximate explanation is a British self-denying ordinance— the 'fiscal autonomy convention' of 1919. Ultimately one must look to the development of Indian political consciousness and organization— and to the evolution of British attitudes toward their own power in the sub-continent.

In 1919 the House of Commons was debating the Government of India Bill—a measure to establish a central Indian legislature though not responsible government. It was widely perceived that the Bill might eventually lead to Dominion status. Reporting on the Bill, the Joint Parliamentary Committee recommended that London should not interfere in Indian fiscal affairs so long as the Government of India and the new Legislature were in agreement, except in relation to the Empire's international obligations and to any fiscal arrangements within the Empire to which the United Kingdom Government were parties. In 1921, Edwin Montague, the Secretary of State for India, took the view that this convention prevented him from interfering in Indian taxation. Though of course the United Kingdom Government could make recommendations and remonstrances, to India as to any other country, it could not force a particular tax or rate upon the Indian people.[3]

Whenever India proposed an embarrassing tariff-increase in the twenties and thirties, the fiscal autonomy convention was appealed to. Admittedly, various Governments took it with varying degrees of seriousness. Labour, nervous about Empire, was especially literal-minded, both in 1924 and in 1930–31. The National Government of the thirties pressed their views upon New Delhi much more vigorously than Labour would have done. However, the documents make it clear that at no time did the United Kingdom coerce the Government of India. Nor does it seem that India's white administrators put Britain's interests before the Indians'.

Besides revenue-need, the Indian tariff rose for explicitly protectionist reasons after 1922. In October 1921, the Indian Government appointed a fiscal commission 'to examine, with reference to all the interests concerned, the Tariff Policy of the Government of India,

[3] For a survey of the convention, see CAB 24/166, CP 299(24), May 24, 1924.

including the question of the desirability of adopting the principle of Imperial Preference'. The Commission reported in July 1922, recommending 'discriminating protection', a Tariff Board, and no general Imperial Preference. It was prepared to countenance specific preferential arrangements, but only if they would neither diminish the needed protection of Indian industries nor cost India any significant amount ... and only on condition that the Indian Legislature would approve each preferential arrangement.

Nothing was done about preferences. But in February 1923 the Government convinced the Legislature to resolve that 'the fiscal policy of the Government of India may legitimately be directed toward fostering the development of industries in India'. In July 1923 a Tariff Board was set up primarily to adjudicate requests for protection.

The Board immediately proceeded to consider protection for the Tata Works—India's only iron and steel plant, established in World War I and already in serious trouble. In February 1924 the Board recommended a stiff dose of protection—three years of duties at 20 to 28 per cent, instead of the existing 10 per cent. Informing the British Cabinet of this recommendation, the Viceroy noted that a preferential tariff would imply heavier burdens for consumers than a simple tariff, but reported that he would try to get the Legislature to accept the idea.[4] Britain's Labour Cabinet, however, was not prepared to make any vigorous effort to that end. While not averse to the idea of a two-tier tariff, the Cabinet resolved to instruct the Viceroy in different terms. They approved a telegram which reminded him that the Labour Government opposed protection on principle, cited the fiscal autonomy convention, and informed him: 'His Majesty's Government would not desire that you should incur any embarrassment whatever for the sake of establishing principle of Imperial preference if there is not the voluntary disposition in your Government to grant it.'[5] It is hardly surprising that the protective iron and steel duties, established in June 1924 for a three-year period, incorporated no special concessions to British goods. When the duties were renewed and extended for a seven-year period in 1927, however, some preferential margins were created. But this seems to have been done because the Tariff Board recommended the step, not because Whitehall insisted on it.[6]

[4] CAB 24/166, CP 256(24), April 11, 1924.
[5] CAB 23/48, April 29, 1924.
[6] The Board noticed that for some products it was British competition that mattered, while for others the competition was continental. British steel prices it thought would be stable, while continental prices might vary. Hence it favoured a basic duty based on the known prices of British steel, and a higher supplementary duty on foreign steel, See CAB 32/104: 'Tariff Structures in the Dominions and India.'

Meanwhile, the Viceroy abolished the domestic cotton-excise. This step had in fact been promised since 1916, and had been delayed until 1926 only because the Government needed the revenue. Proposing its abolition in November 1925, the Viceroy expressed his hope, that, by improving the mill-owners' position, abolition would end the Bombay textile workers' strike. Commending the proposition to the Cabinet, Lord Birkenhead argued that Lancashire was now not opposed to abolition, because the British millowners knew the excise must go eventually, and because they knew that vociferous opposition would damage them in the Indians' eyes. In the Indian market, Japanese competition was now much more to be feared, and the British hoped for joint action with the Bombay owners so as to achieve protection against Japanese goods. Birkenhead therefore proposed to accept the Viceroy's proposal. Cunliffe-Lister agreed that it would be 'unreasonable, and indeed impossible, to refuse to agree'.[7] The Cabinet concurred.[8] Thus the excise died forever. And with it was buried free-trade orthodoxy in India.

Cunliffe-Lister was not always so clearly on the side of Indian protectionism. In his autobiography he reports that he negotiated with the Indian Government on behalf of the Lancashire industry at a time when the Indian Government wanted to raise cotton duties. He says, 'The leaders of the cotton trade trusted me to handle the situation, at the same time giving me the benefit of their knowledge and experience. The outcome was happily successful.'[9] Though he gives no dates or details, his remark must relate to the Tariff Board report of June 1927. This report recommended a three-year increase in the cotton-piece-goods duty from 11 to 15 per cent, the proceeds to be used for a bounty on the spinning of the finer yarn-counts. However, the President of the Tariff Board did not agree with this recommendation, and instead proposed an extra three-year 4 per cent duty on all *Japanese* cotton manufactures, including yarn. As Britain was Japan's only competitor in the Indian market, the President was in effect recommending Imperial Preference. However, this recommendation, which Cunliffe-Lister might have been expected to favour, was not adopted. The Indian Government decided that the Board had not really established a case for general protection. Instead, they put certain machinery and mill stores on the free list, and introduced a specific minimum duty of $1\frac{1}{2}$ annas per pound on yarn. The effect of this duty was to raise the implicit *ad valorem* rate on all the cheaper counts, while still allowing the higher counts to come in at the

[7] CAB 24/175, CP 484(25), November 20, 1925.
[8] CAB 23/51, November 25, 1925.
[9] Swinton, *I Remember*, 33–34.

old rate of 5 per cent. Since the Japanese specialized in the cheaper and coarser yarns, and the British in the dearer and finer, the measure discriminated in favour of British trade, which would have been much more severely hurt if the Government had acted on the Board report. Yet Japanese goods, whose competition the *Indian* mill-owners now most feared, were somewhat impeded.

Early in 1930 the second MacDonald Government was told that the Viceroy proposed to raise the cotton duties. The Cabinet members worried at length about the Lancashire reaction, and agreed to tell the Viceroy about their worries, but they did not try to overrule the proposal.[10] The Secretary of State for India reminded them of the fiscal autonomy convention, and pointed to the weakness of Indian credit and to the prospective budget deficit. Hence the general cotton duty must go up from 11 to 15 per cent. The Viceroy reported that the revenue needs and the troubles of the Bombay mill owners were now so great that India must impose higher duties. However, he suggested:

> While we cannot modify a general application of 15 per cent revenue duty, we are prepared to propose to Assembly that, as regards any additional and temporary protective measures, their application might be limited to non-British goods, and that in these circumstances there should be imposed, in addition to a 15 per cent revenue duty, a 5 per cent protective duty . . . on plain grey goods against all cotton piece goods from outside the United Kingdom. We should propose protective duty for three years only. . . . We cannot ask the Assembly to commit themselves to Imperial Preference as a principle, but merely to adopt a particular course which in our judgment is consistent with India's interests.[11]

Commenting on his proposal, the President of the Board of Trade thought it 'of considerable if not epoch-making importance' because it incorporated the preferential *principle* for the first time. He admitted that, because the preference covered only a small part of British cotton exports to India, its practical effect would be small, though in plain grey goods it might help the United Kingdom mills to win some sales from Japan. Hence he warmly welcomed the Viceroy's idea. He also thought it difficult to controvert the reasons for the increase in the general duties.[12]

---

[10] CAB 23/63, February 7, 1930.

[11] CAB 24/210, CP 68(30), February 25, 1930, pp. 104-5. There was to be an overriding minimum protective duty of 3½ annas per pound on foreign grey goods. Thus on really cheap grey goods the protective duty would exceed 5 per cent *ad valorem.*

[12] CAB 24/210, CP 51(30), February 14, 1930.

On February 19, 1930, the Cabinet approved the Viceroy's suggestion, and subsequently cabled that 'the Cabinet has received your telegram and recognizing the position of India under the Tariff [*sic*] Autonomy Convention is precluded from offering any further comment on your proposals'.[13] The Indian Government then argued its case before the Indian Legislature, claiming that the extra 5 per cent on British goods would hurt consumers while bringing little immediate benefit to Indian mill-owners, who would be unable significantly to increase production of the finer goods during the three-year period for which protection was proposed. The Legislature agreed to pass a Cotton Textile (Protection) Act, which would give such protection till March 31, 1933. But it imposed the $3\frac{1}{2}$ annas per pound minimum levy on all plain grey goods —not merely on foreign ones. And it extended the minimum yarn duty of $1\frac{1}{2}$ annas per pound.

Early in 1931 the Indian Government again proposed to raise cotton duties—once more for revenue reasons. The result was a major row in the British Cabinet. The Secretary of State for India pleaded with his colleagues not to make any representations on behalf of Lancashire, noting that past representations had merely led to a more intense boycott of British goods. The same, he said, would certainly happen again. But Lancashire politics compelled the Cabinet to draft a telegram of complaint. The cable pointed out that the 1930 increases had been followed by 'a most serious decline' in Britain's cotton-export to India, and noted that any further decline would exacerbate political ill-feeling between the two countries—something to be avoided when Britain was so sharply divided on the question of Indian political evolution. The Cabinet asked the Viceroy whether it would not be possible to grant some sort of increased preferential concession 'by which a larger part of the burden could be placed upon foreign goods, and a correspondingly less burden on goods from this country'.[14] But the Indian Government was adamant: 'I am afraid that we could not allow . . . representations to influence us.' Further, if the surcharge were not applied to cottons the Indian boycotters would receive the gift of an 'effective new cry'.[15]

The 1931 Indian Finance Act raised duties substantially. British cottons now paid 20 per cent, and many other goods also paid much more than in 1930. But this was not the end. During 1931 the Indian

[13] CAB 23/63, February 19, 1930; CAB 24/210, CP 68(30), February 25, 1930.
[14] CAB 23/66, January 28, 1931; CAB 24/219, CP 22(31), January 30, 1931.
[15] CAB 24/219, CP 35(31), February 2, 1931. The Secretary of State for India had already noted that the Indian millowners would welcome the new duties, but that it was politically impossible to reimpose countervailing excises. CAB 24/219, CP 18(31), January 22, 1931.

Legislature passed specifically protective measures which raised the duties on many iron and steel products, heavy chemicals, gold thread and salt. The British Cabinet does not seem to have complained of these measures. And in the autumn the Indian Government, stricken with a budgetary crisis and strongly pressed from London, proposed further increases in its revenue duties.

By this time the National Government ruled in London. Such a government, formed in an effort to cut expenditure and balance the United Kingdom's budget, could hardly take grave exception when a dependent government was trying to do the same thing. Indeed, the evidence suggests it was the United Kingdom Government which insisted that the Indian Government must put its financial house in order. However, the result was highly unpalatable. 'Nothing short of a 25 per cent uniform increase in all Import Duties would suffice.' The India Office was pressing for a countervailing excise, but it expected howls of Indian protest should any such thing be attempted. Nevertheless, the British Cabinet decided to ask for one.[16] But the Government of India would not agree. The Cabinet then asked the Indians to impose a differential tax on cottons—a 40 per cent rate on foreign goods, and 31 per cent on British goods.[17] A further appeal was made three days later.[18] But to no avail: the surcharges were imposed, and many specific increases were also introduced. By the end of September 1931, foreign cottons paid 30 per cent at the Indian frontier, and British cottons 25 per cent. A far remove from 1915s 5 per cent rate!

During 1930 and 1931, no British Government could argue convincingly for an Indian preferential concession. In 1930, Philip Snowden had made it perfectly clear that he would abolish all tariffs and all preferences as soon as he could. By September 1931, though the British Government had changed British policy had not. Most Indian exports were raw materials and foodstuffs—the things on which Britain was most reluctant to impose a duty. Churchill had already removed the only really worthwhile preferential concession, when he abolished the tea duty in 1929.

The Import Duties Act of 1932 treated Indian goods like Dominion products: free entry was granted until November 1932, unless satisfactory preferential trade agreements could be signed. Further, in restoring the tea duty, Chamberlain seems to have had India in mind: he offered a much wider margin of preference than any Chancellor had offered between 1919 and 1929, saying that 'the old preference of

[16] CAB 23/68, September 17, 1931.
[17] CAB 23/68, September 22, 1931.
[18] CAB 23/68, September 25, 1931.

two-thirds of a penny seems to be totally inadequate to the present circumstances'.[19]
The Indian Government appears to have taken the hint. In April 1932, it referred the question of its cotton and rayon duties to its Tariff Board. The Board was asked whether the Indian cottons industry had established its claim to protection; if so what the protection should be, and whether there should be Imperial Preference on cottons. In May 1932, Indian representatives reached London on their way to Ottawa. The delegation, led by Sir Atul Chaterjee, the former Indian High Commissioner in London, contained two ex-presidents of the Tariff Board. Welcoming them at a meeting of the Cabinet's Ottawa Committee, Baldwin emphasized the scope for complementary trade—for a planned division of markets between producers.[20] This theme was natural in the circumstances: Indian cotton weaving was concentrated at the coarser end of the spectrum, and British weaving at the finer. However, it soon became clear that India could do nothing for British cottons until its tariff board had reported. Further, on iron and steel the protective duties were 'bound' by the existing legislation, and could not readily be changed—though here too there might be scope for intra-imperial specialization and 'rationalization'. On many other items, it seemed, some progress could be made. Britain had asked for many specific concessions, and some seemed possible—especially in 'general merchandise'.[21]

These preliminary talks revealed a puzzle which does not previously seem to have worried the British, but which was to perplex Anglo-Indian trading relations for the rest of the decade. This was the question of Indian raw cotton. It was a problem because of the pattern of world trade in raw cotton. India was one of the world's largest cotton producers. But she sold very little to Britain, which drew only 10 per cent of her supply from India in 1930. Most of India's production was consumed at home; the rest went to continental Europe, China, and especially Japan, which was taking more and more Indian cotton as her own textile exports expanded. If Britain could take more Indian cotton, India might be more able to restrict her import of Japanese textiles, which were chiefly made from Indian fibre. Unfortunately, Lancashire machinery was ill adapted for the relatively short-stapled Indian cotton, which was perhaps inherently unsuitable for the finer counts on which Lancashire now concentrated. Indeed, the Indian spinning industry itself imported, largely, from Uganda, the longer-staple material which the finer counts required.

[19] 264 HC Deb 5s, April 19, 1932, 1437–8.
[20] DO 35/237/8531/157.
[21] DO 35/242/8831N/36; CAB 32/105, O(B)(32)135.

In September 1931 India imposed its first raw-cotton tariff. In May and June 1932, the Indian representatives asked the United Kingdom to impose a preferential tariff on raw cotton.[22] Sir Horace Wilson immediately retorted that this was impossible. But how could India give a preference to Lancashire, thus displacing Japanese textiles which used Indian raw cotton, if the United Kingdom would not buy more of the Indian material?[23]

At Ottawa this nettle was not firmly grasped. The delegations agreed that Britain could use more Indian cotton in the future than in the past, and decided to confer further with respect to the means—research, propaganda, improved marketing. As for British piece goods, no decision could be taken until the Tariff Board had reported, but it was agreed that where the Board did not recommend protective duties the British articles would get the 10 per cent preference.[24]

The Indian Government also agreed at Ottawa that it would give a 7½ per cent preference on certain motor vehicles, and a 10 per cent margin on many other items—including building and engineering materials, chemicals, drugs, hardware, tyres, various metallic manu-factures, and many items of food, drink and clothing. However, the margin was far from general. It extended only to those iron and steel goods which did not pay protective duties, and in machinery it covered only those items which paid the ordinary rate of 25 per cent. Further, the Agreement did not preclude a rise in Indian tariffs—preferential as well as general. It merely guaranteed some *margins* of preference. As the British had already found in their Canadian and Australian trades, wide margins meant little when the general tariff level was high. High rates were especially likely in India, where the Government could not afford to cut many tariffs for the sake of creating preferential margins. In many cases, the margin was created by raising the general tariff, while British commodities continued to pay the same rate as before.

In exchange, Britain guaranteed free entry for all the Indian goods that had temporarily enjoyed it under the Import Duties Act. She guaranteed margins of preference on a wide range of Indian exports, including tea, jute, cottons, and tobacco. She promised a new and higher margin of preference on coffee. And she imposed new duties on six vegetable oils, linseed, rice and magnesium chloride.[25] She had also worked hard on the Dominions, to win preferential concessions for India in their markets also.

---

[22] They also asked for such duties on hemp, tungsten, linseed, rice and coffee. Nothing specific was requested for tea.

[23] DO 35/242/8831N/26.

[24] Article 11 in Doc. 28, Indian Agreement.

[25] Schedule A of Anglo-Indian Agreement (Doc. 28).

British ministers publicly defended the Agreement because, they said, India had now accepted the principle of Imperial Preference. But she had not conceded very much. If we did not know that India was a British possession at the time, we should probably say that the clever and powerful Indians had forced a disadvantageous trade treaty upon the weak and inept English. The most obvious hole in the Agreement, from the British standpoint, was its indecisiveness with respect to iron, steel and cottons. On these products negotiations continued intermittently until after the outbreak of war.

Lancashire quickly began to honour its commitment with respect to Indian raw cotton. But in the winter of 1932–33 the Indian Tariff Board recommended higher protective cotton duties, and no Imperial Preference.[26] This report was suppressed; the Secretary of State for India told his colleagues that the India Office would work out an alternative within six months.

As for iron and steel, a British delegation went to India in November 1933 to explore cartel arrangements with Tata; his operations, the Tariff Board judged in 1934, had become so much more efficient that he could operate with much reduced protection, and with free entry for some British products. The cartel scheme was moderately successful. And the Indian Assembly legislated along the lines of the Board report.[27]

These things were gratifying, and could be ascribed to the Ottawa discussions. But British cottons went downhill steadily after 1932. Indian tariffs were not coming down. And Japanese competition was increasing in a fashion which frightened the millowners in India at least as much as in Lancashire. We have already seen that it was worrying the Indian Government as early as 1930.

As the depression deepened, competition increased from month to month. As boycotts shut Japanese textiles out of China, the millowners sought new markets. In this they were aided after December 1931 by the floating and depreciation of the yen, which fell nearly 40 per cent by early 1933, sharply depreciating relative to sterling—and therefore to the Indian rupee, whose sterling exchange rate remained unchanged. Further, Japanese industry was almost certainly benefiting from cost-reducing innovations which her millowners were rapidly applying in production. Hence Japanese textiles penetrated into new areas—East Africa, Australia, and even West Africa and the Caribbean. In older markets, sales rose quickly. It was British mills which suffered most from Japanese competition . . . not only in India but in colonial areas

---

[26] CAB 23/75, February 1, 1933.
[27] For details, see United Kingdom Department of Overseas Trade, *Conditions and Prospects of United Kingdom Trade in India*, 1933–34 (London, HMSO, 1935).

and in Australia. Early in 1933 the problem of Japanese competition was increasingly seen as a single question, and in London Indian trade policy was increasingly considered as an aspect of it.

In August 1932, following anti-Japanese representations by British and Indian millowners, and after reference to its Tariff Board, the Government of India raised the duties on non-British cottons from $31\frac{1}{4}$ to 50 per cent. Shortly thereafter, the Japanese and Indian Governments began desultory trade discussions.

Early in 1933 the British began their own defensive measures. On March 3rd, Runciman proposed that the Japanese should be told the United Kingdom would abrogate its trade treaty and impose quotas unless the Japanese would agree to quantitative controls.[28] A few days later he pointed out that in its colonies Britain could deal with the Japanese in another way: by unilaterally withdrawing the West African colonies from the coverage of the Anglo-Japanese trade agreement, Britain could use quotas there without abrogating the treaty.[29] At a Cabinet meeting on March 8th, Cunliffe-Lister pressed for this course.[30] The matter was deferred for three weeks. When it came up again, on March 29th, Runciman argued that things had got much worse even in this short period. He 'hoped eventually to arrive at a position where cartel arrangements might be discussed with the Japanese, but these must be preceded by action such as he had proposed'. The Cabinet agreed, deciding to withdraw West Africa and the West Indies from the Anglo-Japanese Commercial Treaty, and also authorizing India to denounce the Indo-Japanese Commercial Convention of 1904,[31] so that she too could discriminate against Japanese goods. On April 10th India did so. But as the action would have no effect until October 10th, she also proposed to raise her foreign-cottons rate from 50 to 75 per cent!

The United Kingdom Cabinet discussed the Indian tariff proposal on May 24th. The Foreign Office, believing it would infuriate the Japanese and worsen Anglo-Japanese relations, opposed the step. But the India Office staff thought that it should be allowed, because a refusal would damage an Indian industry and inflame feeling against England, while Lancashire would benefit from the more severe taxation of foreign cottons. The Secretary of State for India 'was convinced that on political and commercial grounds a refusal to allow the Government of India to increase these duties would cause serious and possibly

---

[28] CAB 24/239, CP 54(33), March 3, 1933.
[29] CAB 24/239, CP 55(33), March 6, 1933.
[30] CAB 23/75, March 8, 1933.
[31] By imposing quota controls and by allowing India to raise the foreign-cottons duties the British Government was, other things being equal, reducing the real incomes of colonials and Indian residents.

irreparable damage'. And so the Cabinet agreed that the increase should occur.[32]

Japan immediately began a partial boycott of Indian raw cotton.[33] But she also started serious trade talks for the first time.

At this stage both British and Indian Governments hoped for some sort of market-sharing arrangement with the Japanese. Runciman explained this idea to the Japanese Ambassador on April 25th[34]— twenty-three days before the Anglo-Japanese Treaty was denounced as far as it concerned West Africa and the West Indies. Since the denunciation would not take effect until May 16, 1934, there was plenty of time for an accommodation.

To this end, the chairman of the Bombay Millowners Association visited London in the summer of 1933, and the British cotton and rayon magnates made a pilgrimage to India. Such commercial diplomacy between textile industrialists was prominent in Anglo-Indian trade discussions for the rest of the decade. On most later occasions it was unsuccessful, but this first time it yielded the 'Lees-Mody Pact', signed on October 28th. The Bombay millowners accepted preferences as 'fair and desirable'. They promised not to oppose a reduction in the duty on British cottons from 25 to 20 per cent. The British also talked helpfully but vaguely to the Japanese industrialists who were simultaneously in India. The Indian officials told the British that there would be a new cotton agreement between India and Britain as soon as the Indo-Japanese negotiations were over. The Tariff Board report on cottons had been totally buried: it had been neither published nor acted upon, and the Lees-Mody Pact had superseded it. Summing up the industrialists' adventures, Runciman wrote: 'The work of the Delegation . . . has gone some way to justifying the Government in their belief that the best approach to the problems of international industrial cooperation is by the method of discussion between industrialists.'[35] Later, announcing the arrival of Japanese textile magnates in Britain, he said that such conversations were 'the only hopeful way of escape he had been able to see from the present difficulties'.[36]

However naïve we may find this faith, we know how characteristic of British governmental attitudes it then was. Still, even then, when thinking of cottons nobody was really prepared to put his entire trust in the industrialists. The British industry was still too ill-organized for

[32] CAB 24/241, CP 137(32); CAB 23/76, May 24, 1933.

[33] She maintained it until a trade protocol was signed in January 1934.

[34] DO 35/293/9301/73: Foreign Office memorandum F 3920/583/10/, June 12, 1933.

[35] CAB 24/243, CP 421(33)(Revise). See also CAB 23/77, November 29, 1933.

[36] CAB 23/78, January 31, 1934.

easy and stable cartelization, and other industrialists might not be trustworthy. Hence Government would have to support businessmen's commitments. In cottons, as in iron and steel, tariff-ingenuity would help 'rationalize' the world industry and prevent undue competition. Further, quotas could be used to divide markets for piece goods, and to create markets for Indian raw cotton.

On this basis the Indo-Japanese negotiations proceeded during 1933. The British Government assisted their progress by guaranteeing the Indian Government against any loss which might eventuate if it should have to take 1·5 million bales of Indian cotton off the market.[37] Given this assurance, the Indian Government could withstand the Japanese threat of a total cotton-boycott. Japan was told that her quota-proposals were unacceptable. The Japanese quickly gave way, agreeing to buy a definite amount of Indian cotton and accepting a quota for their cottons in the Indian market. In return, the Indian Government immediately lowered the foreign-cottons duty from 75 to 50 per cent.[38]

Having handled the Japanese, the Indian Government proceeded to deal with the British. In accordance with the Lees-Mody Pact, it introduced new cotton duties during 1934. These continued the British preferential rate of 25 per cent and the foreign rate of 50 per cent for two years, after which time the rates might be adjusted. Protection was to continue until 1939. On yarn, the Act raised the foreign duty to $6\frac{1}{4}$ per cent while fixing the preferential duty as 5 per cent.[39] Specific minima were fixed for the coarser yarn and for plain grey goods, but because Britain did little trade in these qualities the specific duties were of much more significance for Japanese than for British goods.

These arrangements, incorporating the principle of Imperial Preference on cottons, were obviously more favourable to Britain than the discarded Tariff Board report. British cottons still faced enormously higher barriers at the Indian frontier than they had faced in 1915—or

---

[37] CAB 23/77, December 6, 1933. For the background, see CAB 27/556. The guarantee was offered to convince the Indian Government that it should reject the current Japanese quota-proposal.

[38] The agreement was to last until March 31, 1937. It provided a minimum quota of 325 million yards, and a maximum of 400 million yards. The allotment was to rise in step with Japanese purchases of Indian raw cotton; if Japan did not buy the stated 'minimum' quantity, she would lose some of ther 'minimum' quota, while as she bought more her allowables would rise toward her 'maximum' quota. In 1937 the protocol was renewed until March 31, 1940, on the same general terms, but with reduction in the maximum and minimum quota to 356 million yards and 283 million yards. The quota allotment was to rise by $1\frac{1}{2}$ million yards for every 10,000 bales of raw cotton, in excess of one million bales, that Japan might buy. If Japan should buy less than one million bales, the minimum quota would be reduced by 2 million yards for every 10,000-bale shortfall.

[39] There were also provisions for silk and artificial silk.

1929. But the Indian millowners, recognizing that Japanese competition was even more deadly than British, were prepared to tolerate a very large preferential margin so long as the foreign-cottons duty was high enough.

As for the Anglo-Japanese conversations, these did not go nearly so well. Early in 1934, Japanese textile magnates arrived in Britain and began to talk to Lancashire. But by mid-March the talks had broken down. Britain had made some conciliatory gestures. In particular, she had forced certain colonies to delay the imposition of tariff-increases which, partly to widen preferential margins and partly for revenue reasons, they had introduced in 1933. She had also delayed the revision of her own silk duties. Nevertheless, the Japanese businessmen made demands which the British businessmen and the British Government thought unreasonable. By early April, Sir Horace Wilson saw no point in continuing the conversations, as the Japanese Government seemed to have no practical scheme in view. 'If negotiations were not pursued, then we should be left with a free hand, and measures to deal with Colonial markets should be put in hand at once.'[40] By mid-April a Cabinet committee had reported in similar vein, and the Cabinet decided to proceed with the introduction of quotas in Ceylon and other colonies. Still, for political reasons Runciman was urged to explain the policy to the Japanese Ambassador 'in the most friendly way'.[41]

The result was a most frustrating interview. Runciman begged the Ambassador to suggest some alternative, reminding him that the Japanese Government had been asked to do so in mid-March. The Japanese, believing that it was up to Britain to find a solution, had nothing to suggest. Runciman, regretting that the industrialists had not found any agreement, said that the United Kingdom could delay no longer, but was still willing to discuss alternatives to the quota scheme if any counter-proposal should emanate from Japan.[42] But nothing came forth.

As both inter-industrial and inter-governmental diplomacy had now failed, on May 7th Runciman was obliged to announce that the United Kingdom would ask all the appropriate colonies and protectorates to impose quotas on all foreign textiles, the basis being average shipments in 1927–31. In West Africa, where other nations enjoyed special rights but where, with respect to Japan, the most-favoured-nation problem did not arise, quotas would be on Japanese goods only.[43]

---

[40] DO 35/294/9301/90: minute by J. Wiseman, April 9, 1934.
[41] CAB 23/79, April 18, 1934.
[42] CAB 24/249, CP 130(34), May 3, 1934. Further details are in CAB 27/568.
[43] 289 HC Deb 5s 1933–34, col. 717. Quotas covered cottons and rayons. In West Africa the treaty problem was somewhat simplified in 1936, when the French denounced the relevant sections of the 1898 Anglo-French convention.

In fact the quotas were never applied in as wholesale a fashion as Runciman had suggested. All the mandates were held on terms which precluded such discrimination in favour of the mandatory power. In East Africa and half of Northern Rhodesia, the Congo Basin treaties prevented such quotas in Britain's favour. For other reasons, Hong Kong, Tonga, Gibraltar, St Helena, and the Falkland Islands were excluded from the system. Further, in Ceylon and perhaps elsewhere the quotas had to be imposed over considerable local opposition and resentment.[44] But the results were dramatic.

Explaining the quotas to the Empire Prime Ministers in May 1935, Cunliffe-Lister noted that the colonies were now buying 64,000,000 yards of British textiles, instead of 25,000,000. He also asserted, rather strangely, 'the conclusion was that when the Japanese knew that something was regarded as essential, they were prepared to accept it'.[45] Later, in Cabinet, Runciman argued that the quotas 'had saved Nigeria for the Lancashire trade'.[46]

Whitehall then began to negotiate with New Delhi on the subject of Indian *protective* duties, in an effort to supplement though not replace the Ottawa Agreement, which had ignored them. Runciman successfully extracted the same sorts of commitments with respect to 'domestic competition' which three Dominions had given at Ottawa. He also got the Indian Government to recognize that she herself might need higher protection against foreign than against British goods—an implicit admission that, especially in cottons, iron and steel, Britain was no longer competitive. India agreed that 'wherever possible, lower duties will be imposed on goods of United Kingdom origin'. Both Governments made promises with respect to iron, steel and cottons duties, and quotas for cottons in the Dependent Empire.[47]

[44] For the proceedings over Ceylon, see CAB 24/249, CP 172(34), and CAB 23/79, July 4, 1934, and July 25, 1934. As there was no prospect of passing the required measure through the Ceylonese State Council, the measure had to be carried by order in council from London.

[45] CAB 32/125, PM(35), 2nd meeting of British Commonwealth Prime Ministers, May 7, 1935. This statement was presumably meant to strengthen Australia's resolve in its own battle against Japanese cottons and rayons.

[46] CAB 23/87, March 10, 1937.

[47] The Agreement was published as Cmd. 4779, January 9, 1935. See also United Kingdom *State Papers*, Vol. 139(1935), (HMSO, 1939). For Runciman's report on the final stages of the negotiations, see CAB 24/253, CP 1(35). At the last moment, the United Kingdom Cabinet still hoped to obtain a concession with respect to the level of cotton duties—though when deciding to seek it the Cabinet ministers suspected that India might never be able to spare the revenue. See CAB 23/81, January 9, 1935. The Agreement itself provided, in an exchange of notes, that 'as soon as the second surcharge comes off as a general measure', and subject to other conditions, the duty on British cottons would fall from 25 to 20 per cent.

Unfortunately on March 30, 1936, the Indian Legislative Assembly asked the Indian Government to denounce the Ottawa Agreement. The Government was pledged to accede, and did so on May 13th. However, the Agreement was subsequently extended, subject to three months' notice on either side, while the British and Indian Governments tried to work out a replacement.

The prospective loss of the Ottawa commitments was especially alarming in Whitehall because, in the spring of 1936, the Indian Tariff Board had just produced a rather dreary report on the protective cottons-duties. While implying that rates should come down on some British cottons, the report was less favourable to Lancashire textiles than had been hoped. Further, India was bound to act on the report only in the context of the Ottawa Agreement. In other words, after denunciation had taken effect, the rates could be different from those the Tariff Board had recommended.[48]

But a new agreement was hard to construct. Talks dragged on through 1937 and 1938. In 1937, the Indian delegation visited Lancashire on its way to London and marshalled considerable Lancashire support for unspecified cottons-concessions in exchange for very specific adjustments: the loss of preferences on 80 per cent of British exports to India, a guarantee of unrestricted free entry for Indian jute manufactures on the British market, and certain important administrative concessions on duties at the British end.

Reporting on the negotiations, Oliver Stanley explained that the demands were unreasonable and asked for permission to break off negotiations.[49] However, Lord Zetland, the Secretary of State for India, thought that Stanley was not prepared to concede enough and begged him to avoid a breakdown, stressing the ill-feeling in India if negotiations should cease. Lord Halifax took the same line: 'It would be worthwhile to go a long way to secure the goodwill of India'. The Cabinet recorded no definite conclusion, but the sense was that Stanley should make further concessions, and should not end the talks.

By March 1938, matters were not much advanced. Considering the situation, the Cabinet members were not prepared to countenance the loss of all preferences: if there was no preferential trade agreement, India would simply buy elsewhere. However, though Chamberlain believed no further concessions would be made, the proffered agreement was still very unfavourable to the United Kingdom. It was resolved to send a delegation of Lancashire cotton industrialists to India. 'If nothing useful resulted from that visit, the negotiations would not be

[48] CAB 24/262, CP 111(36), May 1, 1936.
[49] CAB 24/271, CP 219(37); CAB 23/89, September 29, 1937.

proceeded with.' Meanwhile, Scots industrialists should also visit India to set up a jute cartel.[50]

The cotton mission failed. Lancashire was met with a 'stone wall'. Too little was offered on piece goods, and too much was asked with respect to raw cotton. Oliver Stanley doubted that Lancashire would support such an offer, but the industry now said that *government* must decide. 'As a result of the present negotiations we were being asked to give up half of the preferences which we enjoyed under the Ottawa Agreements.' He favoured refusal, because the only beneficiary, the textile industry, would oppose the agreement, making the Parliamentary position impossible. However, Chamberlain thought that the proffered agreement was better than none, and the Cabinet agreed that Stanley should again consult the Lancashire interests. He should explain the probable alternatives to them; if they then favoured acceptance he should accept the Indian offer, but if they favoured rejection 'they should be asked to state what terms they would accept; a counter offer might then be suggested and an attempt made to continue negotiations'.[51]

In March 1939 Stanley reported that a new Anglo-Indian agreement was ready. 'Looked at purely from the trade point of view, the Treaty was unfavourable to us; as his colleagues were aware, however, the negotiations had been carried out on lines decided by the Cabinet from the wider political point of view,'[52] that is, the appeasement of India and Lancashire.

At long last, on March 20th, the new Anglo-Indian trade agreement was signed to replace the 1932 and 1936 arrangements. The British were still guaranteed some preferential margins of 10 and 7½ per cent. But the list of 1939 was much shorter than that of 1932. Some electrical equipment was added, but many manufactures, most textiles, and many semi-manufactures were removed. As before, *rates* of duty were still not fixed. Britain continued to guarantee the preferential margins on almost all the Indian goods for which they had been fixed in 1932. Only bran, rice meal and lead were taken off this list. In a few cases, most strikingly cotton and some jute manufactures, Britain widened her guaranteed margins from 10 to 20 per cent. For the time being, Indian iron and steel could still enter Britain duty-free, while British iron and steel still faced protective duties at the Indian border.[53] With respect to

---

[50] CAB 23/92, March 2, 1938.
[51] CAB 24/278, CP 186(38), July 27, 1938; CAB 23/94, July 28, 1938.
[52] CAB 23/98, March 15, 1939.
[53] In an exchange of notes the agreement provided that Britain could impose duties on Indian iron and steel after March 31, 1941, if the Indian Government should raise its own iron and steel duties on the expiry of the Indian Iron and Steel Protection Act, 1934.

cottons and raw cotton, there was a clause of Byzantine complexity elaborating the 1934 Indo-Japanese Agreement.[54] The more Indian raw cotton Britain bought, and the smaller her shipments of piece goods to India, the lower the duty these cottons would pay.

The 'cotton clause' makes the 1939 agreement look rather like a 'capitulation'—the sort of thing which Marxists tell us the evil imperialist Western governments force on the weak and helpless countries of the Third World. But in this case, as at Ottawa and at the subsequent negotiations with Canada and Australia, it was Britain who had capitulated, sacrificing most of her preferential advantages to win a doubtful benefit for her cotton trade, and a most uncertain 'goodwill'. The reader is left to ask himself who was exploiting whom.[55]

[54] The smaller Britain's sales of cotton piece goods in India, the lower the *ad valorem* duty in the following year. If Britain bought less than 450,000 bales of Indian cotton in 1939, or less than 450,000 in any calendar year thereafter, India could tax Britain's cottons *as she liked*. If Britain should buy less than 500,000 bales in 1939, less than 550,000 bales in 1940, and less than 600,000 bales in 1941 and thereafter, Britain's purchases would be 'deficient'. Such 'deficiencies' would cause notional adjustments in Britain's actual exports of cotton cloth. The notional result, not the actual export, would fix the cotton-cloth tariff for the next year. British cottons would pay 17½ per cent, 15 per cent, or 2 annas 7½ pies a pound, depending on type, so long as total sales had been more than 350,000 yards the preceding year. If *current* sales should rise past 425,000 yards, in the next year the Indian Government could raise its cottons duties 'to such rates as may be deemed necessary for the purpose of restricting imports of such goods to 500,000 yards'. If sales should fall below 425,000 yards, duties would revert to the basic scale in the following year. If sales should be under 350,000 yards, the following year all the rates would be 2½ per cent lower than the basic rates.

[55] For more information about Indian protectionism and its effect, with special attention to cotton, steel, and sugar, see H. L. Dey, *The Indian Tariff Problem in relation to Industry and Taxation* (London, 1933). D. H. Buchanan, *The Development of Capitalist Enterprise in India* (New York, 1934) devotes thirty-six pages to the cotton industry (pp. 194–230) without mentioning the tariff. Wm. Roger Louis, *British Strategy in the Far East 1919–1939* (Oxford, 1971, 219 ff) gives passing attention to the Anglo-Indian cotton negotiations in the context of Anglo-Japanese relations. But his main concern is with China. And his account is marred by errors. Sir Frederick Leith Ross was not 'one of the world's foremost economists' (p. 231). Iraq and Egypt were not part of the British Commonwealth during the crucial years. The first measures against Japanese textiles were taken by India, not by Egypt. The outer Commonwealth countries did not 'suffer' from Japanese textiles; their consumers gained, and it was only the producers in India and Britain who were hurt. Finally, any account of Anglo-Japanese commercial diplomacy must be accounted incomplete if, like Louis', it omits all mention of Runciman's efforts to cartelize the Anglo-Indo-Japanese textile industry.

PART II:
DOCUMENTS ON IMPERIAL ECONOMIC POLICY

1. The United Kingdom Government commits itself to Imperial Preference and Empire Settlement at the Imperial War Cabinet[1]

FROM Public Record Office, CAB 23/40, Imperial War Cabinet April 11 and 12, 24 and 26, 1917.

... The following resolution was submitted by Mr. Massey for discussion by the Imperial War Cabinet:

That the time has arrived when all possible encouragement should be given to the development of Imperial resources and (consistent with the resolutions of the Paris Conference) especially to making the Empire independent of other countries for the food supplies of its population and raw material for its manufactures. With these objects in view this Conference expresses itself in favour of:

(1) A system by which each country of the Empire will give preference through its Customs to the goods produced or manufactured in any other British country; and

(2) An arrangement by which, in the case of intending emigrants from the United Kingdom, inducements may be offered to such emigrants to settle in countries under the British Flag.

Mr. Massey pointed out that the question of Imperial Preference had been considered on many occasions, more particularly at previous Imperial Conferences, where it had been twice agreed to without opposition, so far as the Dominions were concerned. The difficulty had been due to the views of the electorate of the United Kingdom. But in that respect a very important change in public opinion had taken place, a striking proof of which was afforded by the recent report of Lord Balfour of Burleigh's subcommittee. The War had undoubtedly made people realise the dangerous extent to which the United Kingdom had been dependent on foreign countries. This

---

[1] The members of the Imperial War Cabinet were Prime Ministers Lloyd George (United Kingdom), Borden (Canada), Massey (New Zealand), and Morris (Newfoundland), together with J. C. Smuts (South Africa), J. G. Ward (New Zealand), George H. Perley (Canada), and Earl Curzon, Viscount Milner, Walter Long, and Austen Chamberlain (United Kingdom). A political crisis prevented the Prime Minister of Australia from attending. Eight other British and Dominion ministers also attended for the discussion of the matters reported here, and four officials were present for some or all of the discussions. Sir Maurice Hankey was Secretary.

dependence was unnecessary, as the Empire could produce all it required, so long as it retained control of the sea. The Dominions had already adopted Preference so far as they were concerned, and New Zealand was prepared to go further if necessary. He did not think that it was fair or possible to go back to the condition of trade with enemy countries as it existed before the War. Moreover, owing to the great additional burden of taxation which the War would leave behind, there were certain to be considerable increases in Customs Duties, and these two factors would facilitate the establishment of Preference. He did not consider, in view of the productive capacities of the Empire, that any measure of Preference in this country would add to the cost of living.

With regard to the second part of his resolution, Mr. Massey pointed out that there was plenty of room in the Dominions for emigration. The population of the United Kingdom was 370 to the square mile, whereas in New Zealand it was 10, in Canada 2, and in Australia 1½. The South African War had been followed by a very large wave of emigration, and that experience and his own conversations with soldiers convinced him that there would be a large emigration after the War, which it was very desirable to guide into British channels. In the Dominions they would welcome not only farmers, who were the most useful type of settlers, but immigrants of every suitable class. He pointed out that between the period 1876–1913, of a total net emigration from the United Kingdom of 5,149,000, over 2,770,000 (i.e. 53 per cent. of the total) had gone to the United States and had been lost to the British Empire. It was impossible for us to expect that other countries should be content to see the British Empire possessing vast areas which it was not properly occupying. Emigration could not be forced to stay within the Empire; what was necessary was to give inducements, and he urged that the Governments of the Empire should join together to arrange a scheme of financial assistance.

Sir Robert Borden stated that the whole fiscal system of Canada had been designed for national and Imperial purposes, and it was largely owing to its fiscal system that Canada was now a portion of the British Empire. He considered Preference a valuable and fundamental principle. He also realised, however, that it was not only an Imperial, but also a domestic question. In so far as it was the latter, he had always avoided interfering with it. The Dominions would be resentful of interference in their own internal affairs, and were not disposed to interfere in controversies which the United Kingdom had to settle for itself. No one in Canada would desire a Preference that was felt to be oppressive or unjust by the population of these islands. Any such feeling would injure the Imperial aspect of Preference. He considered that the Empire could produce all the food it required. As regards Canada more particularly, whose chief exports were wheat, cheese, and bacon, a Preference which did not deal with the question of food supplies would be illusory and unsatisfactory. One of the difficulties which had confronted Canada in the past, and raised the greatest measure of outcry from her farmers, had been the increased costs of transportation across the Atlantic, and he suggested that it might be possible for the United Kingdom and the Dominions to get together in some great enterprise which would restrict the cost of transportation within the Empire. Transportation was quite as important to all the Dominions as Customs Preference.

With regard to the second part of Mr. Massey's resolution he entirely agreed, though he considered that emigration to the United States, both from the United Kingdom and from Canada, had not been wholly a loss in so far as it had affected the United States' feeling towards the British Empire. He was prepared to support any Imperial scheme of emigration.

The Prime Minister, speaking not in his official capacity, but as one who had taken a leading part in discussions on this question, began by declaring that his general attitude had been altered by things which had happened since the War. The War had undoubtedly revealed certain fundamental facts which it was necessary to take cognisance of in our Imperial and domestic arrangements. There were industries essential to defence which we had been compelled to build up at great cost in the middle of the War, and which might not be able to hold their own unassisted at the end of the War. It would be great folly, in view of the expenditure we should still have to incur upon the Army and Navy, if we neglected to maintain industries essential to the efficiency of those Forces.

Again, there was the Imperial point of view. The value of cohesion and co-operation between the nations of the British Commonwealth had been revealed in an extraordinary way; it had been the great surprise of the War to our enemies and largely to ourselves, and had made us the most important factor in the War. Consequently, from the selfish point of view of the United Kingdom alone, the development of the Empire would be an essential point in British policy. The figures Mr. Massey had quoted showed that if more trouble had been taken over the development of the Empire in the past, the Dominions might possibly have had double their present population and proportionately increased the strength of the British contribution to the present War. These were fundamental facts which were bound to produce an essential change in the policy of the United Kingdom with regard to the Dominions, and *vice versa*.

With regard to the methods to be adopted, he wished to point out that the war had revealed, more particularly in the case of Russia, the peril which might arise from dear food. That issue was one which had somehow or other obsessed the minds of the working classes in the United Kingdom ever since the Corn Laws, and the memories of the present war would revive that dread. He concurred in Sir Robert Borden's statesmanlike view, that it would not do for the prosperity of Canada to be based on the want of the workmen of England. He wished the working-classes to regard the Empire as something that meant not only glory, but also material advantage.

He was all for Preference, and would personally assent to any resolution laying down the principle, but he asked Mr. Massey to leave out the three words "through its Customs," which specified a particular method. He was inclined to consider that Sir Robert Borden's method of subsidised transit through the Empire would give a more substantial Preference. He was all for the old Roman method of binding an Empire together by its roads—in our case by shipping. Another argument in favour of this particular method was that the principal wheat- and meat-producing countries besides the Empire were not our present enemies, but our Allies, Russia and the United States, and a declaration in favour of a Customs Preference might look as if we were attempting to do them an injury. It was quite true that improved shipping would also take trade away from them, but that was a matter which could be justified on grounds of Imperial defence, and was a recognised method of development employed by the United States, Russia, and France.

He did not rule out the remission of dues on the Suez Canal, or the possibility of subsidy on the actual goods sent over, but trusted that for the moment the precise method should be left open for future discussion. The United Kingdom had got to consider the question of its own industries after the War. This was not a matter of Free Trade or Protection but of stern Imperial necessity for defence. Subject to this, he would personally agree to the resolution.

Lord Robert Cecil agreed with the resolution as amended by the Prime Minister, but suggested that, as it would have to be published in some form or another, and as there was a real feeling (more particularly in the United States), that we might make use of our victory to injure American trade, it might be desirable to put in some phrase such as "having due regard to the legitimate interests of our Allies".

Mr. Massey said that he was prepared to accept this suggestion, and in that case to omit the reference in his resolution to the Paris resolutions.

Mr. Austen Chamberlain stated that India would certainly endeavour to conform to any general system of Preference adopted throughout the Empire, though the particular methods would have to be matters of special consideration. While India would undoubtedly welcome low rates of shipping freight, he wished to point out that she had not the revenue which would provide large subsidies. She had also important markets in foreign countries which she could not afford to lose without securing fully equivalent markets elsewhere.

Lord Milner wished to make it clear that Preference on Customs Duties was not excluded by the resolution as amended. He did not absolutely accept Sir Robert Borden's contention that Preference on foodstuffs would be the only one of value to the Dominions, for it certainly did not apply to all parts of the Empire, and he doubted if it applied wholly even as regards Canada. He regretted that the path of Preference had been made difficult by the assumption that it was necessary to put on duties which were not required in themselves in order to grant Preference. All he had ever contended for was that whatever duties should be imposed in any part of the Empire for its own interests, the rest of the Empire should be treated differently in respect of those duties from foreign countries. He placed the principle of Preference as something much higher than either tariffs or shipping; it was an absolutely vital matter: *Articulus stantis aut cadentis imperii*. He could imagine a policy of Preference without tariffs or without shipping subsidies, but he could not, in his conception of the Empire, imagine a policy that had tariffs and gave no Preference on these tariffs.[2]

The Prime Minister quite accepted that view; the only stipulation he wished to make was that it should be made clear, when the resolution was published, that we had not actually committed ourselves to taxes on food.

The Secretary of State for the Colonies[3] expressed his agreement with Lord Milner. He was quite content with the amended resolution, as long as it did not preclude any of the methods by which Preference could be granted. He was continually being pressed in this matter, not only by the Dominions, but by people in this country of very varying political view. It would create profound dissatisfaction if it became known that the utilisation of tariff Preference was to be excluded from the Cabinet scheme of Imperial Preference. With regard to Canada, he felt sure that Sir Robert Borden would agree with him that the exports of Canada would in the near future or at no distant date include a great volume of manufactures. All he wished was to make sure that the door remained open.

Mr. Henderson entirely agreed with the views expressed by the Prime Minister and Sir Robert Borden. His own personal views differed from those of some of the members of the Cabinet, but he was prepared

---

[2] As neither the United Kingdom nor India gave tariff preferences at this time, Lord Milner apparently could not conceive of the British Empire as it actually existed.

[3] Walter Long.

to go to the extent suggested by the Prime Minister, and considered that the value of the resolution as amended was that it would secure agreement between those who differed as to the particular methods of carrying it out.

Mr. Chamberlain wished to register the fact that he was still an utterly impenitent adherent to the policy of food duties, which he believed to be the right one for the country. He considered that the question of food supplies was now being taken by the country far more seriously than before the war.

Mr. Massey wished to make it clear that he had brought forward this matter not on behalf of New Zealand only, but in the general interest of the Empire, and that he certainly would not have brought it up if he thought that it could possibly put the working classes of the United Kingdom in a worse position.

The Imperial War Cabinet accepted the resolution in principle, subject to settlement of its precise wording. The Secretary of State for the Colonies was requested to convene a small Sub-Committee, consisting of Lord Milner, Sir Robert Borden, Mr. Massey, Mr. Henderson, Lord Robert Cecil, [and] Mr. Austen Chamberlain, to settle upon the wording and bring the matter up before the next meeting of the Imperial War Cabinet.

* * *

... The Imperial War Cabinet considered Mr. Massey's resolution on Imperial Preference as amended by Mr. Long's Drafting Committee ... The amended resolution was in the following terms:

> The time has arrived when all possible encouragement should be given to the development of Imperial resources, and especially to making the Empire independent of other countries in respect of food supplies, raw materials, and essential industries. With these objects in view the Conference expresses itself in favour of:
>
> (1) a system by which each part of the Empire, having due regard to the interests of our Allies, will give specially favourable treatment and facilities to the produce and manufactures of other parts of the Empire.
>
> (2) Arrangements by which intending emigrants from the United Kingdom may be induced to settle in countries under the British Flag.

General Smuts pointed out that the instructions with which he had come to the present Conference had not included the settlement of a definite Imperial Tariff system on this occasion, and he considered that the wording of the resolution went further than really was intended. All that was required, in his opinion, was to recognise the principle, namely, that in any future arrangement which included tariffs, Preference should be granted, and not to lay down a policy. South Africa certainly had no objection to the principle of Preference, inasmuch as she had already applied it herself. He suggested that it might be possible to draft the resolution in a form which more clearly expressed the situation.

The Prime Minister suggested that a new draft resolution might be drawn up, emphasising, first of all, the complete freedom of each Government in the Empire to adopt any economic system it chose; secondly, that where there are customs duties those duties should be more favourable to the produce and manufactures of other countries in the Empire; and thirdly, that the principle of Preference should be carried out in any arrangements for the improvement of communications and transportation, or in any other way in which it could usefully be applied.

It was pointed out that a draft on these lines had been before the Committee but had been objected to by Mr. Henderson on the ground that it recalled too vividly past controversies.

The discussion was interrupted in order that a draft resolution should be drawn up on the lines suggested by the Prime Minister, and to enable Mr. Henderson to be present.

On Mr. Henderson's arrival the discussion was resumed on the draft resolution so drawn up. Mr. Henderson stated that if the resolution were adopted in this form he would be obliged to record his dissent, as he could not countenance the Government holding out the hope of a wider range of duties, which the amended resolution did by implication.

It was also pointed out that the amended resolution, in so far as it stated the situation in more definite terms, might not only evoke more direct controversy in the United Kingdom, but also create anxiety among our allies, more particularly in the United States.

Mr. Massey also drew attention to the possibility of an interval occurring immediately on the conclusion of the war, during which the principle of Preference might not yet be in operation; but it was pointed out in reply to this that the provisions of the Paris resolutions, as well as the general situation that was likely to continue for some time after the immediate conclusion of hostilities, would preclude such a possibility.

Lord Robert Cecil suggested that General Smuts' objection would really be met if for the words "a system by which" at the beginning of sub-head (i) of the resolution, were substituted "the principle that". This would make it clear that what was contemplated was not the establishment of a rigid system, but the application by the different Governments, in their own fashion, of a common principle.

In view of the desirability of securing a unanimous decision, General Smuts stated that, though he still preferred the more explicit draft, he would not stand on his objection, more particularly if Lord Robert Cecil's suggested amendment were adopted.

The Imperial War Cabinet agreed that:
the resolution as framed by the Colonial Secretary's Committee should be amended so that sub-head (i) should read—
The principle that each part of the Empire, having due regard to the interests of our Allies, shall give specially favourable treatment and facilities to the produce and manufactures of other parts of the Empire.

2. The Cabinet Committee on the Trade Relations of the United Kingdom with the Empire[1] broods upon a system of Imperial Preference

FROM Public Record Office, CO 532/114, eighth meeting, January 2, 1918.

... Mr. Hewins presented the Sub-Committee's Report on Dutiable Articles. He said that the Sub-Committee recommended an Empire Preference of $33\frac{1}{3}\%$ in respect of every article except tea and wines. He now learned that the Board of Trade were disposed to favour a flat rate of $33\frac{1}{3}\%$ without exception.

The Chairman read a letter from Dr. Addison taking exception to the special rates of preference proposed on wines, and supporting the principle of a flat rate.

The Chairman said that an exceptional preference on wines had been proposed by the Sub-Committee in order to make that preference substantial. He did not think that the bulk of our Dependencies were concerned about the rate of the preference to be granted; though in certain cases no doubt a substantial preference would be required to

---

[1] The chairman of the Committee was Walter Long, the Colonial Secretary. Members present at the meeting were W. A. S. Hewins (Colonial Undersecretary and former Secretary of Chamberlain's unofficial Tariff Commission), Stanley Baldwin (Joint Financial Secretary to the Treasury), Christopher Addison (Minister in charge of Reconstruction), Lord Islington (Under-Secretary of State for India), and Sir Albert Stanley (President of the Board of Trade).

rehabilitate the trade of some of the Crown Colonies. Otherwise the question of preference was regarded by the Dependencies and Dominions as one of sentiment.

Lord Islington thought that a preference of $33\frac{1}{3}\%$ on tea would be of material advantage to India; but generally speaking, the preferences proposed would be of little advantage to the Dominions and India. He thought that there was a good deal to be said for the flat rate.

Mr. Baldwin thought that a preference of $33\frac{1}{3}\%$ to Empire tea would be a heavy burden on the Treasury, though it might be mitigated by raising the rate of the duty.

Mr. Hewins favoured the flat rate. If the Treasury objected, those objections could be discussed at a later stage.

The Chairman thought that the recommendation of a flat rate, if it were adopted by the Committee, should be accompanied by two reservations. First, that if, in the case of any particular article, the flat rate imposed an undue burden on the Treasury, that case should be open to reconsideration. Secondly, that if the flat rate led, for example, in the case of wines, to a preference which seemed ineffective, here again the special case should be reconsidered.

Mr. Hewins said that the Board of Trade took exception to the preferences which the Sub-Committee proposed giving to certain of the Allies. These proposals had been inserted in deference to the views of Lord Robert Cecil.[2]

Sir Albert Stanley thought that, in the matter of preferences to the Allies, the Sub-Committee's Report was too definitely worded and might tie the hands of the Government in an undesirable way at some later stage. He hoped that the Government would take the Board of Trade into consultation when the time came for negotiating with the Allies. He thought it better for the Committee to accept in principle the position that preferences might be granted to certain Allies, and to leave detailed proposals to be framed in actual negotiations with the Allies.

Mr. Hewins hoped that the Committee would not make a recommendation so generally worded that it would be possible to give to Allies even greater preferences than were accorded to the Empire.

Sir Albert Stanley proposed that Mr. Hewins and the Secretary should be empowered to alter Recommendation (5) in S.3 of the Draft Report in accordance with the views which had been expressed in the discussion. To this the Committee agreed.

Mr. Hewins then proposed the adoption of the Draft Report subject to (a) the insertion (with a caveat) of the principle of the flat rate, for

[2] Under-Secretary of State for Foreign Affairs and Minister of Blockade.

Empire Preferences, of 33⅓%; (b) alteration of S.3 in the sense of Sir A. Stanley's proposal.

The Committee agreed to this motion . . .

Mr. Hewins said that many plans were being evolved for the organisation and control of raw materials after the war. The Colonial Office possessed a good deal of information on the subject, which it was desirable to lay before the Committee. The Economic Offensive Committee had decided that the policy to be adopted in respect of raw materials ought to be settled before the organisation of the control was discussed. The first question of policy . . . was obviously the policy of the British Empire towards its own raw materials.

Dr. Addison said that a considerable number of Committees were already working on this question, and that it was essential to consider each material separately.

Sir Albert Stanley said that the question of control bristled with difficulties; as yet he saw no light upon it; and he personally desired that it should be considered by everyone who might be able to offer suggestions.

The Chairman thought that the Committee must investigate the question, though he thought that the Dominions would never agree to surrender the control of their own raw materials.

Dr. Addison argued that the business problem involved—how to get control of raw materials—must be separated from the further political problem—how the supplies are to be allocated when obtained. The first point was one for the business man to consider. The second point affected the Colonial Office, India Office and Foreign Office.

Mr. Hewins said that in practice the commercial and political problems must be discussed together. No one Committee could settle the whole subject of Empire raw materials, involving as it does vast interests in every part of the world.

The Chairman said that overlapping could be avoided if there were continuous communications beween the Sub-Committee and the other Committees engaged on the same subject.

It was agreed that the Sub-Committee should take up the question of the control of raw materials.

DUTIABLE ARTICLES
(final report)

s.1: The Committee are of opinion that it would be extremely desirable, if it were practicable, to abolish all Customs barriers within the Empire. They recognise, however, that financial and other reasons make it impossible, both for the United Kingdom and for the Self-Governing Dominions, to remit all customs duties upon Empire produce and manufactures, at least in the immediate future. They therefore confine themselves to recommending that preferential treatment should be given by the United Kingdom to dutiable imports from other parts of the Empire.

The Committee recommend:

(a) That a preference should be given to imports from Empire sources of every article which is at present subject to duty, except where (as in the case of Beer and Spirits) an excise duty corresponding to the import duty is in existence and is of importance to the revenue of the United Kingdom.

(b) That it is desirable to grant an Empire preference, subject to the above exceptions, in all cases where a new import duty is imposed, whether on manufactured or on unmanufactured goods.

(c) That it is undesirable to create new import duties for the sake of granting an Empire preference.

(d) That it is desirable to grant such preferences in the form of a percentage rebate on the ordinary duty.

(e) That it is desirable to take as the standard rate of Empire preferences $33\frac{1}{3}\%$ of the general rate of duty on each commodity (but in exceptional cases it may be found desirable to adopt *either* (a) a higher rate of preference on the ground that, for the commodity in question, the standard rate of $33\frac{1}{3}\%$ would not give a substantial preference *or* (b) a lower rate, on the ground that a preference of $33\frac{1}{3}\%$ on the article in question would involve a serious loss of revenue).

s.2: *Recommendations as to Particular Duties:* The Committee recommend the following preferences on the existing list:— . . . [beer, cider, perry, spirits: nil; all others: $33\frac{1}{3}\%$]

s.3: *Preferences to Allies—Recommendations.*

(1) The Committee are of opinion that H.M. Government should be in certain cases empowered to grant preference to some of our allies who have made great sacrifices in the common cause. The claims of France, Belgium, Italy, Roumania and Serbia to special consideration are obvious. The claims of Greece and Portugal also call for examination.

(2) The grounds for which any preference should be granted are that we recognise our obligation to assist our Allies in repairing the ravages of war; and that to grant preferences to the Empire without extending them to the Allies might in certain cases aggravate their financial or commercial difficulties. Preferences should only be given to the Allies in cases where these reasons apply, and should be usually confined to trades or territories which have suffered direct damage resulting from the war.

(3) The Committee do not recommend that preferences should be granted solely for the benefit of the colonies of the Allies.

(4) The Committee recommend that any preference given to Allied products or manufactures should be temporary (i.e. for the reconstruction period); they should in no cases exceed, and should not necessarily · be as substantial as, the preferences granted to the Empire on the same commodities.

s.4: *Cost of the Imperial Preference Suggested Above.* The cost of the Empire Preferences may be roughly estimated as follows (on the basis of the 1913[1] figures at the present rates of duty):—chicory, chloral hydrate, chloroform, cider and perry: nil; playing cards £17; cinematograph films £202; clocks £8; musical instruments £630; watches £310; cocoa £209,0000; coffee £19,000; dried fruits £29,000; motor cars £24,000; motor spirit £97,000; tobacco £120,000; wine £23,000; sugar £1,500,000; tea £4,400,000.

3. The Government Emigration Committee[2] transmits L. S. Amery's[3] Memorandum on Empire Settlement in connection with a revised draft of the Emigration Bill

FROM Public Record Office, CAB 24/75, GT 6846, February 20, 1919.

... The development of the population and wealth of the whole British Empire is the key to the problem of postwar reconstruction. The heavy burden of war debt upon every part of the Empire makes this development an immediate and urgent necessity. The growth of population in the Dominions, in so far as it adds directly to their strength and prosperity, and consequently to the strength and prosperity of the whole, and in so far as it increases the number of our own best customers

---

[1] The figures for cinema film, clocks watches, and dried fruits are 1916 figures, and those for motor cars relate to 1915. In this reproduction the list of items has been rearranged for compactness. Emphasis added to sugar and tea. Total 'cost of preferences' £6,422,179. Total customs revenue in 1912–13: £35,200,000; in 1914–15: £39,200,000.

[2] Shortly to be renamed the Overseas Settlement Committee.

[3] Chairman of the Committee, and Parliamentary Undersecretary of State for the Colonies.

and purveyors of essential food-stuffs and raw materials, is so obviously desirable that it is assumed throughout this memorandum that emigration should be directed to countries within the confines of the British Empire. On the other hand . . . it is essential that [the United Kingdom] manpower and taxable capacity should not be weakened in the process of imperial development . . .

4. Members of the Government[1] discuss unemployment and the state of trade, February 25, 1919

FROM Public Record Office, CAB 24/75, GT 6887: Shorthand Notes of a Conference of Ministers.

THE PRIME MINISTER: I will ask Sir Auckland Geddes to start today's proceedings.

SIR AUCKLAND GEDDES: I have been presiding over a good many conferences recently of representatives of the different Government Departments, all suggesting lines of policy and executive acts, and it appeared to me as we went on that there were four really separate and main lines of thought running through the action or suggested action of the Government Departments. There is first of all a policy—and I do not refer to the Chancellor of the Exchequer himself here for the moment —which has been very strongly pressed at many meetings by representatives that the main interest of the country at the present time was to get

---

[1] The participants were Lloyd George (the Prime Minister), Bonar Law, Austen Chamberlain (the Chancellor of the Exchequer), Sir Auckland Geddes (Minister of Reconstruction and National Service), Sir Eric Geddes, Sir A. Stanley (President of the Board of Trade), L. S. Amery (Parliamentary Under-Secretary, Colonial Office), R. Munro (Secretary for Scotland), A. W. Samuels (Attorney-General, Irish Office), Lord Sinha (Under-Secretary of State for India), Sir L. W. Evans Minister of Pensions), Winston Churchill (Secretary of State for War), Sir Robert Horne (Minister of Labour), Dr. Christopher Addison (President of the Local Government Board), H. A. L. Fisher (President of the Board of Education), Lord Inverforth (Minister of Munitions), Lord Ernle (President of the Board of Agriculture and Fisheries), A. H. Illingworth (Postmaster-General), and Sir A. Steel-Maitland (Under-Secretary of State, Department of Overseas Trade).

back to the gold standard, and to stop every possible form of Government expenditure. We have a policy, which is being very strongly pushed really by the big combination of manufacturers which forms the Federation of British Industries, and that policy is that everything must give way to getting the trade of the country going. We have a third policy, which is represented by the housing scheme, the land settlement scheme, the scheme for ways and communications, and so on. We have got a fourth policy, which is being very strongly urged by at least one Department, and affects the actions of others—what I might call the Imperial policy, which seeks to regard the Empire as an undivided whole, which compares our position today with that of America 60, 70, or 80 years ago when there was an industrial nucleus and a great undeveloped territory, and that policy calls for a great mass of emigration within the Empire. There is no doubt that the Government is pledged by every possible election pledge to the social policy. But that carries with it, it seems to me, certain things which I do not think are perhaps fully recognised by all Departments when they put forward recommendations for executive action. There is no doubt that if we are to have this great development of social amenities in the country, improved housing, land settlement,[2] health, and all the rest of it, a very great deal of national capital is going to be locked up in what is going to be a slow-maturing investment.[3] Just so long as that capital is locked up it will be unavailable for trade purposes, as it seems to me. I have looked at the thing very carefully, and have looked at all the Reports of Reconstruction Committees, and so on, and I do not find anywhere that what appears to me to be an absolutely essential consequence of adopting that policy recognised.

THE PRIME MINISTER: Will you tell me this? Up to the present you have not pointed out to me in what respect the policies are inconsistent. Is there any reason to believe that trade is not starting because there is a lack of capital?[4]

SIR AUCKLAND GEDDES: I think there is a good deal of reason to believe that trade is not starting because there is a lack of capital that can be made available. I was going on to indicate where it seems to me the clash is coming. In connection with the social policy we have got this locking up of capital, and that appears to me to make it absolutely

---

[2] That is, settlement on the land in Britain.

[3] In modern terminology, a high proportion of current gross and net physical capital formation will consist of housing and social amenities whose annual yield is low and whose lives are long. Geddes is implicitly making the incorrect assumption that the annual total gross and net physical capital formation is fixed.

[4] Lloyd George means capital *funds*—essentially, credit to finance current production.

essential that we should recognise that the trade position of the country cannot be what it was before the war, and that the country cannot carry the food population which it did carry before. We have had during the last four years by recruitment what is, in so far as its social effects are concerned, really the same as emigration on a great scale. We have had the places of those who have gone filled, and a social reorganisation has taken place which has profoundly modified the whole conditions as they existed in 1914. It seems to me that with this social policy—I have looked at it carefully, and I think there is no doubt about it—we cannot possibly hope for years to come to carry the food population which this country did carry before, because the development must be slow if we are to get the agricultural development which is necessary to produce the food in this country. It is not going to happen this year or next year; it will be a matter of slow development. The development of the agricultural policy, the production in our own country, seems to me to be essential if we are to carry the population, and for this reason, that the markets of the world are entirely transformed, so far as trade is concerned, from what they were before the war. We cannot possibly have the same sort of markets. Central Europe is practically shut out. Our Allies, France, Italy, and so on, are not in a position to pay for goods that they receive from us to a great extent. They owe us amounts of money which it is likely they will never pay for in food, and the trade position cannot go back. Therefore it seems to me that what we have to realise is that the minute we embark upon this social policy—as we have embarked—we have done two things: really we have made it essential that there should be great emigration, and we have also recognised the fact that trade is not going to go back—the conditions and the organisation of trade and industry in this country cannot go back to a pre-war state ...

THE PRIME MINISTER: I read your paper this morning, and I really did not see where the clash came in. How can there be a clash between the Board of Trade and the Minister of Agriculture? What clash is there between the Board of Trade and the President of the Local Government Board about housing? I really do not see it ...

MR. BONAR LAW: I think the Prime Minister's first question is, is there any shortage of capital? I do not think there is.

THE PRIME MINISTER: No doubt businesses are not starting. There is raw material, which is rather high, and they think it is coming down. There is a shortage of orders, and I daresay there is a shortage of capital in France and elsewhere. We have lent them money to give orders there. Do you know of any business which is unable to start here because there is a lack of capital in that particular business?

SIR ALBERT STANLEY: No, there is not. On the contrary, there is an abundance of capital[5] for all the railway demands. It is only that business is nervous. Capital[6] is hiding itself. . . .

MR. CHAMBERLAIN: Our cry is, "Go to the market and raise more". If you wanted to do nothing but your own internal trade development there is capital enough, but there is not capital enough to find for the State the funds it needs to borrow for the war, for the Government reconstruction schemes, and to find all the capital which is required for Empire development, either in the old Empire or in new territories of which we may become a mandatory, and to find the capital for general foreign enterprise which many people wish to do. In these circumstances we have passed our new Order in Council in order, while we relax certain of the restrictions which have been in force, to make those which we preserve really effective, and to secure that such capital as there is shall be allotted to those purposes which best serve the national interest.[7]

MR. BONAR LAW: Is not this the fact? Ultimately there will be a shortage of trade. The difficulty Mr. Chamberlain speaks of is a different one. It is that firms have spent so much in excess profits duty that they have not the courage, with that big burden on them, to go to the public and ask for big sums of money.

SIR AUCKLAND GEDDES: The high value of material comes into the excess profits question. It[8] is not entirely excess profits.

MR. CHAMBERLAIN: Every business, owing to the rise in prices and wages, wants more working capital.[9] Every business has to incur capital expenditure in transferring itself to its new peace work, or a great number are. What they say is that the 20% left them under the excess profits duty is a sufficient reserve for those purposes.

THE PRIME MINISTER: I agree with Sir Auckland Geddes that if you have got trade going you would find a shortage, but I do not think it exists at present. Supposing the war had gone on for another year, which is what we contemplated, and was very probable, could we not

[5] Capital funds.
[6] Either the banks are unwilling to lend, or businesses are reluctant to buy raw materials and undertake production because of uncertainty about the future, or the new-issue market is not eager to subscribe for new industrial issues. We cannot be sure which of these three things Sir Albert Stanley might mean.
[7] Chamberlain is talking about the new-issue market, hence about the raising of capital funds thereon. His analysis is defective in that the flow of funds to the market is something which in principle and in practice the government could have controlled.
[8] In 'real' terms profits were smaller than they seemed, because materials could not be replaced at the old prices.
[9] Capital funds to finance stocks and wage payments.

have borrowed the necessary 2,000,000,000 £? We were spending money freely on public works, so if you create a sort of prosperity there is no doubt that you could find the money . . . Let us see what the problem means. Take public works. How much money could you spend this year upon your scheme? Supposing you get your bill through in three weeks, how much money could you spend this year?

SIR AUCKLAND GEDDES: I have no idea.

THE PRIME MINISTER: Comparatively little. I want to know why this problem should be such an appalling one for a nation that has been spending 2,000,000,000 £. . . .

MR. CHAMBERLAIN: We cannot live by taking in one another's washing. What we want to do is to get a healthy trade started. That is far more important than stocking a great lot of expensive relief work. If you could get the businesses to move the rest would follow. . . .

THE PRIME MINISTER: I have heard many reasons given why business has not started. This is the first time I have heard it suggested it is lack of credit, and it is not even approximately accurate. There is plenty of money, and if there were business and confidence on other grounds business would start. I say there is no incompatibility between these two things.

MR. BONAR LAW: I should like you to realise the difficulties. I have not got the figures, but I always thought we had difficulty in getting the money absolutely necessary for the State during the transition period, for this reason. The money came to us largely from profits made by war industries and such like, and it came in the form of Treasury bills. If the industries are slack, how can we get it?

THE PRIME MINISTER: Take the banks.

MR. CHAMBERLAIN: I have had it all already, in bonds and Treasury Bills. As businesses get active they will not renew their Treasury Bills.

THE PRIME MINISTER: All I know is this. I always used to hear from Mr. McKenna, when he was Chancellor of the Exchequer, that we could not borrow beyond the 31st March, and that then there would be an end. Then he brought it up to September.[10] . . .

---

[10] Lloyd George correctly perceives that there is no limit to the market's willingness to absorb new Government flotations so long as the monetary authorities provide enough monetary reserves to the banking system. Chamberlain and Bonar Law do not understand this fact, nor its corrollary: it was the expansion of reserves, not excess profits, which made it possible for the British Government to borrow so much during the First World War.

SIR AUCKLAND GEDDES: . . . The points I wanted to make are these. Are we, or are we not, going to try and get back rapidly to the gold standard basis, because that policy is being urged at the recent Conferences, not in so many words but in effect, by the representations that are made? That is the first thing. If we are going to get rid of the inflation[11] I see enormous social difficulty and political difficulty. The next point is this. Are we going to adopt the sort of policy which is urged by the Federation of British Industries, that their losses on stocks, their losses on contracts entered into by them before the war, are to be met by the State? . . . The next is, are we to recognise—what I believe to be the case—that this social development programme which is adopted by the Government and to which the Government is absolutely pledged, carries with it, as I am sure it does, the need for organising emigration on a large scale? This is coming on to the fourth policy, because this country cannot absorb the full mass of people if we are going in for long-range investments on a great scale not only this year, but next year and the year after. Then, if that be recognised, are we also recognising that by going in for this policy at the present moment we are destroying the basis of private enterprise in such an industry as the building industry? How shall we deal with that situation? Those are the points on which we have no policy. There is the general overshadowing money difficulty . . . I agree that the amount of money wanted this year can be got, but it is going to have effects, and the effects will vary as we move along certain lines of policy. I wanted to . . . get an indication as to what is your general mind and the mind of the Government with regard to the lines of policy on which we are moving. . . .

MR. BONAR LAW: Sir Auckland's point . . . is this. It is a question of trying to get rid of the inflation. That seems to me to be the thing. At present, apart altogether from any other consequence, the loss of markets is one thing, and there are our expenses, and in addition to that the scale of wages; and, if along with that you want to get back to the gold standard business, it is obvious you cannot do it. Inflation must be kept up.

SIR AUCKLAND GEDDES: Inflation is absolutely essential. This policy which has been urged of getting rid of it is unsound. We have to keep inflation.

MR. BONAR LAW: It is a right thing to have as a hope, but that is all.

SIR AUCKLAND GEDDES: It seems to me we have to keep inflation, and we have to realise it.

---

[11] A return to the gold standard at the prewar gold-parity would require a reduction in the British price level and in the British money supply.

MR. CHAMBERLAIN: Will Mr. Bonar Law develop his idea? He says it is obvious we shall have to maintain inflation. I think even if we try to get rid of it we cannot. What happens then? At the present time we maintain the dollar exchange in New York, as we maintain other exchanges, by artificial means. The Government buys exchange and sells exchange. In other words, it subsidises the importer from those countries and to some extent penalises the exporters to those countries. If we let the exchange go, import would become more difficult and export would become easier. Does Mr. Bonar Law contemplate that it is the proper policy for us to pursue to let the exchanges go?[12] If we do, then of course gold will be shipped.

MR. BONAR LAW: That implies two things. If the exchange goes, it means the inflation here is higher than in America. That is not sound, to begin with. In the second place, whether we like it or not, it is obvious you cannot stop inflation if you have to go on borrowing money;[13] and you can do nothing else if we are to go on with our policy at all. When we come to the exchange we must do our best to keep it up. . . .

COLONEL AMERY: Might I come back to the point Sir Auckland Geddes raised about emigration? He said that, owing to the immense number of people who went out, and the length of time they have been abroad, the war has been in its social effect on enormous emigration. It has lasted so long, and things have transformed themselves so much at home that I do not believe you can get all the war emigrants back into this country any more than you can put Australia back into this country. The army includes hundreds of thousands of men who would have emigrated but for the war, and others whose attitude has changed, who, if they come back, will be restless and will want to go. I think it is essential that they should not be discontented by having no machinery for seeing that when they do go they go to the right places and that there are arrangements for receiving them at the other end. I mention that because I think it is of tremendous importance that before they all come back and want to start off again, as they are bound to do, they should find the machinery ready and will not be rushing off to cities like Montreal and other cities which they would congest, and create a lasting feeling against emigrants at the other end.

There is this also. Not only has industry transformed itself completely in a period of reduced industrial population, owing to war emigration, but this has taken place under non-competitive conditions. There has

---

[12] That is, allow the dollar-sterling exchange rate to float freely.
[13] Not necessarily true; the envisaged scale of *post-war* borrowing might not have been inflationary in any sense, though wartime borrowing certainly had been—in all senses.

been no question of price in competing markets with other countries. We are now on a different industrial basis, and I believe that, apart from the immediate requirements of neutral markets at this moment which the rising [sic] of the blockade might enable us to fulfil, you will find a little later that the old market for British industry on the Continent and in neutral countries no longer exists. Those countries, for their own reasons, will restrict their imports. France is doing so now, and Germany will have to do so in order to keep up the exchange.[14] We are in fact no longer the sort of country that can compete industrially in the open market except in certain industries. We are more in the position the American industries were in a generation ago, capable of doing tremendous things in our own area where we compete with our own kind of conditions, but not capable of competing in the open market.[15] It really comes to this, that we can both carry out our social reform and develop an immense trade, but mainly if not almost entirely within the Empire. That hangs together with the emigration question in this sense, that every man who goes out to other parts of the Empire not only creates trade in equipping himself but becomes a new source of trade and development when he has arrived there. Apart from the immediate question of capital, and whether you can ease the trade situation by opening the blockade, I do believe over a longer period of years, the only chance of keeping up the population and the prosperity of this country is by developing the population of the Empire outside as rapidly as we can. The immediate thing is that we must not have an appalling congestion of people in this country, who want to emigrate and cannot find the proper conditions to do so.

THE PRIME MINISTER: Have you a scheme prepared in the Colonial Office?

COLONEL AMERY: Yes, we have had an Emigration Committee, and the question was to have come up yesterday before the Cabinet. We have a bill for machinery, and definite projects as to dealing with the ex-soldier, who is going to be the chief factor in emigration, because he is the man who would have gone if there had not been a war, the type of man who will be unsettled if his place has been taken, the man who has mixed with colonial soldiers. . . . I do strongly ask the Cabinet to allow us to introduce the proper machinery, because we cannot possibly go to

---

[14] That is, the exchange rate.

[15] A country can be non-competitive in everything only if its exchange rate is over-valued, as Britain's almost certainly was before its flotation later in 1919 and after the return to the gold standard in 1925.

High Commissioners[16] and Agents-General[17] and begin any sort of negotiations without machinery or even an outline of what the Government would be prepared to do for the ex-servicemen. If the Government would let me introduce a Bill and get the machinery started, I could get in touch and find out what the Canadians would do for us, what Australia and each State of Australia would do for us, and so on, and we should be ready ... and we should be able to say, "Yes, this is all right, we can send so many here, and so many there". The thing would proceed evenly, and you would not have the Bolshevism and the very real trouble you will have if you are not prepared to cope with this period of congestion which must come ... Public social works, taking off the blockade, and suchlike remedies should ease the situation for some months to come. But I am sure a period is coming within six months, and will last for two or three years, when you will find England cannot absorb the men who emigrated for the war, unless it is prepared to come back to the pre-war wages and pre-war conditions of labour; in fact, we should have to be the old European competitive England instead of what it is now, an England almost on the American basis of high wages.[18]

MR. ILLINGWORTH: I would stake my existence that there will be a great shortage of labour in this country, and the emigration business ought to be discouraged.

MR. CHURCHILL: I quite agree.

THE PRIME MINISTER: It is a dangerous thing to put forward. If there is anything to be done in the way of, I will not say promoting it, but making arrangements for it, I hope it will be done by private conferences with the Colonies, to begin with. If you introduced an Emigration Bill now it would have the worse effect upon the labour situation I am sure, and I am doubtful about it.

COLONEL AMERY: I cannot carry on the Conferences without your authority.

THE PRIME MINISTER: Authority, yes; but it is a Bill I am against.

COLONEL AMERY: The Bill creates the authority, but not the emigration.

[16] The representatives of the Dominions in the United Kingdom.

[17] The representatives of the Australian States and Canadian Provinces in London.

[18] The argument is correct if we assume Amery to mean that only by making labour as scarce relative to land and capital goods in Britain as in the United States can the British economy pay American real wages. Amery may or may not mean this.

DR. ADDISON: I share Mr. Illingworth's opinion as to the future and all the prognostications. We have lost the best producers in the war, and if we are going to encourage the next best producers to emigrate, how are we going to be solvent in the future? . . .

SIR AUCKLAND GEDDES: It will help us if you would state what the policy is. You wish to discourage emigration, and you wish to retain the inflation. Is it to be taken as the policy of the Government that all the money that is required for these social improvements is to be found? Is that to be a first charge?

THE PRIME MINISTER: It is not merely that we are to be pledged. I want to look ahead and see how we can guarantee the peace of this country. Nothing struck me more, in the conversations I had with the miners, that the part this plays in the general irritation which has made them unreasonable.

SIR R. HORNE: Have you seen the way they live? . . .

MR. CHAMBERLAIN: Mr. Prime Minister, I do not want you to think that I differ from you, where, in fact, there is no difference. I should like to say that there are two distinct problems which are getting mixed up in our discussion. . . . There is the question of unemployment, and the question of what our social policy is to be, for the social and political reasons which you have put forward.

THE PRIME MINISTER: And the economic policy.

MR. CHAMBERLAIN: . . . Far more important than these Government schemes from the point of view of unemployment is the setting to work of trade. That really is only incidentally affected by our social programme; it is rather dependent upon individual men and people placing orders with individual manufacturers, and manufacturers finding a market for their goods. . . .

THE PRIME MINISTER: There are here four business men in front of me who are engaged in trade and business on a considerable scale. I will put two questions to them . . . would they feel any despair about finding sufficient employment for everybody in this country provided the right course were taken to set the machine going? . . . What course would they adopt in order to get the machine going?

LORD INVERFORTH: On your first question, I should have more employment than men to employ. . . .

MR. ILLINGWORTH: . . . in twelve months' time I would stake my existence upon the shortage of labour in the country. . . .

SIR ERIC GEDDES: I think there will be a period of unemployment, and I think it is most desirable to get emigration arrangements going for that reason. I do not know whether that period will last over twelve months or not. I think it is desirable for two reasons: one, that there will be a large body of men who will be dissatisfied and want to get to the colonies. The present home-life they will not like, and I think it will be a valuable safety-valve to get emigration arrangements in being. Personally, I do not fear that after it may be 12, 18, or 24 months the country cannot support its population. I do not think emigration will be so great as really to have much effect of that kind, but it ought to be provided for as a safety-valve. I think it is inevitable that those two years of the post-war period you should treat from the point of view of expenditure as years during the war. You must be prepared to spend money and treat it as part of war expenditure in order to employ people. The best way to employ them is upon the schemes which we are all agreed are essential—these social schemes. I think during that period you will have to allow people to get out of the country or employ them, because you cannot keep giving them doles and keep them contented. You must be prepared to spend money on after-the-war problems as you did during the during-the-war problems. That must be found, and added to our war debt if necessary. It is the period of reconstruction, and money has to be spent generously, and on those schemes. If we get over that period I think the trade of the country will revive. There is no reason why it should not. . . .

SIR ALBERT STANLEY: First of all, I think there will not be the measure of unemployment that some people fear. I think we are unduly apprehensive at the present time. Trade will substantiate itself in time. . .
We must go through a period when there will be considerable unemployment, because there is so much uncertainty as to how and when trade will establish itself. Capital is not being attracted into trade at the present time; it is very nervous now. . . .

THE PRIME MINISTER: I think we have had a very valuable discussion, and, so far as I am concerned, an enlightening discussion. I was glad to hear from those who have met the business associations, being men of affairs themselves, that they are able to assure the Cabinet that, in their judgement, there is no real apprehension as to the future of British trade and British industry. I must say that that is the view I had formed, but I do not feel that I am as qualified to express an opinion as they are. I thought the needs of the world so great that somebody would have to supply them, and ourselves and America must do it. There are four things which, as far as I can gather from all those who have spoken, have got to be set right in order to get a real start. First of all, there are these restrictions[19] . . . The second is this: government orders[20] . . . Thirdly there is a question of excess profits.[21] All these things give confidence to capital, and is essential to give confidence to Labour as well. That is a much more difficult business, because they are thoroughly rattled and are greatly suspicious. . . .

MR. FISHER: Can anything be done to bring down food prices through Government action? That is a very important thing.

THE PRIME MINISTER: Yes. They are going to bring meat down by 4d. a pound. That is very substantial.

SIR R. HORNE: I am getting out the effect of the proposed reduction now.

THE PRIME MINISTER: You must tell the people something of that sort in order to show that we are not merely talking. They are getting sick of talking.

2, Whitehall Gardens, SW, 26 February, 1919.

5. The Cabinet Unemployment Committee urges the subsidization of emigrants

FROM Public Record Office, CAB 23/115, CP 2145, November 1920.

The Committee has considered certain proposals in relation to overseas settlement as a means of relieving abnormal unemployment during the coming winter which were submitted by the Chairman of the Overseas Settlement Committee. At present overseas settlers are assisted by the Exchequer with free passages for ex-servicemen and women, and by grants from the National Relief Fund to those who have suffered direct hardship as a result of the War. As at present arranged, applications for free passages must be sent in before December 31 next [1920], and the whole of the National Relief Fund has been allocated. The funds in the hands of the Overseas Settlement Committee will probably last till the end of this calendar year, and no funds are available after that date.

---

[19] The blockade restrictions which hindered trade not only with former belligerents but with Continental neutrals.
[20] The giving of government orders to purchase, so as to create business confidence.
[21] The continuance of excess profits taxation was believed to hinder business revival.

The Committee[1] recommend:

(a) that the time for receiving applications from ex-servicemen and women for free passages should be extended for one year

(b) that grants in aid of settlement within the Empire should be placed at the disposal of the Overseas Settlement Committee, in so far as they may be required, at a rate not exceeding £50,000 a month from January 1, 1921 to March 31,1921, with preference to ex-servicemen

(c) that the Colonial Office, after negotiation with the Dominions, should formulate a scheme of assisted emigration on a large scale, for submission to the Cabinet.

6. The British Government warns certain Dominions that they will be asked to contribute to migration schemes

FROM Public Record Office, CO 532/167, November 11, 1920: telegram from the Secretary of State for the Colonies to the Governors-General of Australia and New Zealand[2] and to the Governors of the Australian States, November 29, 1920.

I desire to take this opportunity of explaining that the adoption in future of any scheme of a similar nature [to the scheme of free passage for service personnel] must, in my view, be contingent upon the participation of the overseas governments to a greater degree than heretofore in the policy which the grant of free passages represents ... any increase in expenditure in connection with overseas settlement could only be defended if it were shown to be required in connection with an Imperial policy of Empire development with which the overseas governments were in full sympathy, and in which they were prepared to share ... [as for ex-servicemen, the overseas governments should undertake] a reasonable part of the cost of settlement ... The same considerations would apply to the question of extending the scheme to other classes of settlers ... for whom there is a special demand in the self-governing Dominions.

---

[1] That is, the Unemployment Committee.

[2] Until much later in the interwar period, the United Kingdom Government and the Dominion Governments normally communicated with one another via the Governors-General and the Colonial Office (after 1925, the Dominions Office).

7. A Cabinet decision

FROM Public Record Office, CAB 23/23, Cabinet Minutes of December 6, 1920.

[the Cabinet] concurred in ... recommendations of the [Unemployment] Committee for encouraging overseas settlement as a means of relieving abnormal unemployment.

8. The United Kingdom asks the Dominions to help with Empire Settlement

FROM Public Record Office, CO 532/158, December 21, 1920: telegram from the Secretary of State for the Colonies to the Governors-General of Canada, Australia, New Zealand, South Africa, and Newfoundland.

His Majesty's Government are anxious to consult at an early date with the Governments of self-governing Dominions as to possibility of initiating a large-scale policy of state-aided settlement within the Empire based upon mutual cooperation between Governments concerned. The objects in view would be to meet exceptional conditions which have arisen from the war; to distribute and use the population of the Empire to the best advantage; to develop cultivation of the land and other natural resources and to ensure that largest possible proportion of population likely to leave U.K. in near future should be attracted to the Dominions and available to strengthen and build up their national life, and not be diverted into foreign countries. His Majesty's Government trust that it may be possible to arrange special conference upon this question early in the new year.

9. The Empire Settlement Act of 1922[1]

12 & 13 Geo.5, Ch. 13.

1. (1) It shall be lawful for the Secretary of State, in association with the government of any part of His Majesty's Dominions, or with public authorities or public or private organizations either in the United Kingdom or in any part of such Dominions, to formulate and cooperate in carrying out agreed schemes for affording joint assistance to suitable persons in the United Kingdom who intend to settle in any part of His Majesty's Oversea Dominions.

(2) An agreed scheme under this Act may be either (a) a development or a land settlement scheme; or (b) a scheme for facilitating settlement in or migration to any part of His Majesty's Oversea Dominions by assistance with passages, initial allowances, training, or otherwise, and shall make provision with respect to the contributions to be made, either by way of grant or by way of loan or otherwise, by the parties to the agreed scheme towards the expenses of the scheme.

(3) The Secretary of State shall have all such powers as may be necessary for carrying out his obligations under any scheme made in pursuance of this Act: provided that:

(a) the Secretary of State shall not agree to any scheme without the consent of the Treasury, who shall be satisfied that the contributions of the government, authority, or organization with whom the scheme is agreed to the expenses of the scheme bear a proper relation to the contribution of the Secretary of State; and

(b) the contribution of the Secretary of State shall not in any case exceed half the expenses of the scheme; and

(c) the liability of the Secretary of State to make contributions under the scheme shall not exceed beyond a period of fifteen years after the passing of this act.

(4) Any expenses of the Secretary of State under this Act shall be paid out of the moneys provided by Parliament: provided that the aggregate amount expended . . . shall not exceed one million five hundred thousand pounds in the financial year current at the date of the passing of this Act, or three million pounds in any subsequent financial year, exclusive of the amount of any sums received by way of interest on or repayment of advances previously made.

[1] Omitting the formal opening and Clauses 2 and 3, which relate respectively to protectorates and mandates and to the Act's short title.

10. Lord Milner's Tariff Advisory Committee[1] Reports

FROM Public Record Office, CAB 24/164, C.P.7(24), December 22, 1923.

MOST SECRET (circulated by direction of the Prime Minister[2])
1. The Tariff Advisory Committee have held in all ten meetings and have made considerable progress in examining the material submitted to them by the Board of Trade, the Customs and other Government Departments.

2. The Committee were given to understand that the Government desired to have their recommendations at the earliest possible date and in any case not later than the middle of January . . . Thanks to the assistance . . . afforded them, the Committee had, in the course of their sittings, already come to conclusions on some of the main points involved in their inquiry and were beginning to see their way about the rest. They had also made a certain amount of progress in framing a schedule of rates and it seemed possible that, by holding almost continuous sittings during December, they might be able to submit their recommendations to the Government early in the New Year.

3. When, however, the Committee met on December 7, it was felt that, in view of the result of the General Election, the Government would probably have no further need of their services. In that case, it seemed to them that all they could do was to leave a brief record of their proceedings, without attempting to make a formal report or to submit recommendations on a subject, their investigation of which they had not had time to complete. The Chairman of the Committee . . . subsequently ascertained that the views of the Government were in accordance with these anticipations. . . .

---

[1] Chairman Lord Milner. Members Wm. Ashley, Algernon F. Firth, W. A. S. Hewins, Lord Kylsant, Arthur Pugh, W. Peter Rylands, and Edward G. Strutt. A Committee containing neither public officials nor ministers, but made up instead of interested academics, businessmen, and Tariff Reformers.

[2] Baldwin. The Committee had been formed in pursuance of Baldwin's declaration that he would fight the 1924 election on the issue of protective tariffs. As the Conservatives lost the election the Committee report was presented to the outgoing Conservative ministry and ignored by the incoming Labourites. Hewins had pressed for an executive committee under his personal control; the Milner Committee, he feared, could not work fast enough. Hence he would not allow the Committee to use the materials which his Tariff Commission had collected. See University of Sheffield, Hewins Papers, diary entries for October 30, and November 2, 1923.

4. The deliberations of the Committee were necessarily limited by the declared policy of the Government. Thus duties upon staple articles of food were excluded from consideration, while the Committee themselves had no hesitation in recommending that no duty should be placed upon raw materials. They therefore confined their attention to manufactured and semi-manufactured articles.

5. With regard to the tariff upon these, the Committee took the view, that it should, in the first instance at any rate, be an *ad valorem* tariff. It was felt that, at present, the material did not exist which would enable the Committee to decide whether or not specific rates of duty should be imposed at a later date.

6. The Committee were agreed that the rates of duty should, as a general rule, be graduated according to the amount of labour expended at the several stages of manufacture.[3] They were further agreed that, on the first introduction of a tariff system, it would be impracticable to have a great number of rates, or to attempt to differentiate too nicely between the amounts of duty chargeable upon different articles of the same general character. They therefore, favoured the inclusion of all articles, upon which they might recommend the imposition of a duty, in one of three classes, to be taxed respectively 5%, 12½%, and 20%. It was reserved for further consideration whether in the middle class—by far the largest and comprising goods in more or less advanced stages of manufacture—there should not be a further subdivision into two or even three sub-classes, subject to duties of 10% and 15%, or of 10%, 12½%, and 15% respectively. Side by side with these classes of dutiable articles, they held that there should be a Free List including not only staple articles of food and raw materials, but also any other articles, such as pig iron, which, though partly manufactured, it might be desirable, for special reasons, to place in the same category as raw materials. At the other end of the scale there would be a special category, including commodities which are already subject on importation to duties of a protective character, but exceeding 20%—such as the so-called "McKenna Duties"[4] or the duties imposed under the Safeguarding of Industries Act.[5] These special duties it was, in the opinion of the Committee (having regard to their proved value in preserving or stimulating the industries affected by them), desirable to retain.

7. Besides considering the general character of the Tariff and the rates of duty to be imposed under it, the Committee had arrived at

---

[3] That is, the Committee wanted to impose a heavier *ad valorem* duty, the higher the ratio of labour-cost to materials-cost in the cost-structure of the good.

[4] The duties on motor cars, clocks, watches, and cinema film imposed in 1915.

[5] Special protective duties imposed under the Safeguarding of Industries Act, 1921.

agreement on certain points of fundamental importance, to which it seems desirable to refer.

8. Thus it was agreed to recommend that a rebate of one-third of all duties imposed under the Tariff should be accorded to goods produced in and consigned from any part of the British Empire.

9. The Committee were also in general agreement with the proposals, submitted by the Departments, on the subject of Valuation and of the provisions to be made for allowing dutiable goods re-exported in their original condition to obtain exemption from payment of duty. The Committee were fully alive to the great importance of maintaining the entrepot trade. . . .

12. A more difficult question arises with regard to goods which have paid duty on importation into this country and are subsequently re-exported after having undergone some manufacturing process here. These can only be dealt with under a system of drawback, and there is room for difference of opinion both as to the extent to which drawback should be allowed and as to the best method of determining the amount of it. . . .

14. . . . the Committee felt that the comparative labour conditions prevailing in this country and in the competitive countries and the efficiency of the various industries in this country were relevant to the subject under consideration.[6]

15. The Committee further considered how far it might be possible to use a Tariff for the purpose of making commercial bargains with foreign countries. It was recognised that with such moderate normal rates as the Committee were prepared to recommend—viz. from 5% to 20% *ad valorem*—there was not much scope for obtaining reciprocal concessions from foreign countries through lowering our own duties. This consideration pointed to the conclusion that it might be necessary to include in the Tariff Act another scale of duties, somewhat higher than those recommended above, which might be used for the purpose of negotiation with countries which did not grant fair terms to British trade.[7] . . .

[6] This seems to mean that the less efficient a given British industry is, relative to its foreign competitors, the more protection it should have. Such a prescription is in violent opposition to *laissez-faire* economic thinking with respect to the gains from an international division of labour. Its application would be bound to impoverish Britain as a whole, though it might benefit some Britons.

[7] In other words, for purposes of retaliation Britain should impose a specially high General Tariff. If in these circumstances British, 'favoured' foreign, and 'unfair' foreign firms all supply the British market, the effect of this strategy is to reduce total British sales, while increasing the sales of the British and 'favoured' foreign suppliers; users in Britain will pay a price equal to the world price plus the *highest* tariff rate, and this rate will also raise the 'economic rents' to British producers.

17. It may be argued that, where it can be proved that any sound British industry of sufficient importance to constitute a real national interest is threatened with ruin from any abnormal cause, especially if the danger be of a temporary character, the Government should be in a position to take prompt and vigorous action for the defence of that industry, whether by imposing special duties or by any other means, such as a limitation of imports. This principle, if adopted, would involve fresh legislation, on the lines of the Safeguarding of Industries Act, but greatly extending its present limits. To a thorough investigation of this problem, however, which is obviously one of great difficulty, the Committee had not time to devote themselves, though it had become apparent that, at some stage of their proceedings, it would have been impossible to avoid the consideration of it.

18. In this connection, but not in this connection only, the Committee were led to the conclusion that it would be necessary to create a permanent Tariff Board to assist the Government in the administration of the Tariff Laws. Such a body, composed, perhaps, on the Australian model partly of officials and partly of representatives of Industry and Commerce, would be in a position to investigate and advise upon the appeals of particular industries for protection, which are already numerous under existing statutes. It would also be competent to adjudicate upon the many disputes about classification, valuation, and so forth, which are bound to arise under any extended system of import duties. The creation of such a body appeared desirable for two other and weighty reasons. It would defend the Government and Parliament from undue pressure from sectional interests, and it would inform the Government, as to the cases, should they arise, where the consolidation of business enterprise—which is so rapidly taking place in this country, as in other countries, and is generally conducive to economy of manufacture— might, under a restriction of import, operate to the disadvantage of consumers.

19. The Committee were impressed with the extent of the information as to the magnitude and organisation of the several British industries, which is already in the possession of the Board of Trade. They regret, however, that the exact statistical knowledge, which was secured by the Census of Production for the year 1907, has not been brought more nearly up to date by a subsequent Census of the same character.

22 December 1923.   [eight signatures]

11. Lord Arnold[1] urges the Labour Cabinet to eschew Imperial Preference

FROM Public Record Office, CAB 24/165, C.P. 112(24), February 15, 1924.

It is important to call the attention of the Cabinet to the necessity of taking an immediate decision on the Resolutions regarding Imperial Preference passed at the [Imperial] Economic Conference last October.[2]

The Secretary of State has been receiving representations from several quarters, especially from the West Indies, asking for a detailed statement of the Government's views regarding those Resolutions, and the need for a decision has become most urgent because a Debate on Imperial Preference in the House of Commons has now been fixed for Tuesday, February 26th.

It is also desirable to emphasise that the Dominions must be informed of the Government's intentions well in advance of any statement in the Press or in Parliament, so there is no time to lose.

The whole of the Resolutions which were passed at the Imperial Economic Conference dealing with Preference are appended hereto. . . .[3]

The present memorandum is written by me on the assumption that the Government, though leaving the Resolutions to the vote of the House, will have to state its own views on them in detail before long.

The most important of the Resolutions are those relating to Sugar and Dried Fruits. To take sugar first. The duty is at present 2¾d a lb. and the preference is 1/6th, or nearly ½d per lb. If the sugar duty were halved and became 1⅜d, it is urged that the preference should still be the present amount of nearly ½d and should not be 1/6th of the present duty, which would mean a preference of nearly ¼d. This plan of maintaining the preference at the present amount of nearly ½d is now always called 'stabilisation'.

The most important point for the Cabinet to consider, in relation to stabilisation, is that it clashes with the Labour Party policy of abolishing, as soon as it can be done, the sugar duty altogether. A further difficulty arises owing to the undertaking given by the Coalition Government in February 1922 that the proportional rate of preference would last for ten years. It is true that this undertaking only applied to the *rate* of preference i.e. 1/6th, and not to the existing *amount* of preference of nearly ½d.

---

[1] Under-Secretary of State for the Colonies.
[2] During Stanley Baldwin's first Government.
[3] Omitted from this version.

The undertaking meant that, if the sugar duty were reduced by one-half, the rate of preference would still be one-sixth, and in such an event the actual *amount* of preference would have been reduced from nearly $\frac{1}{2}$d to nearly $\frac{1}{4}$d.

The words of this ten-year undertaking are set forth in a reply given by Mr. Churchill in the House of Commons to a question on the 23rd February, 1922. . . . It should be noted that the undertaking applied not only to the duty on sugar, but to all preferences as prescribed by the Second Schedule of the Finance Act, 1919, that is to say, to all articles on which preference is given. This ten-year undertaking has been counted upon, particularly in the West Indies. . . . Naturally, the sugar growers and others wish to know whether the ten-year undertaking holds good now that there is a change of Government. Also, they wish for more than that. It is here necessary to make it clear that this ten-year undertaking was carried a distinct step further at the Economic Conference last autumn because, as already stated, the stabilisation now proposed is that the present *amount* of preference shall not be reduced. . . .

To return . . . to the Churchill undertaking, I will summarise very briefly what seems to be the position of that matter:—

(1) Constitutionally, it would appear that no such undertaking could have been given and that therefore it ought not to have been given.

(2) No undertaking of this kind could have any definite moral obligation unless it had been agreed to by the other parties in the State. . . .

(3) In these circumstances, it cannot really be contended that the undertaking is binding upon the present Government. . . .

It is quite impossible for the Labour Government to renew the ten-year undertaking in a specific form, particularly as amplified in the Economic Conference Resolution, because:—

(1) To do so would assume that the sugar duty would probably remain in existence for ten years, even though at a reduced rate. Any such assumption goes counter to Labour Party policy, and would mean embarrassment in propaganda and for Labour candidates at Election times.

(2) It seems probable that the Liberals would not be a party to any such undertaking and would vote against the Government on the point in the House of Commons. The result would be that this undertaking would have to be carried by Labour and Tory votes against the Liberals. Nothing could be more disastrous for the Government that that. Labour would at once be represented in the country as thoroughly unsound on fiscal matters, and it would be difficult to deny the charge. Also, the relations between Labour and Liberals in the House of Commons would be greatly strained, which might, on another issue, mean that the Liberals would decide to vote with the Tories and bring the

Government down. It would be in the last degree unfortunate if the Government got into serious difficulties, leading perhaps to its eventual defeat, not because it had boldly adhered to a point of principle, but because it had given way on a matter on which it should have stood firm.

In all the circumstances, the utmost that the Cabinet should consider is agreeing to stabilisation as long as there is a sugar duty. .... But it should also be clearly stated in Parliament that the Labour Party adheres to its policy of abolishing the duty altogether as soon as the finances of the country will allow. .... If the Cabinet decides to make the foregoing announcement about stabilisation it would probably go a very long way to satisfy the West Indies. Certainly stabilisation should be represented in Parliament as a very great concession, and only made because of the extremely difficult position in which the action of the late Government and Economic Conference have placed the present Government.

Dried Fruits

The Government will be pressed to remit altogether to the Dominions the present duty on dried fruits. The duty on foreign dried fruits is now 10/6d per cwt. and those of Empire origin enjoy a preference of 1/6th, i.e. 1/9d per cwt., making the duty on Empire products 8/9d. It is now proposed that this 8/9d shall be remitted altogether, the foreign duty remaining 10/6d as at present. Financially, this would involve a loss of revenue of about £90,000 a year. Such remission would operate mainly for the benefit of Australia and South Africa, and there is considerable demand from those Dominions to give the remission.

As regards Australia, it is argued that the remission would make possible increased emigration from the Mother Country for fruit growing. It is doubtful if there is really much substance in this point. In any case, emigration could probably be stimulated by other means at less cost to the Mother Country.

A chief objection to the remission of the dried fruits duty is the fundamental one that it would operate inequitably as between the various parts of the Empire. It would help Australia and South Africa but would do nothing for Canada, New Zealand, and Newfoundland. Another grave objection is that remission would in effect give increased protection because if, by reason of it, more capital is employed in the fruit growing industry in Australia and South Africa, it would be extraordinarily difficult, in fact almost impossible, subsequently to abolish the 10/6d duty on foreign dried fruits. In short, whereas it may plausibly be argued that the remission is a step in the direction of Free Trade because it means the removal of a duty, it is unfortunately equally true that it almost certainly means the perpetuation of the foreign duty, and that is anything but a step in the direction of Free Trade.

It is also contended that if the Mother Country refuses to give this remission she may hereafter be disadvantaged in certain obvious ways in respect of Australian preferential duties on imports of British manufactured goods.

This latter point raises a most fundamental principle, and similar considerations arise in regard to the request to the Mother Country to give the ten-year undertaking with a view to 'bolstering up' the sugar industry in the West Indies.

The simple fact is that in all these preferences and reciprocal arrangements the Mother Country is on a slippery slope. The appetite of the Dominions and Colonies grows up on what it feeds on. Unless the Empire is eventually to break up, it will be necessary, sooner or later, to take a firm stand and to say 'no' to these Dominion and Colonial importunities and threats. Schemes of Dominion and Colonial development such as those which the Government has in view will do more to help the Empire than all the Tariffs in the world.

The whole policy of preference is economically unsound, and is really based upon the principle of protecting Dominion and Colonial interests at the expense of the people of the Mother Country, and that means mainly of the worker, because preference involves, certainly if it is to be maintained, dearer sugar and tea and so forth.

Preference and these reciprocal trade arrangements with the Dominions and Colonies are bound to break down in course of time. As a matter of principle, therefore, it would undoubtedly be best to take a firm line now rather than be dragged further along the evil path. Whenever such a stand is taken it will be said that Dominion and Colonial interests are being flouted, and that the Empire is being ruined, and so forth. But these things should be faced, more particularly as they would not be really true, and such criticisms are much less harmful than going further along wholly wrong lines. Quite apart from anything else, it is necessary to emphasise that all these requests from the Dominions and Colonies are a clear violation of the doctrine of economic equality, and this policy, if it is pursued further, will undoubtedly in course of years lead to great international friction and not improbably to war. It is the height of unwisdom to try and enclose within tariff fences such large parts of the world's surface, more especially as the various countries are scattered all over the globe.

Nevertheless, in view of the extraordinarily difficult position in which the Cabinet is placed, it may be decided to remit the dried fruits duty. . .

The latter part of the Economic Conference Resolution on currants, about considering an increase in the duty on foreign currants, should not of course be entertained.

The remaining Resolutions for *increased* preferences are in respect of tobacco and wine, but the pressure regarding them has been less than in the cases of sugar and dried fruits.

All the other Resolutions dealing with Imperial Preference which were passed at the Imperial Economic Conference would require the imposition of new duties, and I have assumed that the Cabinet would not assent to any such proposals. . . .

If it is decided to agree to sugar stabilisation and the remission of the duties on dried fruits and currants, the dangers of this course must again be stressed. Such concessions are wrong in principle, they would be inequitable in operation, and they can be, and in all probability would be, riddled by the criticism of the Liberal Party in Parliament.

It would obviously be of great assistance to the Cabinet if it were possible to ascertain in advance with some exactitude what view the Liberals are likely to take about these various matters. It may be the case, in view of the situation created by the Resolutions of the Economic Conference, that the Liberals will be more inclined to compromise than would otherwise be the case.

12. Colonial Development Act

20–21 Geo. 5, 1929, ch. 5
[Formal opening and some clauses omitted.]

1. (1) The Treasury, with the concurrence of the Secretary of State for the Colonies and on the recommendation of the committee to be appointed for the purposes of this Act, may make advances to the Government of any colony or of any territory to which the section applies, for the purpose of aiding and developing agriculture and industry in the colony or territory, and thereby promoting commerce with or industry in the United Kingdom, by any of the following means:

(a) Encouraging the adoption of improved machinery and equipment for cultivation and for the preparation of agricultural produce for the market;

(b) The improvement of internal transport and communications and the provision of equipment therefor;

(c) The construction and improvement of harbours and the provision of equipment therefor;

(d) The development and improvement of fisheries;

(e) Forestry;

(f) The reclamation, drainage, and irrigation of land;

(g) Promoting the discovery and improvement of water supplies and the development of water power;

(h) Promoting the development of mineral resources;

(i) The promotion of scientific research, instruction and experiments in the science, methods and practice of agriculture and industry, the organisation of co-operation, and instruction in the growing and marketing of produce;

(j) Assisting the Government of the colony or territory in defraying in whole or in part during a period not exceeding ten years from the raising of the loan, the interest payable by the Government on any loan raised after this section comes into operation for any purpose for which an advance might have been made under this section, including any loan raised under the Palestine and East Africa Loans Act, 1926;

(k) Any other means (including surveys) which appear calculated to achieve the purpose aforesaid.

(2) Advances under this section may be made either by way of grant or by way of loan, or partly in one way and partly in the other, and on such terms and subject to such conditions as the Treasury may think fit, and may be applied by the Government to which they are made either directly or through any person or body of persons.

(3) For the purposes of this section there shall be paid out of moneys provided by Parliament such sums, not exceeding one million pounds in any one year, as Parliament may from time to time determine.

(4) All sums issued on account of moneys provided by Parliament under this section shall be paid into a fund to be called 'The Colonial Development Fund', and all advances made under this section shall be made out of that fund. . . .

(10) The territories to which this section applies are territories which are under His Majesty's protection and territories in respect of which a mandate on behalf of the League of Nations has been accepted by His Majesty and is being exercised by His Majesty's Government in the United Kingdom.

(11) In this section the expression 'colony' means a colony not possessing responsible Government.

2. (1) The committee for the purposes of this Act shall be appointed by the Secretary of State for the Colonies subject to the approval of the Treasury. . . .

3. (1) His Majesty may, if a representation is made to him by the Treasury and the Secretary of State that it is desirable to do so, make an

Order in Council directing that the Colonial Stock Acts, 1877 to 1900, shall be extended, subject to such modifications and to such conditions as may appear expedient to His Majesty, so as to apply to stock issued after the passing of this Act and forming part of the public debt of any territory specified in the Order which is under His Majesty's protection or in respect of which a mandate on behalf of the League of Nations has been accepted by His Majesty and is being exercised by His Majesty's Government in the United Kingdom. . . .

4. The Palestine and East Africa Loans Act, 1926, shall have effect in relation to any loan raised thereunder after the commencement of this Act by the Governments of Kenya, Uganda, Northern Rhodesia, Nyasaland or Tanganyika as if—

(a) there were included under each of the heads 1, 2 and 3 in the Second Schedule to the said Act the purpose of paying (during such period, not exceeding five years from the date on which the loan was actually raised, as may be determined by the Secretary of State with the approval of the Treasury) interest on so much of the said loan as is to be applied under that head;

(b) in paragraph (b) of subsection (2) of section one of the said Act a period not exceeding sixty years were substituted for a period not exceeding forty years.

13. The Prime Minister of Canada explains his strategy with respect to Imperial Preference

FROM Public Archives of Canada, William Lyon MacKenzie King Papers.

PERSONAL AND CONFIDENTIAL   Ottawa, June 14, 1930.

A. C. Morton, Esq., President, the Herald Printing House, Montreal.

My dear Mr. Morton:

I have read with much interest your note of June 5,[1] and have made some examination of the pamphlet which you enclosed, and which I plan to go into more fully at the first opportunity.

[1] Morton had urged that Canada should take a bold lead in advocacy of preferential trade, and had asked King to indicate the Liberal Party position.

I wholly concur in your view of the importance of trade between Great Britain and Canada, and in your belief that there is a wide range of products which might be exchanged between the two countries without doing any injury to the industries of either country.

The budget introduced by Mr. Dunning[2] is an effective and practical demonstration of the truth of this view. It confers very substantial advantages on British industry without doing injury to Canadian industries.

As to mutual preferences, it is our view (and our practice) that where Great Britain or any Dominion establishes duties for protective purposes, preferences should be granted to Canadian products. It is, however, quite another matter to demand that Great Britain should change its fiscal policy[3] for the express purpose of granting preference to Canada or other Dominions. It should not be assumed, as too frequently is done, that our position would be better if Great Britain were to establish a protective tariff with Empire preference. It is quite conceivable that in some cases the interests of home producers would result in even the preferential tariff eventually being made sufficiently high to reduce imports from the Dominions competing with their products.[4] If Great Britain has not given us a preference over the foreigner, she has at least given us equality with her own producers.[5] One of your editorial confreres remarked the other day that since Confederation Great Britain had bought five billion[6] dollars worth more of goods from Canada than Canada had bought from Great Britain.

To your inquiry 'whether the Canadian preference for British products has no other purpose than to meet strictly domestic needs without any concern for the future of Canadian trade in the markets of the United Kingdom,' I should say emphatically no. On the contrary, we consider that there is no more effective means of securing a favorable attitude towards Canadian goods in the British markets than the action which the Government has recently taken. It is essential to increase, not to decrease, imports from Britain if we wish to increase our exports to Britain,[7] and the Budget ensures this by diverting trade from the United

[2] Charles Dunning, Canadian Minister of Finance in 1929–30 and 1935–39, had made substantial unilateral increases in the British preference in his 1930 budget.

[3] That is, basic policy with respect to protective tariffs.

[4] King is here describing Canada's own practice with respect to the tariff-protection of manufactures.

[5] More than King's Government was prepared to give Britain in the Canadian market.

[6] In British terminology, five thousand million.

[7] King's statement is untrue in the environment of general currency-convertibility which then existed. Canada would not necessarily sell more to Britain by buying more from Britain.

States to Britain. Further, every observer agrees that the extension of the British preference has created an extremely friendly attitude in the minds of all parties and individuals in Great Britain towards Canadian trade, an attitude which will undoubtedly bear fruit in both collective and individual action, whether that action take the form of tariff preferences or of some other means of increasing imports from Canada. I have not the slightest doubt that, particularly at this juncture, this policy will be much more effective in increasing Canadian exports to Great Britain than the policy[8] of bargaining and dictation.

I trust that these views will commend themselves to those who, like yourself, are concerned in the development of the most friendly and profitable trade relations between Canada and the Motherland.

Yours sincerely,
W. L. MacKenzie King

14. J. H. Thomas begs his Cabinet colleagues to take some decisions and make some concessions to the Dominions at the 1930 Imperial Conference

FROM Public Record Office, CAB 24/216, C.P. 366(30), October 27, 1930.

SECRET. THE IMPERIAL CONFERENCE: Memorandum by the Secretary of State for Dominion Affairs

The Imperial Conference has reached a crisis on the economic side, and unless the crisis is resolved within the next few days, I see no prospect of saving the Conference from shipwreck.

In these circumstances I think it due both to my colleagues and to myself to set out, as frankly as possible, the situation as I see it.

We have in the first place to keep very clearly before us the fact that the people of this country, as indeed of the whole Empire, are hoping for, and indeed are demanding, real and tangible economic results from this Conference. If those hopes are disappointed—if, so far from producing any beneficial results, the Conference breaks up in confusion—they will certainly visit their resentment on the Government, and it will

---

[8] Already espoused by R. B. Bennett and the Canadian Conservative Party.

be no use to say that the failure was not our fault. Conversely if we can achieve positive results, which can reasonably be held out as offering some chance of increasing trade within the Empire, our position in the country will be strengthened. The fate of the Government, in my opinion, may well be bound up with the fate of this Conference.

Now there is no difference between us and no misunderstanding on the part of the country or of the Dominion delegations attending the Conference, as to our main tariff policy. We are definitely opposed to any new taxation on foodstuffs and raw materials. This must have been clear to the Dominions from the first meeting of Heads of Delegations when the economic position was discussed, and I am confident that the country will support us in maintaining that policy.

It is however insufficient for us to rest on this purely negative policy. The country is looking for positive results from this Conference and if our sole contribution to the discussion is merely to reject the proposals of the Dominions, the Conference has failed. It is therefore up to us to offer alternative proposals, and alternative proposals which can be made to appear sufficiently acceptable to enable the Dominions to put forward acceptable counter-offers.

Now we have already in fact discussed one such proposal which seems likely to fall within this category. This is the quota proposal[1] as applied to Empire wheat. I am well aware that in the previous discussions in the Cabinet on the subject of the quota system the plan was limited to wheat grown in the U.K. and that no agreement was reached even on that limited proposal. I am also well aware that in his statement at the meeting of the heads of Delegations the President of the Board of Trade was careful not to suggest that the quota system was already accepted and agreed upon by His Majesty's Government in the United Kingdom. It seems to me however that we should put ourselves in a false position by refusing to go on with the quota system if it should prove acceptable to the Dominions. If Canada and Australia now say (as indeed they have already gone far towards saying) that they are prepared to accept a quota system in lieu of a tariff on foreign wheat, and we then turn it down, what else can they think but that we have been fooling them for the last fortnight, and what else can they say but that if all the time we meant to refuse not only a tariff on foreign wheat but also every alternative to such a tariff, why didn't we say so at once and let them go home?

It seems to me therefore to be abundantly clear that we are bound not only to agree to a quota system for Empire wheat, which, it should be

---

[1] This particular quota-scheme involved a guarantee that the Dominions would enjoy a certain stated minimum percentage of the market for wheat in the United Kingdom, whose millers would be obliged to use at least this percentage of Dominion wheat.

remembered, involves no guaranteed price, but to advocate such a system as an alternative proposal which will benefit the Dominions more directly and more certainly than a tariff, and will moreover remove from the arena of discussion the very troublesome question of the dumping of Russian wheat. I must press my colleagues most earnestly to make up their minds to this course.

A quota system for wheat is however an alternative only to the tariff proposals of Canada and, to a less degree, of Australia. What alternatives can we offer to the proposals, likewise for a preferential tariff involving the taxation of foodstuffs, and raw materials, put forward by the other Dominions?

I have no doubt whatever that in the first place it is essential that we should put an end to the existing uncertainty as to the continuance of the preferences which we at present accord to a limited number of commodities produced within the Empire. It cannot be questioned that the fact that we have announced it is part of our policy to remove the taxes, and with them the preferences, as soon as possible has a most depressing effect on the industries concerned in the Dominions: no business could be carried on successfully with such an uncertainty.[2] If we really intended to carry this declaration into effect, I might have nothing to say. But every one of us knows that in fact we have no intention of carrying it into effect within the next three or four years at least. Then why, in the name of commonsense, should we not say so? Is it not plain folly to risk breaking up this Conference and thereby cutting our own political throats by refusing to say what we and everyone else here know to be the truth, namely that the preferences will certainly remain for the next few years—at least until the next Imperial Conference? We certainly stand to gain by making a concession which costs us nothing and is likely to be effective as a bargaining counter.

On this point, therefore, I must earnestly ask my colleagues to reach a decision forthwith.

These are the two most important points for decision. If we can agree upon these, as I greatly hope we can agree, I feel confident that we can build up on them a policy which will give us a real chance of saving the Conference, or, at worst, of defending ourselves effectively against the charge that we ourselves have wrecked it. . . .

---

[2] True only in the sense that several Empire industries were insufficiently competitive to maintain themselves without the artificially elevated export prices which the preferential system offered. The Empire sugar, canned and dried fruit, and wine industries seem to have been in this position; loss of preferences would have so lowered profits that they would have contracted a great deal.

My colleagues will remember that one of the things which we had hoped would result from this Conference was a system of inter-Imperial [sic] economic machinery; and I believe that our consent to 'imperialise' the Empire Marketing Board would not only be very welcome to the Dominions but would go far towards providing precisely the sort of permanent inter-Imperial economic machinery which we had in mind. . . .

What do we hope to get in return? First some striking declaration by the Imperial Conference in favour of economic co-operation which, I suggest, would of itself be of no small political advantage to ourselves. Secondly and most important the practical revision of Dominion tariffs. . . . There can be no possible doubt that such a revision would be of the very greatest value to our export trade. The Dominions have made it clear that they mean to protect their own industries, but that, subject to that proviso, they are anxious, if [they can, to help our industries] by readjustment of the existing tariffs. . . . On the other hand, Mr. Bennett[3] and General Hertzog[4] have stated, in very plain terms, that if they receive no encouragement from the United Kingdom at this conference towards continued co-operation in the endeavour to increase inter-Imperial trade, they may find it impossible to retain their existing preferences to the United Kingdom. That may well be a threat which public opinion might prevent them from carrying out. But it is a possibility, the effects of which—political as well as economic—I do not care to contemplate.

We are within days of the end of the Conference. We can no longer postpone our decision. It is for the purpose of making it clear that we not only have a policy on the economic side, but that that policy is a definite and practicable one, that I submit this memorandum.

Dominions Office.   (Intd) J.H.T.
27 October 1930.

[3] Prime Minister of Canada.
[4] Prime Minister of South Africa.

15. South Africa's pessimism with respect to British Tariff Policy

FROM Harriet Irving Library, University of New Brunswick, R. B. Bennett Papers, 100, 389–10.

A handwritten note from N. C. Havenga, the South African finance minister, to R. B. Bennett, on the note paper of the United Kingdom Prime Minister. Though undated, almost certainly written during a session of the 1930 Imperial Conference—either a plenary session or, more probably, a meeting of heads of delegations.

Re proposal for further conference at Ottawa, or any other place, in the near future, is anything to be gained by agreeing to this, unless we are prepared to face the fundamental difference as regards policy? What are the chances of agreeing later on, in view of the very definitive views with regard to the taxes on food and raw materials?

16. The Permanent Undersecretary in the Dominions Office[1] explains British tactics to the British High Commissioner in Ottawa[2]

FROM Public Record Office, DO 35/236/8831/69.

Secret and Personal   17th December, 1931.

My dear Clark:
    In my Secret and Personal letter of today regarding our preparations for the Ottawa Conference I said that I was writing to you separately with regard to the question of tariff concessions from the Dominions which formed the subject of our Secret telegram to the Dominions . . . of the 10th December, and of the Secret telegram sent to you on the same date. . . .

[1] Sir Edward Harding.
[2] Sir William Clark.

You will see from my account of their work that the Ottawa Cabinet Committee are preparing for the Conference on the basis that any concessions which we may be ready to make must be conditional on corresponding concessions from the Dominions. As you know a great deal of detailed investigation into the nature of the concessions which we would like to obtain from the Dominions was carried out by the Board of Trade at the instance of the late Government. The new Ottawa Cabinet Committee have had before them shorter versions of the memoranda and schedules indicating possible concessions from New Zealand, the Union, and Newfoundland. .... They have also before them new Documents which have been drawn up, in a similarly shortened form, in respect of Canada, Australia, and Southern Rhodesia. The material regarding the Irish Free State will be in a different form from those prepared in respect of the other Dominions and will not be ready until after Christmas.

All this material, with the exception of that regarding the Irish Free State, has been handed to the Federation of British Industries and the Association of British Chambers of Commerce and have been considered by those Bodies during the last few weeks. We have, this week, obtained the views of the Association, and the general concurrence of the Federation of British Industries, subject in the latter case to the right to raise a certain number of further points of detail at a later date. The suggestions of the Association are now being embodied in the schedules and we will send you, as soon as possible, the document in respect of Canada in its final form, subject only to possible further observations by the Federation of British Industries.

You will see from our Circular telegram of the 10th December that the intention is that, subject to the concurrence of the Canadian Government, this schedule should be available for discussion between the Canadian Expert Advisors and yourself and our Senior Trade Commissioner in Canada, it being understood, of course, that these discussions would be on a non-committal basis. In the same telegram Dominion Governments were invited to nominate representatives to discuss in London with our Expert Advisors here the material available. Pending replies from the Dominions, we do not as yet know the precise procedure which will be employed. It is, however, the feeling here that preliminary discussions should be carried as far as possible before the Ottawa Conference meets, since otherwise, i.e. if there were to be a mass of detailed discussions at Ottawa as between the United Kingdom on the one hand and the six Dominions and Southern Rhodesia on the other, it would be extremely difficult to reach agreements in the time likely to be available.

Instructions are now being prepared as to how you should proceed with regard to the discussions in the event of the Canadian Government wishing them to take place in Canada. These instructions will be sent to you with the final version of the schedule in respect of Canada. In the meanwhile I send you two copies of the Memorandum and schedule in the form in which they were handed to the Trade Associations in this country. As I understand that the amendments made by those Bodies are not likely to be extensive, you will no doubt be glad of an opportunity of studying the material as it stands now.

We are of course arranging with the Department of Overseas Trade that you shall have the assistance of the Senior Trade Commissioner for any discussions.

Yours sincerely,
E. J. Harding

17. Sir William Clark reports a telephone conversation with the Prime Minister of Canada

FROM Public Record Office, DO 35/239/8831G/36: telegram, Sir William Clark to Dominions Office, March 26, 1932.

After holding out some rather indeterminate hope of some information next week he began to develop the following thesis. The Conference, he felt, should concern itself with principles rather than detail. The principles should be that tariffs in each part of the Empire should be adjusted so as (a) to give all Empire producers or manufacturers advantage over foreign so far as possible admitting Empire products free when non-competitive with domestic products, (b) to provide in respect of competitive products equality of competition as between domestic producers or manufacturers and those of the rest of the Empire. . . . The value to each of us of these principles would, I pointed out, be in fact wholly dependent on their application and therefore it seemed very desirable that details should be explored first if only that all parties might know what principles would mean. . . . Further the public which was expecting concrete results from the Conference might, however unreasonably, be critical of mere enunciation of principles. . . . Prime Minister agreed that examination of tariff items must continue in any case but his judgement in arriving at this new theory of Conference has been, I fear, influenced in part by his difficulties in getting down to preparatory work. . . . I presume you will wish me to continue to press for expediting of tariff examination. . . .

18. The British Government tells the Dominions to speed their Ottawa preparations and to make reasonable requests and concessions

FROM Public Record Office, DO 114/42, pp. 112–114: telegram, Dominions Office to Canadian, Australian, New Zealand, and South African Governments, May 9, 1932.

... We are somewhat disappointed at slowness of progress made in these preliminary discussions. ... His Majesty's Government in the United Kingdom desire that no misunderstanding should exist as to their position ... their view throughout has been that continuance of concessions within framework of Import Duties Act after 15 November could not be justified to public opinion and affected interests here unless balanced by reciprocal concessions, and for this reason they have through their representatives in Dominions, pressed view that that in order to facilitate work of conference itself, interval before conference opens should be used to secure full and searching exploration of possibilities as regards reciprocal concessions. They are somewhat concerned that, though time is running short, there has so far been no real indication of attitude of Dominion Governments as regards concessions which latter might be prepared to give in return for concessions under the Import Duties Act. ...

Furthermore, requests are being made to His Majesty's Government in the United Kingdom by some Dominion Governments for tariff concessions which go beyond the range of the Import Duties Act. His Majesty's Government in the United Kingdom feel that it ought to be made clear that, having regard to domestic interests of the country, concessions in respect of commodities now on free list under Import Duties Act would be far more difficult than continuance of concessions within framework of that Act. Should His Majesty's Governments in the Dominions desire discussion of possibilities as regards items now on free list, His Majesty's Government in the United Kingdom would not desire to rule out any commodity on grounds of principle, but they wish to make it plain that before concessions could be considered, reciprocal concessions of outstanding importance would have to be offered by the Dominions, i.e. over and above those offered in return for continuance of concessions under the Import Duties Act. Similar considerations would apply to any cases where increased duties on foreign goods might be desired by Dominion Governments.

19. A further conversation between Sir William Clark and R. B. Bennett

FROM DO 35/239/8831G/113: letter, Sir William Clark to Sir E. Harding, May 11, 1932. [In the earlier part of the conversation, Bennett cast doubt upon the value of the United Kingdom's new 10 per cent preferential margin under the Import Duties Act. He repeated his earlier suggestion that the Conference should stick to principle and not mere 'vulgar detail'.]

Did he mean by all this that we were to have no discussions on our schedule before the Conference? He hastily repudiated this suggestion. . . . I frankly find it very difficult to say where we stand. . . . Similarly I find it very difficult to make up my mind as to what Bennett is really after. . . . I sometimes wonder whether Bennett isn't deliberately playing for delay in order to have little or no time for pre-Conference examination of tariff schedules. Then at the Conference he would trust to luck . . . and try to get away with it by putting forward his principles. . . . You will see from all this that the first impact of your Circular telegram [of May 9] had not been very promising of results so far as Bennett is concerned . . . but Bennett is after all a business man, and when he thinks it over, will no doubt see our point of view—though it may not convince him. At any rate I will do my best to keep up the pressure as opportunity serves— . . . but the *vis inertiae* has been really formidable.

20. The Australian Prime Minister suggests that Australia and Canada coordinate their schemes

FROM Harriet Irving Library, University of New Brunswick, R. B. Bennett Papers, 115,252. Telegram, Prime Minister of Australia[1] to Canadian Secretary of State for External Affairs[2] May 18, 1932.

[1] J. A. Lyons.
[2] R. B. Bennett, who served as his own minister for external affairs.

In continuation of my telegram of the 30th April, Australia's representative in London ... is in position to fully discuss with your representative Australia's proposals with regard to all commodities of common interest. In view of the great importance of wheat exports, would appreciate direct exchange of views with your government with view to cooperation. We fully realize that wheat being of paramount importance to Canada you will desire to secure greatest assistance obtainable. We entirely share that desire but find practical difficulties which in our view nullify value of suggested concessions by means of quotas or even preferential tariffs. Fact that in any circumstances half the Dominions' wheat must be sold outside the Empire would govern price levels including that protected by quotas in British market. This would prevent any benefit accruing to Empire wheat growers and disturbance to existing trade might be serious. With preferential duties less danger of dislocating trade but we think that no greater likelihood of any price benefits or market security to Empire wheat growers. His Majesty's Government in the Commonwealth of Australia therefore reluctant to press for concessions more apparent than real, which might considerably minimize prospects of obtaining preferences on products in respect of which we consider benefits would be of far greater value. We have informed our London representatives that restriction on imports of Russian wheat desirable because of disorganisation of markets by Russian sales methods and also because large Russian surplus generally in the same year as heavy West European crops and consequently low import quotas for Germany, France, Italy. Our representative in London has been instructed to explore possibility of heavy discriminating duties or other restrictions by anti-dumping regulations. Views of your Government would be appreciated and would be carefully considered.

21. The Agenda for the Ottawa Conference

FROM Public Record Office, DO 114/42. Telegram, Sir William Clark to Dominions Office, June 15, 1932.

I have now spoken to the Prime Minister.[1] In rather vague terms he said that he had not contemplated publishing agenda before end of the

---

[1] R. B. Bennett.

month, but promised to go into question at once. During the conversation I tackled him again on the question of our Schedule and Canada's own requirements, pointing out how serious the delay was becoming. He promised to put everything else aside and get on with it, but he still seems very undecided in his conception of what the Conference is going to do. I have tried to impress on him that His Majesty's Government in the United Kingdom at any rate must get down to details, either now or in August, if our current concessions to Canada are to continue, after November, but he still seems to be toying with the possibility of evading the issue in a cloud of sonorous principles.

Telegram, Canadian Government to Dominions Office, 3 July 1932, transmitting *inter alia* the following trade items for the agenda:

1. Examination of aspects of question of trade and tariff policy and administration affecting Empire trade, including *inter alia* the following subjects:

(a) recognition of principle of reciprocal tariff preference within the Commonwealth

(b) general application of existing and future tariff preferences within the Commonwealth

(c) determination of percentage 'Empire content' necessary to secure preferential tariff treatment

(d) extension to other parts of Commonwealth of tariff advantages accorded to foreign countries

(e) export bounties and anti-dumping duties within the Commonwealth.

2. Commercial treaty policy with respect to foreign countries, including *inter alia*:

(a) relations of inter-imperial Preferences to concessions to foreign countries

(b) interpretation of most-favoured-nation clause, particularly with reference to development of regional preference and of systems of import quotas.

22. The Committee of Officials reminds the British Government that it must decide many things before the Ottawa Conference

FROM Public Record Office CAB 32/105,0.(B)(32)136: 'Revised List of Questions suggested for Consideration of H.M. Government', July 8, 1932.

GENERAL APPROACH

As the Empire meets to promote trade and not to restrict trade—

1. Do we wish Empire prices for agriculture and primary products to rise—(a) if world prices rise (b) even if world prices do not rise?

2. If Empire prices rise and world prices do not rise, are we content to lose our trade with the world, which would seem on this hypothesis to be inevitable?

3. Is the main object of Conference therefore—(a) to enlarge world trade (b) and trade done by British Empire (c) and thereby to increase world price level (d) and maintain standard of living of our own people?

4. Is it a guiding principle in applying our Tariff that we should bring down tariffs elsewhere and promote objects in 3?

5. Has a general statement been prepared to advise—

(a) creditor countries that their tariff policy must admit goods and services from the world and that they must maintain a passive balance in exchange for goods and services;

(b) debtor countries that their tariff policy must not burden their export industry or raise the cost of their local production beyond world level.

MOST FAVOURED NATION

6. Has the unconditional most-favoured-nation clause the effect of keeping tariffs up? Is conditional most-favoured-nation clause open to the same objection?

7. If unconditional M.F.N. has tended to keep tariffs up, what measure should this country adopt alone or in conjunction with Empire and/or Foreign countries to achieve Great Britain's main objective, viz.: reduction of world tariffs, etc. Would it be the establishment of a G.B. four-decker tariff? the adoption of Conditional i.e. Reciprocal M.F.N.? Would the Four Decker Tariff be—Imperial ..., Low ..., Treaty-country ..., Maximum? How can equality of treatment be measured? ...

EXCESSIVE DOMINION TARIFFS

10. Can and will the U.K. protest against the policy of Dominions to foster local manufactures by excluding U.K. exports? . . .

DISCRIMINATION

Will His Majesty's Government refuse to countenance the policy of Canada in Exchange Depreciation Tax?[1]

EMPIRE GOODS DEFINITION

Imperial *content*—has a definition been thought out? Has analysis been made as regards the main U.K. imports [and] exports of the proportion of foreign content that the U.K. trade and/or Board of Trade think should be allowed? Are any products mainly manufactured in U.K. but processed in a foreign country en route for Empire destination? . . .

MACHINERY

Will a Board of Economic Research be maintained to review currently the effect of social and economic, particularly fiscal, policies on the wealth of each Dominion, the cost level of their exports and their power to help in Empire progress and to report confidentially its conclusions to Governments of all nations of Empire?

CONCESSIONS TO DOMINIONS

Agricultural produce—what concessions do His Majesty's Government feel able to give to agricultural produce in the Dominions against what quid pro quo? Corn, butter, eggs and cheese, fruit meat, bacon, mutton, beef, tea, coffee, etc. Can the cost to the consumer [and] value to Dominions (separately) be estimated?
Manufactures and Raw Materials—ditto. . . .

MACHINERY OF CONFERENCE

How will the conference work? Presumably there will be: plenary sessions at which ministers will deliver speeches on general policy to open business; committees for special general items; sub-committees on individual industries or groups of industries; drafting etc; final plenary sessions. Will Chairmen be appointed for these groups? Will they be brought into contact with one another in a Co-ordination Committee, and if not, how will conclusions of Group reach Conference?

---

[1] Canada was levying special exchange depreciation taxes on the goods of countries which had left the gold standard. As the procedure involved the assignment of arbitrary valuations to the several currencies involved, it could and did discriminate against some countries—in particular against the United Kingdom.

23. The Canadian Prime Minister expresses his displeasure with the aid which the Canadian Manufacturers' Association has given him

FROM Harriet Irving Library, University of New Brunswick, R. B. Bennett Papers, 113,405: letter, R. B. Bennett to J. K. Walsh, Manager of Canadian Manufacturers' Association, July 11, 1932.

I think you will agree that the list of items not produced in Canada, comprising several thousand in number, which you forwarded, is not a practical answer to the question that I submitted to your Association last December. . . . I have given some little study to the list, and it is rather disheartening to think that such a list should be submitted to intelligent men as indicating the extent to which Canada might be able to improve trade and commerce with the United Kingdom by the admission, free or at a lower rate of duty, to our markets of the products of Empire countries. I think that the manner in which you have dealt with the items mentioned in Sir William Clark's list[1] is highly satisfactory, but he was very anxious to have had a reply from us some time ago.

24. The State of the Conference: 'Appreciation' sent to London, August 15, 1932

FROM Public Record Office, CAB 32/103,0. (UK)(32) 49.

We shall probably have to take our definite decision today (Monday). . . . Our policy throughout has been to try to secure agreements that embody the principle of the progressive lowering of tariff barriers . . . we have laid great stress on the principle that duties against British goods in Dominions should not be at a higher rate than is necessary to put the United Kingdom manufacturer in the position of a domestic competitor . . . and that Tariff Boards in Dominions should be instructed to review duties in accordance with that principle and that we should have right

---

[1] The 'Canada schedule'. See above, Documents 16 to 19, and below, Document 25.

of audience. . . . We shall insist on this as the most important term in the agreements. . . . Bearing in mind the need for bringing the Conference to a successful end and on the assumption . . . that the tariff and other concessions are of sufficient immediate and prospective value to warrant the expectation of increased markets for United Kingdom goods, we feel justified in making agreements. . . . Apart from Russian question, Canada has made it clear that she expects a duty of 2/– per quarter on wheat. Our difficulty in accepting this was great. . . . Before we left London it was apparent that meat would be the principal question at issue, and everything that has happened here has emphasised this. . . . Australia in particular has reiterated that all her proposals are conditional upon satisfaction in regard to meat. They asked for duties on lamb, mutton, beef, and bacon. We have said we are unable to agree to this. We have prepared a scheme for temporary restriction of mutton and lamb in 1933 pending a conference of meat interests. . . .

Over and above the trade advantages . . . there is the intangible but very important gain to sentiment and confidence (which might well extend far beyond the Empire) in the course of which the Empire had shown unity of purpose and had translated ideals into specific agreements.

We hope, too, to be able to preface the specific agreements by conference conclusions which will form another intangible but very important asset through the adhesion to general principles of a kind that could be represented at home and to the world as committing the Empire to a policy intended to diminish the barriers to trade and to restore world prosperity.

We are unanimously satisfied in the circumstances that the concessions we have been able to secure justify us in making agreements on these lines.

Ramsay MacDonald's Response to the 'Appreciation', August 16, 1932

FROM Public Record Office, CAB 32/103,0.(UK)(32) 54.

Only those who have been through the whole negotiations can value present situation. I have greatest confidence in my colleagues' judgement and though I must reserve a final decision for myself until I know whole scheme and its possibilities my inclination will be to back up you up. Had I been able to get any of important ministers on telephone today for a consultation I should have done so; but all are scattered. Must therefore content myself by strongly urging you all to remember feeling in this Country about food taxes and possible reactions in Cabinet. Do your honest best to secure a rational conclusion and I shall do mine to find reasons for keeping us together though one cannot conceal difficulties.

25. Frederick Field[1] Reports on the Proceedings at the Ottawa Conference

FROM Public Record Office DO 35/237/8831/202. Political No. 213/32/3405, August 24, 1932.

I enclose for your information a confidential memorandum of Canadian tariff items discussed with the Canadian Government by officials of the United Kingdom delegation during the recent Imperial Economic Conference.

2. The memorandum gives the history of the various items and a note of their final disposition, if any.
3. Mr. Griffiths, of the Board of Trade, asked that such a document should be prepared and I shall be glad if you will let him have a copy at your early convenience.

I am, Sir, Your obedient servant,
Frederick W. Field
H.M. Senior Trade Commissioner in Canada and Newfoundland

CONFIDENTIAL
MEMORANDUM WITH REGARD TO TARIFF NEGOTIA-
TIONS WITH CANADA IN CONNECTION WITH THE
IMPERIAL ECONOMIC CONFERENCE, 1932
A letter, dated 15th January, despatched by the Dominions Office to the High Commissioner and containing a 'Canada Schedule',[2] was received in Ottawa early in February. A letter, enclosing a copy of the

---

[1] Senior Trade Commissioner for the United Kingdom in Canada, 1924–48.
[2] One of the set despatched to the various Dominions in January 1932.

schedule was sent by the Department of Overseas Trade to the Senior Trade Commissioner at the same time. The Schedule contained a list of 253 commodity items about which our Government desired to know whether Canada would be agreeable to granting tariff concessions. No information was required as to proposed tariff rates but merely a 'yes' or 'no' on each item. The Trade Commissioner was asked to co-operate with the High Commissioner in the matter.

A short supplementary Schedule was forwarded by the Dominions Office later.

The High Commissioner endeavoured, on a number of occasions to present the list to the Prime Minister who for some time was too busy to receive and discuss it.

After some five weeks' delay, an opportunity was given to the High Commissioner to hand in the list at a Cabinet meeting held in Ottawa on 20th February. A few comments were made at the time with regard to the list and an intimation was given to the High Commissioner that when the Prime Minister was ready to discuss it, the High Commissioner would be informed. On several occasions subsequently the High Commissioner endeavoured to ascertain when it would be convenient to discuss the list with Canadian ministers or officials.

Various reasons were given from time to time (such, for example, as the fact that Parliament was still sitting) as to why the list could not be discussed. In spite of many suggestions that such action would prepare the way for the Imperial Economic Conference, no joint examination of the list took place.

Suggestions were made to the press during the course of the Imperial Economic Conference that the Canada Schedule was compiled in London with the assistance of out of date figures and that many of the tariff rates were inaccurate. Actually the figures in the Schedule were the latest available when it was compiled. In a few cases, old tariff rates were quoted in error. These criticisms, however, do not change the main fact that the list was one of *commodities* upon which the United Kingdom Government desired to know whether the Canadian Government would be prepared to take favourable tariff action. Had the list been compiled without any figures at all, it should have sufficed for the discussions that were desired.

The United Kingdom delegation, therefore, entered the Conference without any knowledge of the commodities on which Canada would be likely to accord tariff concessions.

Shortly after the beginning of the Conference, on 27th July, the Prime Minister of Canada presented the United Kingdom delegation with a large file of documents that had been sent to the Government by the Canadian Manufacturers' Association. On 28th July, Sir Horace

Wilson[3] and other United Kingdom officials met Mr. H. B. McKinnon, the Tariff Commissioner, who was questioned with regard to the documents. He stated that the Prime Minister believed the United Kingdom delegation would like to see the suggestions as to tariff rates, etc., made by Canadian manufacturers. Sir Horace Wilson replied that the United Kingdom delegation had not come 3,000 miles to learn of the opinions of Canadian manufacturers. Mr. McKinnon was asked for a summary of the documents but one was not available and Mr. Wiseman, our Trade Commissioner at Toronto, prepared a summary on behalf of the United Kingdom delegation.

On 4th August, Canada submitted its tariff proposals and these admittedly had been compiled in great haste during the previous few days. The proposals were analysed by Mr. Griffiths and Mr. Taylor[4] and an estimate of their value (in terms of new trade for the United Kingdom) was made by Mr. Wiseman and myself.

A list of goods that were not made in Canada had been prepared by the Canadian Government and checked by the Canadian Manufacturers' Association. The list was open to considerable criticism. An analysis of it was made by Mr. Wiseman for the United Kingdom delegation. A request was made to Mr. McKinnon, Mr. Breadner, and other Canadian officials, for revised copies of the list so that it might be sent to the Board of Trade in London for analysis. The revised copies were not made available. Later I needed a copy to analyse the Canadian Tariff proposals, more particularly those regarding chemical goods. I was informed by Mr. Emery, of the Canadian Customs Department, that I could have a copy. Later, it was refused by the Commissioner of Customs. As a copy was required in order that I might proceed with my work, I approached Mr. D. Sim, Secretary to the Minister of National Revenue, who obtained two copies for me. These were returned as he desired within four days.

A number of meetings were held with the Commissioner of Customs and the Tariff Commissioner (Mr. Breadner and Mr. McKinnon) and Mr. Emery. The United Kingdom delegation was represented at these meetings by three or more of the following: Sir Horace Wilson, Sir Henry Fountain, Mr. Griffiths, Mr. Taylor, Mr. Wiseman, and myself.[4]

We discussed, item by item, the Canadian and the United Kingdom tariff proposals. The United Kingdom proposals were prepared by Mr. Wiseman and by me but the document was not submitted to the

---

[3] Sir Horace Wilson was Chief Industrial Advisor to the United Kingdom Government from 1930 to 1939. He attended the Conference as the senior adviser to the delegation and as coordinator of the officials' negotiations and of the staff work.

[4] All United Kingdom officials.

Canadian Government in its entirety. Items from the document were submitted as occasion offered.

The conclusions reached at these meetings were placed by Mr. Breadner before the Prime Minister and his Cabinet from time to time and progress was made very slowly.

On 16th August, Sir Horace Wilson, Mr. Griffiths and I attended a summons of Mr. Breadner, and upon reaching his office, were told that the Prime Minister and his Cabinet, on the previous evening, had come to a number of decisions with regard to several of the items that had previously been discussed. We were informed that these included withdrawals of several of the original proposals by Canada, of unfavourable amendments to many other items, and the reopening of the steel agreement. Sir Horace Wilson protested and later the United Kingdom delegation placed their objections before the Canadian Prime Minister.

As a result of the negotiations by the United Kingdom, the majority of the tariff items, which had been given unfavourable treatment by the Canadian Cabinet on 15th August, were restored by Canada to their favourable position.

Documents supporting this memorandum are on my files.

22 August 1932   FWF[initialled]

26. R. B. Bennett and Strategy at the Ottawa Conference: Advice and Assumptions

[In late June, 1932, after the British and Canadian textile interests had failed to agree on a cartel arrangement to divide the Canadian market,[1] Bennett was pressed by the president of Canadian Cottons Ltd. to introduce a higher duty on British cottons, with 'a fixed value for duty purposes'.[2] Bennett's rejoinder was sharp:]

I am being strongly pressed . . . to take a firm hand with respect to the cotton industry for it is pointed out that had there been no change in the

[1] The Canadians had favoured higher duties against foreigners, while the British wanted lower preferential rates and a general reduction in Canadian cotton tariffs.

[2] R. B. Bennett Papers, 115,282: letter, A. Dawson to R. B. Bennett. June 21, 1932 (Harriet Irving Library, University of New Brunswick).

original financial structure[3] the profits required to pay a reasonable dividend would have enabled them to compete on more favourable terms. . . . It seems to be quite clear that we cannot get everything and give nothing, and the cotton industry is one in which the British people are tremendously concerned.[4]

[The British delegation criticized Bennett for his tactics at the Conference, and most commentators have attributed them to his personality, or to his lack of interest in the Conference's success. In fact his advisors were urging on him the strategy and tactics which he did follow:]

The committee must be prepared, not only with a statement as to the minimum effective preference to be given, but with a forecast of the increase in exports that will result. They must also indicate the measure of time which must elapse before one or all of these industries is on an export basis. . . . With the estimated value to Canada of the exports selected for preferred treatment, the Canadian delegation will then be in a position to determine what price should be paid for the preference. In other words, it will be necessary to canvass the possibilities of concessions and to decide those which it will propose in exchange for concessions it will ask for . . . as for the Russian question it is one of principle, and to compromise the principle would be to throw away our case.[5]

[After his opening speech, Bennett received at least four memoranda which urged him to make sure that the United Kingdom would commit herself to the *principle* of preference on natural products before beginning to bargain:]

It is essential that the United Kingdom definitely acknowledge the principle. This conference was called on the understanding that the United Kingdom was prepared to grant tariff preferences. The United Kingdom has already by legislation adopted that principle so far as manufactured products are concerned. It now remains to extend the principle to the free list. Until this extension is made, it is idle to discuss particular items on it.[6]

[Such advice, added to the imperfection of his own preparation and staff work, must have exacerbated the initial delays and evasive tactics which so puzzled and annoyed the British. As the Conference

---

[3] The Canadian cotton industry had been reorganized into a few great firms which were believed to be overcapitalized.

[4] Bennett Papers, 115,287: letter, R. B. Bennett to A. Dawson, July 2, 1932.

[5] Bennett Papers, 113,989–993: anonymous and undated memorandum.

[6] Bennett Papers, 113,996–8. See also 113,989–993, 113,999–114,002, 114,003–004.

proceeded, Bennett was urged not to fear breakdown—indeed, actively to strive for it:]

We must realise that any proposal Canada now makes may not be accepted. The United Kingdom delegation will not summarily reject it . . . but will take it home for consideration. This opens the way for Westminster discussion and action. There, the Tory group will attack the remnants of the old Socialist party and will see in this proposal the club with which to drive socialism from the Government. I have never believed that an agreement favourable to Canada would pass the present Unionist Cabinet. Therefore our actions at this time and our future public statements must be governed by this possibility. We shall require the forces of public opinion in England to put through the Agreement, and we can arouse it to our support.[7]

[During the Conference, W. D. Herridge wrote to Bennett:]

. . . purification of the Government of the United Kingdom through elimination of MacDonald and the other socialists is only way in which can be assured stability of Government. . . . This however is prefatory to the main point. . . . Is the agreement which we hope to make the agreement which the Tory Party and the great mass of people in the United Kingdom desire should be made having regard to the inescapable consequences either of complete failure of the agreement or of such ineffectual agreement as will both create dissention discord and recrimination among the peoples of the Empire and drive the Dominions from sheer necessity to immediately supplement this inadequate pact with agreements with foreign countries which will mean something to us . . . it is a question of . . . entering into a contract with the people of the United Kingdom which will assure the continuance of Empire Economic Association.[8]

---

[7] Bennett Papers, 114,041–044. Anonymous and undated memorandum. The Beaverbrook Press is obviously in the author's mind. So perhaps is L. S. Amery, whose unofficial presence so annoyed the official British delegation while confusing the Dominion ministers, especially with respect to meat and wheat duties.

[8] Bennett Papers, 112,534–535: undated note by W. D. Herridge.

27. R. B. Bennett and the Proceedings at Ottawa

Public Archives of Canada, Stevens Papers: excerpts from transcripts of taped interviews recorded in 1966 by H. H. Stevens (MG 27, IIIB9, vol. 163)

[Stevens] drafted the Canadian side of each agreement . . . with the help of some high officials . . . whatever departments were affected [but] the British agreement—Mr. Bennett had asked me not to draft that, that he would do it himself—mind you, this went on for some months prior to the Conference . . . but on Friday previous to the meeting of the Conference Mr. Bennett rang me up and told me that he had been busy and hadn't had time to draft up the British agreements. So I called in Mr. McGregor and two or three others and we worked all day Friday, Friday night, and Saturday and again on Sunday and we drafted up what we thought was a pretty fair form of tariff agreement with Great Britain. And when the Conference met, the British had quite a staff of experts in various lines of business and operation with them, . . . and these met with Canadian officials and myself and we worked out a pretty satis-factory agreement. But after it was worked out, and after it was agreed to by the British, Mr. Bennett made certain changes in it. One was in connection with boiler plates, . . . and . . . there was one in connection with the cotton industry . . . under pressure from Cahan and Sir—the head of the Canada Cotton Company . . . he was the man together with Cahan who did this. And that is what brought about a meeting between the British ministers . . . and Mr. Bennett and myself. And they were very indignant about these changes being made after they had been agreed to . . . they were going to withdraw from the conference but Mr. MacDonald the Prime Minister then in London urged them if the agreement wasn't satisfactory to agree and not let the Conference break up . . . they finally agreed and it was signed.

[Stevens, McGregor, and other Canadian civil servants] for instance had a series of interviews with the [United Kingdom] steel industry. . . . Now we went over the list in the customs schedule covering iron and steel products, generally speaking, and we discussed them and arranged for certain rates of duty . . . the textiles . . . we did the same thing with them. And the same thing applied to others except that in the case of Australia the negotiations were almost entirely with the Minister of Customs . . . and he didn't have any experts with him. . . . In the conference as a whole, whenever the senior delegates would meet, there would be ministers. And of course Mr. Bennett was in the chair and presided over the meetings, and took a very definite part. But he did not take much—or any part—in the negotiation of the details. That was left entirely to me. . . . I had arranged particularly with the United Kingdom iron and steel industry for a certain schedule of customs duties . . . and the British merchants or industrialists went back to London, thinking the matter was settled. But after they left, a Mr. Sherman who was in the iron and steel business in Hamilton, Ontario, came to Ottawa, and saw Mr. Bennett and . . . said . . . that he could manufacture them, so RB changed the schedule, the written schedule, and put a duty on these extra large boiler plates. . . . This very definitely upset the British ministerial delegation . . . and they called a meeting and . . . they in a very dignified way presented their criticism of this action and Mr. Bennett—I can see him now—stood up and literally raved about the whole thing and in a rather unfortunate mood—the British ministers left with what I later learned was the intention to withdraw from the Conference . . . and the next morning I was told by them that they were instructed by the Prime Minister not to break the conference up, to accept anything that had happened[1] . . . our House met later in the Autumn and these items were passed. And in the meantime Mr. Bennett added to the list of duties that had been agreed upon on textiles. . . . It was an arbitrary duty that was imposed above the duty we had agreed upon. This also upset the British very much. . . .

[1] Here Mr Stevens' memory is almost certainly at fault. The British Delegation's minutes, which are extremely detailed, record no such intention and no such instruction. (See CAB 32/102, esp. o(UK)(32), 68th, 69th, and 70th meetings.) They do, however, record a *prior* conversation between Thomas and a Canadian civil servant, who asked Thomas whether it was true that the United Kingdom Delegation had received a message from the Prime Minister authorising them to 'give way on everything, including meat'. Thomas denied the rumour, which was rife in Ottawa, but almost certainly it is the rumour which Mr Stevens is recalling. Middlemas and Barnes (*Baldwin*, p. 680) report a similar rumour but give no source.

28. The Ottawa Agreements with the Principal Dominions and with India, signed August 20, 1932

FROM United Kingdom *State Papers*, vol. 135,1932 (HMSO, 1937).

The Canadian and Australian agreements have been reproduced more completely than the other agreements. Britain's agreements with Southern Rhodesia and Newfoundland have been omitted, as have most of the numerous and lengthy Schedules. The remaining schedules have been combined and renumbered. The footnotes to the agreements show where the contents of each original Schedule are now to be found in these re-arranged condensations. Formal openings, and clauses on termination and variation which conclude each agreement, have not been printed here. The same subjects recur in the various agreements. The following table shows where each subject arises in each. The numbers refer to the Articles in the several agreements

	United Kingdom Agreement with				
	C	A	NZ	SA	I
Commitment by United Kingdom with respect to					
duty-free entry	I	I	I	I	I
duties on foreign goods	2	2	2	2	2
preferential margins	3, 7	3, 4	3	3, 4, 6	3, 4, 6, 13
meat	5, 6	6	4	7	
preferences for India and Dominions in the Dependent Empire	8	7	5	8	9
cotton					8
Russia	21				
Commitment by other governments with respect to					
rate of duty on U.K. goods	9, 17	14	6, 11		
preferential margins	9	8	10	9, 10, 11	10, 11
prices of wheat and metals	4	5		5	5
preferences for products of Dependent Empire	19	15	12	12	12
limits on new protective tariffs	10	9	7		
'domestic competition' and Tariff Boards	11–15	10–13	8, 9		
customs administration	16				
Termination and variation	22, 23	16	13	14	14

1. *Canada*

1. His Majesty's Government in the United Kingdom undertake that Orders shall be made in accordance with . . . the Import Duties Act, 1932, which will ensure the continuance after the 15th November, 1932, of entry free of duty into the United Kingdom of goods consigned from any part of the British Empire and grown, produced, or manufactured in Canada which by virtue of that Act are now free of duty subject, however, to the reservations set forth in Schedule A[1]. . . .

2. His Majesty's Government in the United Kingdom will invite Parliament to pass the legislation necessary to impose on the foreign goods specified in Schedule B[2] . . . the duties of customs shown in that schedule in place of the duties (if any) now leviable.

3. His Majesty's Government in the United Kingdom undertake that the general ad-valorem duty of 10% imposed by Section 1 of the Import Duties Act, 1932, on the foreign goods specified in Schedule C[3] shall not be reduced except with the consent of His Majesty's Government in Canada.

4. It is agreed that the duty on either wheat in grain, copper, zinc or lead as provided in this agreement may be removed if at any time Empire producers of wheat in grain, copper, zinc, and lead respectively are unable or unwilling to offer these commodities on first sale in the United Kingdom at prices not exceeding the world prices and in quantities sufficient to supply the requirements of the United Kingdom consumers.

5. His Majesty's Government in the United Kingdom will invite Parliament to pass the legislation necessary to modify the conditions at present governing the importation . . . of live cattle from Canada on the lines already agreed upon in principle between themselves and His Majesty's Government in Canada.

6. His Majesty's Government in the United Kingdom declare that it is their intention to arrange as soon as possible after receiving the report of the Commission now sitting on the reorganisation of the Pig Industry in the United Kingdom, for the quantitative regulation of the supplies of bacon and hams coming onto the United Kingdom market and undertake that in any legislation . . . provision will be made for free entry of Canadian bacon and hams of good quality up to a maximum of 2,500,000 cwt. per annum.

7. His Majesty's Government in the United Kingdom will invite Parliament to pass legislation which will secure for a period of ten years

---

[1] In schedule 1 below.
[2] In schedule 2 below.
[3] In schedule 5 below.

from the date hereof to tobacco, consigned from any part of the British Empire and grown, produced, or manufactured in Canada, the existing margin of preference over foreign tobacco, so long, however, as the duty on foreign unmanufactured tobacco does not fall below 2/0½d per pound, in which event the margin of preference shall be equal to the full duty.

8. His Majesty's Government in the United Kingdom will invite the Governments of the non-self-governing Colonies and Protectorates to accord to Canada any preference which may for the time being be accorded to any other part of the British Empire provided that this clause shall not extend to any preference accorded by Northern Rhodesia to the Union of South Africa, Southern Rhodesia, and the Territories of the South African High Commission, by virtue of the Customs Agreement of 1930; and further will invite the Governments of the Colonies and Protectorates shown in Schedule D[4] to accord to Canada new or additional preferences on the commodities and at the rates shown therein.

9. His Majesty's Government in Canada will invite Parliament to pass the legislation necessary to substitute for the duties of customs now leviable on the goods specified in Schedule E[4] the duties shown in that Schedule. Provided that nothing in this Article shall preclude ... Canada from reducing the duties specified ... so long as the margin of British preference shown in that Schedule is preserved or from increasing the rates under the intermediate or general tariff set out in the said Schedule.

10. His Majesty's Government in Canada undertake that protection by tariffs shall be afforded against United Kingdom products only to those industries which are reasonably assured of sound opportunities of success.

11. His Majesty's Government in Canada undertake that during the currency of this Agreement the tariff shall be based on the principle that protective duties shall not exceed such a level as will give United Kingdom producers full opportunity of reasonable competition on the basis of the relative cost of economical and efficient production, provided that in the application of such principle special consideration shall be given to the case of industries not fully established.

12. His Majesty's Government in Canada undertake forthwith to constitute the Tariff Board for which provision is made in the Tariff Board Act 1931.

13. His Majesty's Government in Canada undertake that on the request of His Majesty's Government in the United Kingdom they will

[4] Not reproduced here.

cause a review to be made by the Tariff Board as soon as practicable of the duties charged on any commodities specified in such request in accordance with the principles laid down in Article 11 hereof and that after the receipt of the Report of the Tariff Board . . . Parliament shall be invited to vary wherever necessary the Tariff on such commodities of United Kingdom origin in such manner as to give effect to such principles.

14. His Majesty's Government in Canada undertake that no existing duty shall be increased on United Kingdom goods except after an inquiry and upon the receipt of a report from the Tariff Board, and in accordance with the facts as found by that body.

15. His Majesty's Government in Canada undertake that United Kingdom producers shall be entitled to full rights of audience before the Tariff Board when it has under consideration matters arising under Articles 13 and 14 hereof.

16. His Majesty's Government in Canada undertake that Customs administration in Canada shall be governed by such general principles as will ensure (a) the avoidance, so far as reasonably possible, of uncertainty as to the amount of Customs duties and other fiscal imposts payable on the arrival of goods in Canada; (b) the reduction of delay and friction to a minimum; and (c) the provision of machinery for the prompt and impartial settlement of disputes in matters appertaining to the application of tariffs.

17. His Majesty's Government in Canada undertake that all existing surcharges on imports from the United Kingdom shall be completely abolished as soon as the finances of Canada will allow. They further undertake to give sympathetic consideration to the possibility of reducing and ultimately abolishing the exchange dumping duty in so far as it applies to imports from the United Kingdom.

18. His Majesty's Government in Canada undertake to modify the existing regulations governing the importation of pedigree stock from the United Kingdom. . . .

19. His Majesty's Government in Canada undertake to accord to those non-self-governing Colonies, Protectorates, and the mandated Territories to which the benefits of the British Preferential rates are at present accorded and also to Zanzibar the preferences on the commodities and at the rates shown in Schedule F[5] and also any preferences for the time being accorded to he United Kingdom [saving certain exceptions]. . . .

20. Nothing in this agreement shall prejudice or diminish any of the benefits enjoyed by any of the parties thereto under the Canada-West Indies Trade Agreement dated the 6th of July 1925.

21. This agreement is made on the express condition that, if either

[5] Not reproduced here.

Government is satisfied that any preferences hereby granted in respect of any particular class of commodities are likely to be frustrated in whole or in part by reason of the creation or maintenance directly or indirectly of prices for such class of commodities through State action on the part of any foreign country, that Government hereby declares that it will exercise the powers which it now has or will hereafter take to prohibit the entry from such foreign country directly or indirectly of such commodities into its country for such time as may be necessary to make effective and to maintain the preferences hereby granted by it.

2. Australia

1. His Majesty's Government in the United Kingdom undertake that Orders shall be made in accordance with . . . the Import Duties Act, 1932, which will ensure the continuance after the 15th November, 1932, of entry free of duty into the United Kingdom of Australian goods which comply with the laws and statutory regulations for the time being in force affecting the grant of Imperial preference and which by virtue of that Act are now free of duty, subject, however, to the reservations set forth in Schedule A[6] . . ..

2. His Majesty's Government in the United Kingdom will invite Parliament to pass the legislation necessary to impose on the foreign goods specified in Schedule B[7] appended hereto, the duties of customs shown in that Schedule in place of the duties (if any) now leviable.

3. His Majesty's Government in the United Kingdom will invite Parliament to pass the legislation necessary to secure to Australian goods of the kinds specified in Schedule C[8] appended hereto which comply with the law and statutory regulations for the time being in force affecting the grant of Imperial preference, the margins of preference specified therein over similar foreign goods.

4. His Majesty's Government in the United Kingdom undertake that the general ad valorem duty of ten per cent imposed by Section 1 of the Import Duties Act, 1932, on the foreign good specified in Schedule D[9] shall not be reduced except with the consent of His Majesty's Government in the Commonwealth of Australia.

5. The duties provided in this agreement on foreign wheat in grain, copper, lead, and zinc on importation into the United Kingdom are conditional in each case on Empire producers of wheat in grain, copper, lead and zinc respectively continuing to offer those commodities on first sale in the United Kingdom at prices not exceeding the world price.

[6] In Schedule 1 below.
[7] In Schedule 2 below.
[8] In Schedule 3 below.
[9] In Schedule 5 below.

6. His Majesty's Government in the United Kingdom and His Majesty's Government in the Commonwealth of Australia agreed that arrangements shall be made for the regulation of imports of frozen mutton and lamb and frozen and chilled beef into the United Kingdom in accordance with the declaration by His Majesty's Government in the United Kingdom which is appended as Schedule H.

7. His Majesty's Government in the United Kingdom will invite the Governments of the non-self-governing Colonies and Protectorates to accord to Australia any preference which may for the time being be accorded to any other part of the British Empire ... [proviso as in Canadian Agreement].

8. His Majesty's Government in the Commonwealth of Australia will invite Parliament to pass the legislation making the tariff changes necessary to give effect to the preference formula set forth in Part I of Schedule F[10] ... and further undertake that existing preferential margins which exceed those laid down in this formula shall be maintained subject, however, to the right of His Majesty's Government in the Commonwealth of Australia to reduce the existing margins of preference in the case of goods of the kind specified in Part III of that Schedule to an extent not exceeding the amounts shown therein.

9. His Majesty's Government in the Commonwealth of Australia undertake that protection by tariffs shall be afforded only to those industries which are reasonably assured of sound opportunities for success.

10. His Majesty's Government in the Commonwealth of Australia undertake that during the currency of this Agreement the tariff shall be based on the principle that protective duties shall not exceed such a level as will give United Kingdom producers full opportunity of reasonable competition on the basis of the relative cost of economical and efficient production, provided that in the application of such principles special consideration may be given to the case of industries not fully established.

11. His Majesty's Government in the Commonwealth of Australia undertake that a review shall be made as soon as practicable by the Australian Tariff Board of existing protective duties in accordance with the principles laid down in Article 10 thereof, and that after the receipt of the report and recommendations of the Tariff Board the Commonwealth Parliament shall be invited to vary, where necessary, the tariff on goods of United Kingdom origin in such manner as to give effect to such principles.

12. His Majesty's Government in the Commonwealth of Australia undertake that no new protective duty shall be imposed and no existing

[10] Not reproduced here.

duty shall be increased on United Kingdom goods to an amount in excess of the recommendation of the Tariff Tribunal.

13. His Majesty's Government in the Commonwealth of Australia undertake that United Kingdom producers shall be entitled to full rights of audience before the Tariff Board when it has under consideration matters arising under Articles 11 and 12 hereof.

14. His Majesty's Government in the Commonwealth of Australia undertake that in so far as concerns goods the produce or manufacture of the United Kingdom:

(a) to repeal as soon as practicable the proclamation . . . prohibiting the importation of certain goods;

(b) to remove as soon as practicable the surcharges imposed by resolution. . . .

(c) to reduce or remove primage duty as soon as the finances of Australia will allow.

15. His Majesty's Government in the Commonwealth of Australia undertake to accord to the non-self-governing Colonies and Protectorates and [certain] Mandated Territories . . . preferences on the commodities and at the rates shown in Schedule G[11] and also any preference for the time being accorded to the United Kingdom if . . . the United Kingdom so request. Provided that. . . . Australia shall not be bound to accord any preferences to any Colony or Protectorate which, not being precluded by international obligations from according preferences, either (i) accords to Australia no preferences or (ii) accords to some other part of the Empire (in the case of Northern Rhodesia, excepting the Union of South Africa, Southern Rhodesia, and the territories of the South African High Commission) preferences not accorded to Australia. . . .

Schedule H to Australian Agreement [12]

. . . 3. . . . the United Kingdom will, during the currency of the Ottawa Agreement, arrange for the regulation of importations of meat into the United Kingdom, the regulation, in view of the close inter-relationship of all kinds of meat in determining the price level, to be applied to all the meats referred to in Section 5.

[11] Not reproduced here.

[12] The omitted passages committed the United Kingdom to an 'agreed programme' by which British imports of foreign chilled beef would be halted at the level reached in the year ending June 30, 1932 (the 'Ottawa Year'), while British imports of foreign frozen lamb, mutton, and frozen beef would rapidly be reduced in stages to 65 per cent of the 'Ottawa Year' level. Britain also committed herself to impose no restriction upon Australian meat until the middle of 1934, and to arrange for the quantitative regulation of bacon and ham imports.

4. The Policy of . . . the United Kingdom in relation to meat production is, first, to secure development of home production, and, secondly, to give to the Dominions an expanding share of imports into the United Kingdom.

5. . . . . Australia agrees to limit the export of frozen mutton and lamb to the United Kingdom for the year 1933 to an amount equivalent to the total imports from Australia during the year ended June 30, 1932[13]. . . .

6. During the year 1933 and in the light of the experience gained, . . . the United Kingdom will consider, in consultation with . . . Australia, the best means of ensuring an improved price situation and the more orderly marketing of supplies.

7. Should no permanent policy be agreed upon as the result of the consultation, . . . the United Kingdom undertakes, after the expiry of the period named in the agreed programme . . . and during the remainder of the period of the Agreement . . . :—

(a) to arrange for the continuance, unless otherwise agreed between the governments concerned, of the regulation of the imports of foreign meat at the rates in force at the end of the period named in the agreed programme;

(b) in any action affecting the imports of meat into the United Kingdom which the United Kingdom Government may take on behalf of United Kingdom agriculture, to have regard to the policy set out in Section 4 hereof.

8. Should it appear to . . . the United Kingdom after enquiry that, at any time in consequence of the restrictions upon foreign imports, the supplies of meat of any kind are inadequate to meet the requirements of consumers in the United Kingdom, then His Majesty's Government may remove any such restrictions until supplies are again adequate.

3. New Zealand

1. [As Australian Agreement, Article 1]. . . .

2. [As Australian Agreement, Article 2]. . . .

3. [As Australian Agreement, Article 4]. . . .

4. In regard to frozen mutton, lamb, and beef, the understanding between the Governments concerned is set out in the letter dated August 19, 1932, addressed by the Right Hon. J. G. Coates, M.P., to the Right Hon. Stanley Baldwin.[14]

5. [As Australian Agreement, Article 7[15]]. . . .

[13] The 'Ottawa Year' in later meat-talks.

[14] Not reproduced here. In effect the letter gave the same sketch as the meat commitments of the Australian Agreement, Schedule H.

[15] The Australian Agreement, however, specified some goods on which Australia would receive new and increased preferences in colonial markets. The New Zealand Agreement included no such provision.

6. ... New Zealand will invite Parliament to pass the legislation necessary to substitute for the duties of customs now leviable on the United Kingdom goods specified in Schedule D[16] the duties shown in that Schedule and to exempt all United Kingdom goods from the application of the surtax. ...

7. As Australian Agreement, Article 9. ...

8. His Majesty's Government in New Zealand undertake to institute an inquiry into the existing protective duties and where necessary to reduce them as speedily as possible to such a level as will place the United Kingdom producer in the position of a domestic competitor, that is, that the protection afforded to the New Zealand producer shall be on a level which will give the United Kingdom producer full opportunity of reasonable competition on the basis of the relative cost of economical and efficient production.

9. His Majesty's Government in New Zealand undertake that United Kingdom producers shall have an opportunity of putting forward their views in connection with the inquiry referred to in Article 8 hereof.

10. His Majesty's Government in New Zealand undertake that no reduction shall be made in the margins of preference of 20 per cent ad valorem (or its equivalent) or less now enjoyed by United Kingdom goods over those of any foreign country, and that where the margin of preference now exceeds 20 per cent ad valorem (or its equivalent) it shall not be reduced below 20 per cent ... except with the consent of ... the United Kingdom.

11. His Majesty's Government in New Zealand undertake that the existing primage duty of 3 per cent ad valorem now levied on United Kingdom goods which are otherwise duty free shall not be increased and shall be abolished as soon as financial conditions permit.

12. [As Australian Agreement, Article 15]. ...

4. *South Africa*

1. [As Australian Agreement, Article 1]. ...

2. [As Australian Agreement, Article 2]. ...

3. [As Australian Agreement, Article 3]. ...

4. [As Australian Agreement, Article 4] ... and that the existing preferential duties on sugar and wine (except as otherwise provided in this Agreement) shall not be reduced without ... consent.

5. The duty on copper provided in this agreement is conditional on the Empire producers of copper continuing to offer this commodity on first sale in the United Kingdom at a price not exceeding the world price.

[16] Not reproduced here.

6. His Majesty's Government in the United Kingdom will invite Parliament to pass legislation which will secure for a period of ten years from the date hereof to tobacco, which complies with the laws and statutory regulations . . . the existing margin of preference over foreign tobacco so long however as the duty on foreign unmanufactured tobacco does not fall below 2s. 0½d. per pound in which event the margin of preference shall be equal to the full duty.

7. . . . in applying any powers which they may obtain from Parliament for the quantitative regulation of imports of mutton and lamb into the United Kingdom, [the United Kingdom Government] will make provision for the importation of South African mutton and lamb.

8. [Equivalent of Australian Agreement, Article 7]. . . .

9. His Majesty's Government in the Union of South Africa will invite Parliament to pass the legislation necessary to secure to United Kingdom goods of the kinds specified in Schedule E[17] the margins of preference over similar foreign goods shown in that schedule.

10. . . . [South Africa will also] impose on foreign goods of the kinds specified in Schedule F[17] the specific duties shown in that schedule and undertake not to make, or to invite Parliament to pass legislation involving any alterations in the existing rates of duty on similar United Kingdom goods which would result in a decrease in the margin of preference now accorded.

11. His Majesty's Government in the Union of South Africa undertake not to lower the existing margins of preference over similar foreign goods now accorded to the United Kingdom goods of the kinds specified in Schedule G.[17]

12. [As Australian Agreement, Article 15]. . . .

5. India

1. [As Australian Agreement, Article 1]. . . .

2. [As Australian Agreement, Article 2]. . . .

3. [As Australian Agreement, Article 3]. . . .

4. His Majesty's Government in the United Kingdom undertake that no Order will be made, and that Parliament will not be invited to pass legislation which would have the effect of reducing the margin of preference now enjoyed by Indian goods of the kinds specified in Schedule C[18] over similar foreign goods, and further undertake that, in the event of any greater preference being accorded in respect of such goods imported from any other part of the Empire, such greater preference will be extended to similar Indian goods.

[17] Not reproduced here.
[18] In Schedule 4 below.

5. [As Australian Agreement, Article 5: relates to wheat and lead only] . . ..

6. [As Canadian Agreement, Article 7] . . . .

7. His Majesty's Government in the United Kingdom will invite Parliament to pass legislation providing for the admission into the United Kingdom free of duty from all sources of the goods listed in Schedule D.[19]

8. His Majesty's Government in the United Kingdom undertake that they will co-operate in any practicable scheme that may be agreed between the manufacturing, trading, and producing interests in the United Kingdom and India for promoting, whether by research, propaganda, or improved marketing, the greater use of Indian cotton in the United Kingdom.

9. [As Australian Agreement, Article 7] . . . .

10. The Government of India will invite the Legislature to pass the legislation necessary to secure to United Kingdom goods of the kinds specified in Schedule F[19] . . . the margins of preference over similar foreign goods shown in that schedule.

11. The Government of India will consider, in the light of the findings of the Tariff Board, the protective duties to be imposed on goods of cotton and artificial silk according as they are made in the United Kingdom or elsewhere, and will invite the Legislature to pass legislation by which, where protective duties are not imposed as a result of the recommendations of the Tariff Board upon United Kingdom goods of the kinds specified in Schedule G[20] the margins of preference shown in that schedule will be extended to such goods.

12. [As Australian Agreement, Article 15] . . . .

13. His Majesty's Government in the United Kingdom declare that they will maintain their existing policy under which tariff preferences accorded to any Dominion are also accorded to India, and the Government of India for their part declare that it is their intention to extend to the United Kingdom any tariff preferences which they may accord to any Dominion.

SCHEDULES

[1. *Reservation as to certain produce—Schedule A in all Dominion Agreements*]

As regards Eggs, Poultry, Butter, Cheese, and other Milk Products, free entry for produce of Australia/Canada/New Zealand/South Africa

---

[19] Not reproduced here.

[20] Not reproduced here. Consists of cottons and artificial silk goods of all kinds; proposes a 10% rate of preference (that is, ten percentage points between the British preferential rate and the general tariff rate).

will be continued for three years certain. His Majesty's Government in the United Kingdom, however, reserve to themselves the right after the expiration of the three years, if they consider it necessary in the interests of the United Kingdom producer to do so, to review the basis of preference, so far as relates to the articles enumerated, and, after notifying His Majesty's Government in the Commonwealth of Australia/Canada/New Zealand/South Africa either to impose a preferential duty . . . whilst maintaining existing preferential margins, or in consultation with the . . . Government to bring such produce within any system which may be put into operation for the quantitative regulation of supplies from all sources in the United Kingdom market.

[2. *Imposition of New United Kingdom tariffs, showing agreements in which the items are mentioned. Schedule B in all Dominion Agreements; Schedule A in Indian*]

Wheat in grain, 2s. per quarter—Canada, Australia, India
Butter, 15/– per cwt   —all Dominions
Cheese, 15% ad valorem   — „   „
Apples and pears, raw, 4/6 per cwt   — „   „
Eggs in shell, 1/– to 1/9 per great hundred, depending on
    size   — „   „
Condensed milk, whole, sweetened, 5/– per cwt in
    addition to duty on sugar content   — „   „
Condensed milk, whole, unsweetened, 6/– per cwt.—Australia, New Zealand, South Africa
Milk Powder and other preserved milk, not sweetened, 5/– per cwt.—New Zealand, South Africa
Honey, 7/– per cwt.—Australia, New Zealand
Chilled or frozen salmon—1½d per lb.—Canada
Apples, canned, 3/6 per cwt in addition to sugar-content duty—Canada, Australia, S. Africa
Other canned fruits, 15% in addition to sugar-content duty—Australia, South Africa
Dried fruits already dutiable at 7/–, 10/6 per cwt.—Canada, Australia, South Africa
Copper, unwrought, whether refined or not, 2d per lb.—Canada, Australia, South Africa
Oranges, raw, 3/6 per cwt from 1 April to 30 November—Australia, South Africa
Grapefruit, raw, 5/– per cwt from 1 April to 30 November—Australia, South Africa
Grapes not hothouse, 1½d per lb. from 1 February to 30 June—Australia, South Africa

Maize, flat white, 10%—South Africa
Peaches and nectarines, raw, 14/- per cwt from 1 December to 31 March
—South Africa
Plums, raw, 9/4 per cwt from 1 December to 31 March—South Africa
Castor and various other oils, 10% and 15%—India
Linseed, 10%—India
Magnesium chloride, 1/- per cwt—India
Rice, husked but not broken, 1d per lb—India

[3. *British Guarantees of specific preferential margins. Schedule C in
Australian and South African Agreements; Schedule B in Indian*]
Wine not exceeding 27 degrees of proof spirit, 2/- per gallon—South
Africa, Australia
Coffee, 9/4 per cwt.—India, Southern Rhodesia

[4. *British Guarantees that present preferential margins will not be reduced.
Schedule C in Indian Agreement; not present in Dominion Agreements*]
Tobacco, tea, coir, cottons, leather, lead, jute manufactures, oilseed
cake and meal, paraffin wax, spices, teak and other hardwoods now
dutiable, woollen carpets and rugs, bran and pollard, rice meal and dust,
castor seed, magnesite, and sandalwood oil, granite setts and curbs,
groundnuts.

[5. *British Guarantees that present duties on foreign goods will not be
reduced. Schedule C in Canadian and New Zealand Agreements; Schedule
D in Australian and South African Agreements.*]
Timber of all kinds imported into the United Kingdom in substantial
quantities from Canada in so far as now dutiable, canned salmon and
other canned fish—Canada; fresh sea fish—Canada, Newfoundland;
zinc and lead—Canada, Australia; asbestos—Canada, Australia, South
Africa; barley, wheat flour, macaroni, dressed poultry, and eucalyptus
oil—Australia; tallow, canned meat, casein, meat extracts and essences,
dried peas, leather, copra, sugar of milk—Australia, New Zealand;
seeds (grass and clover), gums (other than gum arabic, gum tragacanth,
shellac, sticlac, and seedlac)—New Zealand; sausage casings—New
Zealand, Australia, South Africa; wattle bark and tanning extracts made
therefrom, dried fruits other than currants not specified in Schedule B—
South Africa, Australia; maize products, fruit preserved by chemicals or
artificial heat, fruit juices, whale oil and products, crayfish, fresh hake,
oyster shell grit, ground nuts, goatskins, lucerne seed, kaffir corn and
meal, box wood, potatoes, ostrich feathers—South Africa.

[6. *British Concession of duty-free entry for Empire and Foreign products. Schedule, D in Indian Agreement; not present in Dominion Agreements.*]
Shellac seedlac, and sticlac; jute, raw; myrabolams, broken rice, mica slabs and splittings, crotolaria juncea and any other varieties of Indian hemp that can be distinguished.

29. An Anglo-New Zealand Customs Union?

FROM Public Record Office, DO 114/50, pp. 189–90.
[Telegram, New Zealand Government to Dominions Office, October 25, 1933.]

With reference to question of quantitative regulation of agricultural produce imported into United Kingdom, there is a widespread belief on the part of producers in New Zealand that if we undertook a drastic reduction or removal of New Zealand's preferential tariff on United Kingdom goods, His Majesty's Government in the United Kingdom would guarantee continuance of unrestricted entry of New Zealand primary products. His Majesty's Government in New Zealand would be grateful if His Majesty's Government in United Kingdom would indicate their attitude towards this suggestion.

[Telegram, Dominions Office to New Zealand Government, December 22, 1933.]
I must regret delay in responding to your message, which required careful consideration in consultation with my colleagues.

We desire in the first place to make it clear that the policy adopted by His Majesty's Government in the United Kingdom is designed to promote the planned marketing of agricultural products in the interest of all concerned, and involves where necessary control of home production as well as of home marketing. Its objective is, by correlating supply with demand, to raise the price of the commodities concerned, and to maintain it at a level at which it will become remunerative to all producers supplying the United Kingdom market.

It is true that in present circumstances regulation is likely to involve a check to immediate expansion, but orderly increase of production, as demand increases, with due regard to a remunerative price, is of course contemplated.

The suggestion in your telegram would involve modification of United Kingdom policy indicated above, and could hardly be considered with reference to New Zealand alone. Nor we think could an examination of such a question take place on the basis of a suggestion put forward by particular trade interests. For this reason we feel hardly in a position to give any further indication of our attitude than that outlined above, though we are, of course, at all times ready to give full and sympathetic consideration to any proposals of the New Zealand Government for th development of the mutual trade of the two countries.

30. An Economic General Staff for the Empire? The Canadian Delegation Reports on the Proceedings of the Imperial Committee on Economic Consultation and Co-operation, 1932–33[1]

FROM Harriet Irving Library, University of New Brunswick, R. B. Bennett Papers, 115–704/964–967.

The idea of an economic general staff for the Empire to act as a continuing agency between conferences and to issue advice and make recommendations to the various governments on economic questions was never seriously put forward except by Sir Fabian Ware.[2] The Australian and New Zealand delegations (who in theory favoured this grandiose scheme) realised that it could not possibly receive general support. . . . Sir Fabian Ware . . . submitted a draft charter for the establishment of an Imperial Economic Commission . . . with wide powers of advice and

---

[1] The Ottawa Conference had agreed to set up an ad hoc committee on economic consultation and cooperation which would consider the fates of the various 'Imperial committees' which had been set up in the twenties. It would also consider whether any new measures of organisation were needed. Before 1932, British civil servants seem to have hoped that Ottawa would produce some scheme for continuing consultation between Empire ministers. For this, they thought, a secretariat would be required. See above, Doc. 22. The Ottawa experience seems to have cooled their zeal with respect to consultation. The Dominions Office functioned as the de facto secretariat for the numerous ministerial meetings that bedecked the later thirties.

[2] Sir Fabian Ware had been associated for many years with the Imperial War Graves Commission. In July 1932 he had urged Bennett to push for some sort of Imperial economic machinery free from British treasury control. See Bennett Papers, 115,502–4: letter, Fabian Ware to R. B. Bennett, July 7, 1932.

recommendation on Imperial economic questions and working through standing committees. Sir Fabian, however, got little support for his embryonic economic general staff. . . . The United Kingdom delegation, as a delegation, never at any time submitted any definite proposals for centralisation, though its sympathies were with the Australian and New Zealand delegations. The position adopted by Sir Horace Wilson[3] was that they would accept any plan which the Dominions might agree upon.

31. J. H. Thomas[1] warns Ramsay MacDonald about the Tendencies in British Agricultural Policy

FROM Public Record Office, DO 35/317/9513, April 24, 1934

Dear Prime Minister:

I have read with interest Bledisloe's[2] letter to you and the article from a leading New Zealand paper which he encloses. I return both. I have seen other articles, similar in argument but expressed a good deal more pungently, from the Australian Press. And perhaps you may have seen the remarks bearing on the subject in the speech made recently at a meeting of the F.B.I. by Macdonough. In case you have not, I enclose the relevant 'Times' extract.

I am, I confess, somewhat anxious as to the effect of our present policy in economic matters on our trade relations with the Dominions. I do not believe that the Dominions would dispute for one moment our need to foster our export trade by all means in our power. They would be the first to benefit by any increase in our purchasing strength thereby created; and moreover we made it perfectly plain at Ottawa that this was the course we intended to pursue. Nor would they dispute that we are entitled, and indeed bound, to put our existing agricultural industry on a proper economic footing; that also we made clear at Ottawa. What

[3] The report of the Committee was published as Cmd.4335(1932–33). A Dominions Office administrator minuted upon the report in July 1933: 'It is no secret that the United Kingdom Government would have been prepared to go much farther in the direction of the establishment of machinery for economic co-operation than the Committee recommended, but it is understood that the Report represents the maximum on which unanimity was possible' (DO 35/232/8671/66).

[1] Dominions Secretary.
[2] Governor General of New Zealand.

they *are* afraid of, and what we did *not* make clear at Ottawa (because at that time our agricultural policy had not advanced nearly so far as it has today), is that our own agricultural output may increase so much as to check our imports of primary produce.

Their apprehensions are increased because, in the interests of our export trade, we have limited our freedom of action vis-a-vis their foreign competitors, so that the impact of any such increase seems likely to fall to a large extent upon them. How serious a matter this would be for New Zealand and Australia (Canada and South Africa are less directly concerned) is shown by the fact that 15% of the total exports from Australia and no less than 70% of the total exports from New Zealand, consists of exports of meat, butter, and cheese to this country.

Various aspects of the general question are, as you know, constantly coming up at meetings of the Produce Markets Supply Committee. Hence the suggestion to which Bledisloe refers, that there is a want of co-ordination between Ministers or Departments is not, I think, justified.

But I am bound to say, on the general question of principle, that I think that the Cabinet will soon have to make up its mind within what limits we can properly develop our agricultural policy consistently with the necessities of our Imperial and foreign trade.

Meanwhile you will probably agree that there is not very much that you can say to Bledisloe, but you could certainly assure him that the very important and difficult questions with which his letter deals are receiving constant consideration in the Government here, and I think you might add that you do not feel that he need be apprehensive of any lack of co-ordination between the Departments.

You might perhaps also say that you have been most interested to read in the newspapers of the intention of the New Zealand Government to assume all responsibility for dealing with the problems of the dairying industry. . . .

Yours sincerely, J.H.T.

32. J. H. Thomas and Walter Elliot[1] discuss Levy-Subsidies

FROM Public Record Office, DO 35/317/9513, June, 1934.

My Dear Walter:

I think we may fairly hope that we got a long way nearer this morning a solution of the meat difficulty which will safeguard the position of the U.K. producer without giving rise to very serious friction with the Dominions.

The officials are now working out a scheme to provide a fund out of which deficiency payments may be made to the U.K. producer. It remains, of course, to be seen whether the Dominions will agree to such a scheme, or, for the matter of that, the foreigners. In my opinion the prospect of getting the consent of the Dominions will depend a good deal upon the form which any scheme takes. In your memorandum it is in effect proposed that we shall take the money out of the pocket of the overseas producer and put it into the pocket of the home producer. I mentioned yesterday morning, without elaborating them, some of the objections to which a scheme in this form seems to me to be open. You can imagine how some—probably most—of the Dominion newspapers would write up such a proposal. They would say that if we choose to make their agriculturists subsidise ours, they can make our industrialists subsidise theirs; and we may find ourselves—quite unnecessarily, so far as I can see—involved in almost as much friction and misunderstanding over the levy as seemed likely to arise over the quota.

The alternative—or so it seems to me—would be to impose an import duty (of course with a preference to the Dominions—as I assume would also be the case with the levy) on all imports, and at the same time to pay a subsidy out of the Exchequer to the U.K. farmer. You may say that, assuming that the proceeds of the import duty were approximately equivalent to the cost of the subsidy, there is no difference between this proposal and a levy. I agree that there is not very much difference in substance; but there seems to me to be a great deal of difference in form. There is nothing new about import duties and subsidies; and no legitimate objection could be made—least of all by the Dominions—to our use of them. All that the Dominion producer would know would be that a duty—with a substantial preference over the foreigner—was being levied on his imports; and I feel pretty confident that his dislike of such

[1] Respectively, Dominions Secretary and Minister of Agriculture and Fisheries.

a duty would be considerably less than his dislike of a restriction upon his production. The fact that the U.K. Government had decided to pay a subsidy to the U.K. farmer would be a matter which would not directly concern him. But he would, I feel sure, object to being made to pay that subsidy himself, even though the financial effect of a duty, so far as he was concerned, was the same.

There is a further consideration which occurs to me. If the deficiency payments made to the U.K. farmer are made to depend directly upon the levy, either the payment ot the U.K. farmer, or the levy, must be variable. Surely this would be very undesirable. The U.K. farmer will, I imagine, want to know precisely how much he is going to get: and the Dominion producer will certainly want to know precisely what he is going to pay.

So far as I can see the calculations required for either scheme are substantially the same.

I am sending a copy of this letter to Neville and Runciman.[2]

[J.H.Thomas]

14th June, 1934.

My dear Jim,

Many thanks for your letter of yesterday's date on Levy v. Import Duty. My impression was that the general feeling of the Committee[3] on Tuesday was in favour of the levy principle, but I quite agree that the subject was not fully discussed, and you will, no doubt, raise it again at your next meeting. In the meantime, the examination of the basic figures by the officials, which is now taking place, will not, of course, prejudice the question.

I have no doubt that Neville and Runciman, to whom I note you have sent copies of your letter, will give very careful attention to the points you raise—as, of course, I will myself—in preparation for our next meeting.

Yours ever,
Walter Elliot.

[2] Neville Chamberlain, the Chancellor of the Exchequer, and Walter Runciman, the President of the Board of Trade. Both were members of the Produce Markets Supply Committee, as were Thomas and Elliot.

[3] Produce Markets Supply Committee.

33. Robert Menzies[1] writes to Richard Casey[2] about the Anglo-Australian Meat Talks of 1935

FROM National Library of Australia, Sir George Pearce Papers, MS 213, Ser. 5.

Australia House, London,
18 April 1935.

Dear Dick:

Thomas is shrewd but really has no understanding of the Dominions or of their point of view, and appears to be obsessed with the idea that Australia has behaved dishonestly over the tariff matters dealt with at Ottawa. Walter Elliot impresses me personally very much, but is, of course, hard driven by his primary producers, and is therefore scarcely likely to make bargains which will be of much use to us. Walter Runciman . . . is . . . an excellent type, but he represents the Board of Trade view, and the Board of Trade, for some reason that I have not yet fathomed, is more pro-Argentine than pro-Australian. All things considered, I am not too optimistic, though we have already, as you know, secured pretty good arrangements for the April/June deliveries of chilled beef.[3]

In any consideration of these matters at Canberra, the thing to understand is that the avoidance of any restriction in relation to mutton and lamb[4] is perfectly hopeless. The British ministers point out, unanswerably, that the satisfactory price of mutton and lamb is due to the regulated market, and that no sentimental consideration will induce them to allow Australian supplies at such a rate as will break the market.

I think we might, in the last resort, get the Argentine squeezed[5] by say another 15% which would mean a total reduction of the Argentine of 50% on the Ottawa year, but, as you will realise, this would make merely a trivial difference to the quantities we could export. We must, therefore, resign ourselves definitely to regulation on mutton and lamb.

On beef our great obstacle at present is the Anglo-Argentine Agreement,[6] the significance of which does not appear to be understood at your

[1] Australian Attorney General, in London for the negotiations.
[2] Australian cabinet minister, in Canberra.
[3] That is, the short-term quarterly quota.
[4] That is, some permanent arrangement for the restriction of the Dominions' sales of mutton and lamb in Britain.
[5] Its quota reduced.
[6] Of 1933, expiring in November 1936.

end. We may protest until we are blue in the face but the fact is that the agreement was made and that its effect is to make it impossible for Australia to export more chilled beef, unless it is prepared to accept considerably less frozen beef.

We have been endeavouring to cope with this by discussing with the British ministers how far we could make arrangements with them which would enable them to negotiate with the Argentine a completely revised agreement . . . the difficulty about this is that if such a revised agreement is to be valuable to Australia it must be correspondingly injurious to the Argentine, which country is, therefore, hardly likely to forgo its contractual rights. . . .

One alternative course we might pursue would be to decide that we would not ask for a long term policy until the Argentine Agreement runs out in November of next year, and that, in the meantime, we will bite on the bit as best we can, and submit to such restrictions as the U.K. Government may impose, all with the idea that both we and the United Kingdom will then be in a stronger bargaining position in relation to the Argentine. . . .

34. A Senior Dominions Office Official writes informally to the British High Commissioner in Australia, explaining the Meat Talks

FROM Public Record Office, DO 35/259/1905/3/172

SECRET   Downing Street, 30 June 1936.

My dear Geoffrey[1]:

I am extremely sorry not to have been able to keep you currently informed of the active discussions of the meat question which have been proceeding during the last three weeks. Since, however, we are living in an atmosphere of constant meetings and discussions, it was physically impossible to find time to put the story on paper; moreover, the situation was changing daily, and at times hourly, and it would have been very difficult at any given moment to present an accurate picture. . . .

[1] Sir Geoffrey Whiskard, United Kingdom High Commissioner in Australia.

Dixon's[2] letter of the 5th June took the story to the point when the Commonwealth[3] representatives had presented proposals for quantitative regulation providing for a five-year programme and a reduction of foreign imports of beef into the United Kingdom by $12\frac{1}{2}\%$ on 1935 figures, by a series of progressive cuts. These proposals were discussed at a meeting between United Kingdom and Commonwealth Ministers on the 8th June. . . . You will see that the Secretary of State[4] pointed out certain difficulties in the way of the Commonwealth proposals, but promised that they should be considered, and that we would let the Commonwealth representatives know our views.

Following upon the discussion by the Interdepartmental Committee and subsequently by the Cabinet Committee, a further meeting was held with Commonwealth Ministers on the 12th June . . . at which the Secretary of State put forward tentative proposals with regard to quantitative restriction of imports into the United Kingdom whereby, during the first two years of the existence of the Meat Conference[5], there would be a standstill on 1935 figures of total beef imports into the United Kingdom from each country, the quantities shipped as chilled beef being determined by the Meat Conference on the understanding that foreign countries would, if necessary, agree to reduce their shipments of chilled beef by, say, $2\frac{1}{2}\%$ in each of the two years, with the right to ship frozen beef instead if they so desired. The immediate effect of these proposals was that Dr. Earle Page[6] was apparently struck dumb! He and Mr. Menzies[7] asked one or two questions, but . . . there was practically no discussion, and it was agreed that we should let the Commonwealth Ministers have the tentative proposals in writing.

The Secretary of State accordingly sent to Dr. Earle Page on the 15th June the statement. . . . The immediate result of this letter was that Bruce[8] came to see the Secretary of State and represented that it was useless putting these proposals before the Commonwealth Ministers, and that, if this was the best we could do, the only course seemed to be to abandon discussions, and leave the whole responsibility for the regulation of imports into the United Kingdom to the United Kingdom Government. At the same time, as his own personal and confidential

[2] Another London official.
[3] Here and throughout these two letters, Commonwealth of Australia.
[4] Malcolm MacDonald.
[5] The British were proposing an International Meat Conference of beef-exporters which would regulate the volume of each supplier's shipments to Britain.
[6] Earle Page, leader Australian Country Party and Minister of Commere.
[7] Robert Menzies, Australian Attorney General.
[8] S. B. Bruce, Australian High Commissioner in London.

suggestion, he put forward the idea that the position might be met if it were possible to arrange that, while total imports of beef from all countries taken together would not exceed total shipments for 1935, imports of beef from foreign countries should be reduced in each of the first two years by $2\frac{1}{2}\%$, and the Dominions should be entitled to fill up the gap thus created. . . .

I was authorised by the Secretary of State to discuss the matter further with MacDougall,[9] and I had two evenings' talk with him on the subject, which lasted until nearly midnight. This was followed on the 19th June by a meeting between United Kingdom and Commonwealth officials. . . .

Mr. Lyons'[10] telegram to the Prime Minister[11] had been received on the 17th June, and Dr. Earle Page pressed for an early talk with the Prime Minister on the subject. It was not possible for the Prime Minister to see him, but arrangements were made for him and Mr. Menzies to see the Secretary of State on the 23rd June. . . .

In the meantime, the Inter-Departmental Committee had been considering the position in the light of the talks which were taking place, and put up to the Cabinet Committee proposals whereby

(1) Aggregate shipments of beef of all kinds from all countries taken together should be fixed for the first three years at 1935 figures;

(2) foreign chilled beef shipments would be liable to reduction by 5% (say 400,000 cwts) over the three years, but not more than 2% in any one year, the actual reduction for each of the three years being settled by the Meat Conference;

(3) such reduction would not be replaceable by foreign frozen beef. . . .

The Cabinet Committee on June 24th approved the proposals of the Inter-Departmental Committee, and they were explained by the Secretary of State to Commonwealth ministers at a meeting in the afternoon of the same day. . . .

On the following day, the Secretary of State sent Dr. Earle Page a statement of the proposals, of which I enclose a copy. . . . On the same day, the Prime Minister replied to Mr. Lyons' telegram.

The Commonwealth reply to the proposals was contained in a letter from Dr. Earle Page. . . . It was handed to the Secretary of State at a meeting that morning (Mr. Menzies having already left England). . . .

The proposals have since been explained also to representatives of Canada, New Zealand, the Union of South Africa and Southern Rhodesia, who have been asked to let us have their observations as

[9] A senior official at Australia House in London.
[10] J. A. Lyons, Prime Minister of Australia.
[11] Stanley Baldwin.

quickly as possible. . . . The position in relation to the Irish Free State is, however, full of difficulties, and I foresee a crop of troubles arising from these!

As to the position in relation to the Argentine, you will have seen from the papers enclosed in my letter of the 26th June how discussions with them are proceeding.

If there is general agreement on the proposals, . . . legislation will of course be required to give effect to the new scheme, but this is not contemplated immediately. It is, however, proposed to pass a short Bill providing, as an interim measure, for the continuance of the existing cattle subsidy, until the 31st July 1937, and for the imposition of the levy on foreign imports until the same date, as from the 8th November next, and (always assuming that general agreement is reached), it is at present contemplated that the Minister of Agriculture should make some statement as to the nature of the general scheme in connection with the introduction of the interim measure. It remains to be seen, however, what the developments as to this may be.

The present letter, long as it is, is only an outline of what has been going on, but it will serve, I hope, to give you a general idea of what has been for the officials concerned a particularly harrassing period!

Yours ever,
E. G. Machtig.[12]

SECRET   13 July, 1936
My dear Geoffrey:

You will remember that at his meeting with the S. of S. on 26th June, Dr. Earle Page urged that in view of the existing trade position of Australia in relation to Japan, Mr. Lyons should be enabled to announce at an early date that the meat discussions between Australia and the U.K. were going well. As a result of this, the annexed formula[13] was drawn up here interdepartmentally, as being the sort of thing that Mr. Lyons might safely say, and was communicated on June 29 to Dr. Earle Page, who telegraphed it out to Mr. Lyons. Shortly afterwards a fairly accurate forecast in some detail of the U.K. Government's proposals appeared in the *Manchester Guardian* and the *Evening Standard*. Dr. Earle Page at once represented that this made Mr. Lyons' position even more difficult and urged that he should be authorised to make a fuller statement. In the meantime it had been arranged here that Mr. Elliot[14] should make a statement giving an outline of the U.K. Gvt's proposals on Monday

---

[12] Assistant Undersecretary of State for the Dominions.
[13] Not reproduced here.
[14] Walter Elliot, Minister of Agriculture and Fisheriees.

July 6th in reply to a Question in the House, and, at the time of Dr. Earle Page's representations, the preparation of the statement was in hand inter-departmentally. It was accordingly arranged that Dr. Earle Page's difficulty should be met by sending him an advance copy of Mr. Elliot's statement and suggesting to him that Mr. Lyons should, so soon as the statement had been made here, make public in Australia the material which it contained (but no more). Copies of letters exchanged with Murphy[15] as to this are enclosed. The text of the statement was telegraphed by us to Dominion Gvts. in the S. of S.'s circ. tel[16] E.No. 10 of July 6th. I enclose the Hansard. . . .

Yours,
E. G. Machtig.

35. The Cabinet Committee on Trade and Agriculture[1] discuss the Dominions and Trade Policy, December 17, 1936

FROM Public Record Office, CAB 27/619, T.A.C.(36) 9th meeting.

. . . The Minister of Agriculture[2] recalled that the question [of trade relationships with the Dominions] had arisen out of a memorandum prepared by the Secretary of State for the Dominions on the question of the Agenda for the Imperial Conference next year. At the meeting to discuss that memorandum he, the Minister of Agriculture, had expressed the hope that the agenda would not preclude the discussion of the continuance of the principle of free entry for Dominion products. It had been decided that the agenda should not mention the point but that if, after examination of the matter, it was considered desirable to raise the

---

[15] An Australian civil servant.

[16] Circular telegram.

[1] Members: Neville Chamberlain (Chancellor of the Exchequer), Malcolm MacDonald (Secretary of State for Dominion Affairs), Walter Runciman (President of the Board of Trade), the Earl of Plymouth (Parliamentary Under-secretary of State for Foreign Affairs), Walter Elliot (Secretary of State for Scotland), W. S. Morrison (Minister of Agriculture and Fisheries), and D. Euan Wallace (Secretary to the Department of Overseas Trade). Eight officials also attended from the Dominions Office, the Treasury, the Ministry of Agriculture and Fisheries, and the Foreign Office.

[2] W. S. Morrison.

issue it could be raised on the agenda. At the request of his colleagues he had prepared a memorandum setting out his views, but he wished to make it clear that he was not concerned only with the narrow agricultural aspect of this question. He would not base his plea on the idea that Dominion farmers must subsidise United Kingdom farmers. In fact his view was that the matter was not so much an agricultural one as a revenue one. The expenditure of the home Government on defence had increased very greatly and the Dominions benefited by it. In his view they ought to contribute to this and should not be in the position of claiming the right to free entry for their products for all time. He was anxious to prevent practice becoming principle by course of time. Industries in this country as well as agriculture, he understood, were objecting to Dominion products having free entry; in particular he had seen complaints from the leather industry here about imports from India and a resolution of the Empire Section of the Federation of British Industries calling for re-consideration of the matter at the Imperial Conference. Assuming that it was desired to propose duties on Empire products, he doubted whether the bilateral approach was the best and suggested that the matter should be raised with all the Dominions at once at the Imperial Conference.

The Secretary of State for Dominion Affairs[3] said that he appreciated the Minister of Agriculture's anxiety in this matter, particularly with relation to the protection of agriculture. Although, no doubt, there had been some complaints about manufactured goods, from the practical point of view the problem was mainly an agricultural one. He wished to emphasise in this connection that the Dominions did not dispute the principle that home agriculture must come first and he felt that if we should decide to impose duties on Dominion agricultural products we should do well to give as our reason the protection of our own producers. There were various points of detail in the memorandum by the Minister of Agriculture with which he could not fully agree, but they did not affect the main question. In principle he agreed that it seemed desirable that the Dominions should contribute to a levy, when the home consumer and the home tax-payer were paying, and, in general, that the Dominions should not consider themselves as having a right to free entry. He did not think that we had ever admitted such a right in principle.

As regards the practical possibilities, it would be agreed that nothing could be done about meat before three years owing to the Argentine Agreement, and our position on butter and cheese and other dairy produce had been very carefully safeguarded in discussions with the Dominions, and particularly with Canada.

[3] Malcolm MacDonald.

The Secretary of State for Dominion Affairs went on to say that if an attempt was made suddenly to break into the arrangements for free entry for the Dominions he felt sure that there would be a very big political row. He assumed that it was desired that anything we did should be done by agreement; the Dominions had considerable power of retaliation against us, India and the Ottawa Dominions, apart from New Zealand, being our most important overseas markets. Even if they were approached slowly and steadily on the point the opposition would, he felt sure, be very great. The Canadians had nearly walked out when the possibility of a levy on dairy produce was mentioned, and the Australians had objected strongly to the suggestion of a duty on their meat. These primary products were an extremely important part of the economy of the Dominions, and any action by us involving damage to them would be strongly opposed. At the same time he wished to make it clear that some advance had been made. We had at last got the Dominions to realise that they could not expect free entry for unlimited quantities. It had been extremely difficult to make them accept this position, but he thought that they had now done so. In the case of beef, in particular, the Canadian Government had made great difficulties about our proposal for an International [Meat] Conference but a compromise had been reached. It was hoped that in the next day or two New Zealand would agree to enter the Conference. In the case of mutton and lamb we had also now begun to suggest that expansion must cease, and even that there must be a reduction. He was very unwilling to ask the Dominions to make a further step now, except possibly in the case of some particular commodity.

As regards the method of approach to the Dominions, Mr. MacDonald said he felt it would be definitely undesirable to raise the question at the Imperial Conference, either in principle or in detail, because at that Conference all the Dominions would be together and they would join in resisting our proposal. Even if they were approached one by one it would be a difficult and gradual process to get agreement, and with all together he felt sure we should fail.

The President of the Board of Trade[4] said that the Government was to a great extent committed publicly to having offered the Dominions free entry as a valuable gift, which they should be prepared to pay for. The Ottawa Agreements were their form of payment and now there was the particular case of the renewal of the Canadian Agreement.[5] If duty free admission was to be taken out of this Agreement he felt quite sure that no agreement would be possible. He hoped that the Committee

[4] Walter Runciman.
[5] Then being negotiated with great difficulty.

would feel that, having proceeded so far with our negotiations, we could not now throw them up and start on a new basis at the eleventh hour.

The Secretary of State for Scotland[6] said that he agreed with the Secretary of State for Dominion Affairs that free entry had never been conceded to the Dominions as a principle but only as part of a bargain. On the other hand it was important that the principle of regulated entry had been established, since the effect of this was very much like the effect of a duty. He felt that the most outstanding case where we were likely to want to impose duties on Dominion products was that of dairy produce. One of the reasons why the proposal to impose a duty on Dominion meat had not been pursued was that the revenue involved was very small. In the case of dairy produce the revenue to be derived from Dominion imports would be an important consideration, but equally of course the opposition to the duty would be likely to be more intense. He felt, however, that a proposal to impose a duty on dairy produce might be made more attractive to the Dominions than similar proposals for other products, since it would probably be possible to show that our policy was directed to increasing consumption, which was always attractive to the Dominions. In short he felt that we had a better case to impose duties on Dominion dairy produce than on almost anything else. Unlimited free entry for these products should not be continued and probably a duty would be a better system of restriction than a quota, both for the Dominions and for us.

In reply to a question the Minister of Agriculture and Fisheries said that he attached much more importance to securing his general principle than to seeing it applied in practice in the case of the present Canadian negotiations. He had prepared a formula which would secure the principle; this formula, if it were approved by the Cabinet Committee, would be suitable for inclusion in the Canadian Agreement or in any other trade agreement with a Dominion.

The Secretary to the Department of Overseas Trade[7] thought that any proposal to impose duties on Dominion products could be put to the Dominions as a logical consequence of the principle (already accepted throughout the Commonwealth) that the United Kingdom was entitled to take the commodities it required in a descending order of preference (a) home produced goods (b) Dominion imports, and (c) foreign imports. He did not see how Dominion producers could object to occupying a half-way house between the United Kingdom producer and the foreign producer.

[6] Walter Elliot.
[7] Euan Wallace.

As regards the decision, taken in connection with the Argentine Agreement, to allow Dominion meat to enter duty free, the reason was the lowness of the rate ($\frac{3}{4}$d) finally decided upon as regards Argentine imports. There was no point in having a Dominion preferential rate as low as $\frac{1}{4}$d.

The Chancellor of the Exchequer[8] outlined the recent history of Dominion free entry since the reversal of this country's tariff policy in the early part of 1932. After consultation with his Cabinet colleagues, he (the Chancellor) had decided on Dominion free entry at that stage, as a provisional course. It had been made quite clear that the decision was without prejudice to our future liberty of action.

The next event in the history of our tariff had been the Ottawa Conference, at which our Delegation had conceded Dominion free entry, subject to Schedule A,[9] in return for an assurance that Dominion duties on United Kingdom goods would be competitive, and not protective, during the currency of the Ottawa Agreements. Unfortunately this bargain had not worked out so well for us as had been anticipated.

The Ottawa Conference had been remarkable for progress in one direction—it was the first time that we had been able to shake the complacent Dominion assumption that the United Kingdom would continue to afford an unlimited market for their produce, or at any rate a market in which no limit was in sight. We had been compelled by the expansion of Dominion shipments to take a firm line, and we had made it clear that in future the entry of Dominion produce must be regulated by reference to the consuming power of the United Kingdom market.

A new development had followed upon this. Up to the time of Ottawa all the Dominions, and in particular Australia and New Zealand, had concentrated on the production of agricultural commodities. Our Ottawa announcement had led them to turn to the encouragement of their secondary industries.... The days, however, were gone for good in which it had been a commonplace that we were to supply the Dominions with industrial commodities while they supplied us with agricultural commodities.[10]

[8] Neville Chamberlain.

[9] See Doc. 28, Schedule 1.

[10] Chamberlain had presented a parody of Dominion economic development. Canada had been exporting manufactures to the United Kingdom for twenty years. She, Australia, and South Africa had also industrialized extensively *before* Ottawa—especially in the twenties. It is very hard to see any evidence for deliberate industralization between 1932 and 1936 in any of the Dominions. Only in 1936 and thereafter might Australia be said to have taken any such steps. New Zealand did not do so until she introduced exchange control late in 1938. What Chamberlain was really saying implicitly was that *his father's dream* of Tariff Reform must be discarded for good, because it was no longer in accord with the facts. We can hardly expect him to have added that it never had been.

Mr. Chamberlain was afraid that this meant there were difficulties ahead. The Dominions' secondary industries, which had so far been supplying Dominion demands, might begin to produce for export. When that day came Dominion free entry into the United Kingdom would be very difficult to justify. Since that was the prospect awaiting us he (the Chancellor) found himself compelled to accept Mr. Morrison's conclusion that it would be great mistake to allow Dominion free entry to become crystallized.

Mr. Chamberlain thought that the considerations which he had mentioned must apply also to free entry for India and the Colonies.

The Committee agreed:

1) that it would be dangerous to allow Dominion free entry to be regarded as an established general principle . . .;

2) that the acceptance of Conclusion (1) need not debar us from granting Dominion free entry in cases where it was to our advantage;

3) that similar conditions must apply to imports from India and the Colonies.

. . . The Secretary of State for Scotland said that it seemed to him that the case for a duty on dairy products was much better than any other. At Ottawa the Dominions had been given an absolute right of unlimited free entry for three years, and a guaranteed relative height of preference for two years further; even that guarantee would run out in a short time. It might perhaps be possible, in the course of negotiations for new agreements, to reduce the preferential margin. He quite agreed that it would be extremely difficult in practice to impose a duty in any case, but as New Zealand would be the chief opponent of a duty on dairy products, and she was to have free entry for her mutton and lamb,[11] it was possible that we might be able to get her to agree. He was sure that if we could not carry agreement to a duty on Dominion dairy products we could not carry an agreement to any Dominion duty. . . .

The Chancellor of the Exchequer said that he appreciated the danger, to which the Minister of Agriculture had called attention, of the practice of giving free entry becoming a settled principle.

Mr. W. B. Brown[12] said that, speaking from the point of view of one engaged from day to day in trade negotiations, he felt there must be some practical advantage to offer to the Dominions as Dominions. If questions of expediency alone were considered, it might be desirable in a particular case to have a higher duty on Dominion than on foreign produce.

The Chancellor of the Exchequer said that the political aspect must be recognised. The Dominions must have a preferential position, even

---

[11] Free of duty though restricted in amount by quota.
[12] Second Secretary, Board of Trade (a senior official).

if we had to pay for it. The question still remained, however, whether the preference guaranteed was too high. The Minister of Agriculture indicated assent.

The Secretary of State for Dominion Affairs pointed out that when the Canadian negotiators arrived they had wanted to wipe out many of our preferential margins and that the Board of Trade had attached a great deal of importance to maintaining them, and even to obtaining new ones.

Mr. W. B. Brown added that Mr. MacKenzie King was still saying that our existing preferential margins ought to be reduced. He felt that it would always be the case that a preference which meant anything to the Dominions would be too high to please foreign countries.

The Secretary of State for Scotland said he felt that it might still be that it would be necessary to put a higher duty on, for example, Danish butter than we should have wished, in order to be able to put a duty on New Zealand butter. He felt sure that if we failed to put a duty on Dominion dairy produce the principle of free entry would be definitely established; moreover the revenue would suffer substantially . . . the existing duty on Danish butter was calculated in order to bring in the maximum of revenue.[13] If it was increased it might become protective and bring in less revenue. It was for this reason that the levy subsidy idea had been put forward.[14]

Mr. W. B. Brown pointed out that while it might be said that Denmark had to accept anything we liked to insist upon, if we reduced her exports to us substantially the inevitable corollary was that she would not be able to buy so much from us.

The Secretary of State for Dominion Affairs said that even supposing the Canadians would agree to a reduction of their preferential margin for dairy products, no action could be taken unless agreement was also obtained from other Dominions, particularly New Zealand. Although New Zealand had reason to be pleased with our proposal to leave mutton and lamb free of duty, it was accompanied by an intimation that there was a definite limit to their market for mutton and lamb here, and that it might even have to be reduced.

The Secretary of State for Scotland said he felt the Dominions should take account of the large burden of expense being carried by the home

[13] There is no evidence to support this statement. The original butter duty was imposed in 1932 at the standard rate of 10 per cent which the Import Duties Act levied. It was raised in the negotiations at Ottawa, and subsequently conventionalized in the trade negotiations with Denmark and other foreign countries.

[14] When the levy-subsidy idea was put forward, there was no suggestion that it would safeguard the revenue from the 'ordinary' butter duty.

Government for defence, which was in their interests as well as in ours. He agreed that this did not apply so much to Canada but it certainly applied to New Zealand, from whom the chief objections to a duty on Dominion dairy produce would come. . . .[15]

Mr. W. B. Brown pointed out that an increased duty could not be imposed on foreign imports of, e.g. butter, until eight or nine foreign Trade Agreements had been re-negotiated. These negotiations would take some twelve months, so that nothing could be done at any rate before January 1938.

The Secretary of State for Scotland said his recollection was that the Dominions had not been so averse to duties on dairy products as might have been expected. All they had asked was that before such duties were imposed there should be consultation with them. . . .

The Minister of Agriculture and Fisheries said that he had very little hope of its being possible to impose increased duties, on such a scale as to make Dominion duties effective, on foreign dairy products, owing both to our foreign trade interests and to those of the consumer. He was, therefore, unwilling to accept the position that we must not take the initiative in reopening the Canadian discussions. He felt that it would be possible to approach the Canadians on the ground that since the discussions began there had been a great increase in the calls on the Treasury for defence.

The Secretary of State for Dominion Affairs said that he must emphasise that in his view such action might well lose us the whole agreement. Mr. Dunning[16] had had great difficulty in commending the new Agreement to his colleagues on the present basis, and if that were now to be abandoned even he might lose heart.

The President of the Board of Trade said he attached considerable importance to our avoiding putting Mr. Dunning in the position of having recommended to his colleagues a settlement which afterwards turned out to be no settlement.

The Chancellor of the Exchequer was afraid that the re-armament argument would carry very little conviction in Canada. While sympa-

---

[15] Elliot is really proposing that the Dominions should let the United Kingdom tax them by imposing on their produce an import duty which will be shifted backward to Dominion producers. The political philosophy and constitutional theory of this suggestion are both extraordinary. It is also hard to see how Britain's re-armament could possibly be said to defend New Zealand.

[16] The Canadian Minister of Finance. He had been the most eager Canadian cabinet minister to conclude an agreement, and had persevered through a series of frustrations, both British and Canadian, since the summer of 1936, even entering into private communication with the High Commissioner, unknown to his cabinet colleagues, with respect to the drafting of key passages.

thising with Mr. Morrison's objects he was afraid that it was now too late to recast the Canadian agreement.

The President of the Board of Trade said that he also would go very far with Mr. Morrison on general principles. For the moment, however, his paramount concern was to see the Canadian Agreement signed. He would be anxious until signature was an accomplished fact; Canada was negotiating with four foreign countries at the present time. We could simply not afford to throw away our large and growing Canadian trade. . . .

36. A Civil Servant's Parody of the Ottawa Negotiations, 1932

FROM University of Newcastle upon Tyne, Walter Runciman Papers, Box 3, File 'Ottawa'

Recent Russian plans for the development of the emu industry have caused alarm in Australia. From a report in *The Times* for Wednesday, August 10th, it appears that the Russians hope in the course of 1932 to produce 30 emu chicks.[1]

As Ministers are aware, it is proposed to appoint a Commission to examine the possibility of organising emu production at home. This industry, if properly developed, should play a valuable part in the systematic organisation of our agriculture generally, and incidentally should provide a valuable market for surplus Canadian offals. It is important that its future should not be jeopardised by a Soviet attack while it is still in its infancy.[2]

Strong representations have naturally been made to us in this matter by the Australian Delegation, and those representations have now been reinforced by the demands of the Canadian Minister of Agriculture. From figures placed before us, it appears that the possible Australian exportable surplus is 20 emu eggs a year.[3] Canada at present produces no

[1] Both Australians and Canadians were terrified of Soviet *wheat* exports; Canada also feared Soviet *timber*, and the British market was the focus of both countries' concern.

[2] The United Kingdom Government was already committed to reorganise and increase *bacon* production at home; pigs would eat offals from British wheat-milling.

[3] Australia normally discussed all food exports, especially meat, sugar, dried fruits, and canned goods, in terms of a surplus over home consumption.

emu eggs, but she hopes in the course of the next three years to work up to an annual exportable surplus of 10 emu eggs.[4] Preliminary enquiries by the Ministery of Agriculture officials show that the total consumption in the United Kingdom in the year 1935 is likely to amount to 40 emu eggs.

It is obvious that on a market of this size Russian imports, if unchecked, will be sufficient to ruin the market for both the home and the Dominion producer. It is proposed, therefore, to give an immediate guarantee that no Russian emu eggs will be imported into the United Kingdom[5] and that the home industry will be so organised as to provide for an annual production of 15 emu eggs. Of the remaining 25 emu eggs necessary to supply home needs, Australia will be guaranteed 20 and Canada 5, though if hard pressed on the point we might concede to Canada 5 1/2.

It should be noted that the conditions of the Canadian industry make it probable that all their exportable surplus will be addled.[6] With the consent of the Treasury, however, the Empire Marketing Board propose to devote a sum of £50,000 to a campaign of education to induce the United Kingdom public to eat addled Empire emu eggs.[7]

---

[4] Canadian bacon production was too small to generate many exports, and she did not produce timber in grades and sizes suitable to the British market, but her ministers had high hopes for both commodities.

[5] Britain was willing to bar Soviet goods in certain carefully circumscribed conditions; see Article 21 of the Anglo-Canadian trade agreement.

[6] The quality problem with respect to Canadian timber.

[7] British ministers were already preparing to wind up the Empire Marketing Board, whose publicity campaigns had little obvious effect on British consumption of Empire goods; the Treasury fought long, hard, and consistently to limit the Board's spending.

INDEX